PRAISE FOR
YOU CAN'T CATCH US

"Shannon McKenna Schmidt's indisputable storytelling talents are on full display in her latest book, *You Can't Catch Us*. Schmidt's captivating narrative flow, impeccable research, and novelistic pacing bring readers along for Lady Bird Johnson's groundbreaking whistle-stop tour through the southern states in October 1964. In the wake of her husband's signing of the Civil Rights Act, Lady Bird Johnson took to the rails to support her husband's presidential campaign, shattering the First Lady mold in the process. *You Can't Catch Us* is 1,682 miles, forty-seven stops, eight states, four days, and one powerful story masterfully captured in delectable detail and buoyed by Schmidt's fluid style. An exhilarating and important read. All aboard the Lady Bird Special! This is one ride you won't want to miss."

—Denise Kiernan, *New York Times* bestselling author of *The Girls of Atomic City* and *Obstinate Daughters*

"Shannon McKenna Schmidt's captivating storytelling brings this extraordinary chapter of presidential campaign history into vivid relief with rich detail and illuminating cultural and political context."

—Christy Carpenter, Liz Carpenter's daughter and codirector and coproducer of *Shaking It Up: The Life & Times of Liz Carpenter*

"Important, compelling, and profoundly researched. Shannon McKenna Schmidt has gifted us with a reconsideration of our ongoing activist struggles for civil rights and feminism. A powerful book most needed now!"

—Blanche Wiesen Cook, *New York Times* bestselling and award-winning author of the definitive three-volume biography *Eleanor Roosevelt*

"Surprising, gripping, and hilarious, this inspiring journey through the American South never derails. Shannon McKenna Schmidt has written a gem of American campaign history. All aboard!"
—Margaret McMullan, author of *Where the Angels Lived: One Family's Story of Exile, Loss, and Return*

"The story of Lady Bird Johnson's railroad journey through the South in the wake of her husband signing the 1964 Civil Rights Act is a largely unheralded slice of history. Thankfully, Shannon McKenna Schmidt's *You Can't Catch Us* changes that, bringing the remarkable story forward with vivid, compelling detail."
—Mark K. Updegrove, president and CEO of the LBJ Foundation and author of *Indomitable Will: LBJ in the Presidency*

"In lively prose, Schmidt takes readers along on Lady Bird Johnson's historic whistle-stop tour through the American South, a region reeling over civil rights and segregation. This action-packed account captures the Southern charm and steely courage of Lady Bird Johnson during the most dramatic days of her political life. It is the most panoramic attempt yet made to put the Lady Bird Special in perspective."
—Jill Abraham Hummer, author of *Laura Bush: Texas Roots, Global Impact*

PRAISE FOR
THE FIRST LADY OF WORLD WAR II

"Shannon McKenna Schmidt fully and captivatingly depicts the journey in *The First Lady of World War II*... McKenna Schmidt puts the trip in context and provides a lively account of an often overlooked, inspiring journey."

—*Shelf Awareness*, Starred Review

"The author's ability to combine place with subject is unsurpassed here... This work provides numerous details and the context needed to understand the trials and difficulties of Eleanor Roosevelt's historic undertaking. Readers interested in World War II or women's roles in the war effort will likely appreciate this enjoyable read."

—*Library Journal*

"Eleanor Roosevelt's legacy of activism and mettle continue to inspire. Recommended."

—*Booklist*

"I thoroughly enjoyed getting to know this remarkable woman, friend of the downtrodden and celebrated alike... Highly recommended."

—*Historical Novel Society*

"As Schmidt powerfully conveys, it was a trip that changed many lives, especially Roosevelt's."

—*BookPage*

"This action-packed and suspenseful wartime drama vividly captures the selfless grit and tenderness of Eleanor Roosevelt's battle-zone leadership."

—David Michaelis, *New York Times* bestselling author of *Eleanor*

ALSO BY
SHANNON McKENNA SCHMIDT

The First Lady of World War II
Novel Destinations
Writers Between the Covers

You Can't Catch Us

Lady Bird Johnson's Trailblazing 1964 Campaign Train and the Women Who Rode with Her

Shannon McKenna Schmidt

Copyright © 2026 by Shannon McKenna Schmidt
Cover and internal design © 2026 by Sourcebooks
Cover design by Lucy Kim
Cover images © LBJ Library photos by Frank Muto and UPI (Norfolk, VA)
Back cover images © LBJ Library photo, LBJ Library photos by
Frank Muto (New Orleans, LA and Selma, NC)

Sourcebooks and the colophon are registered trademarks of Sourcebooks.

All rights reserved. No part of this book may be reproduced in any form or by any electronic or mechanical means including information storage and retrieval systems—except in the case of brief quotations embodied in critical articles or reviews—without permission in writing from its publisher, Sourcebooks.

No part of this book may be used or reproduced in any manner for the purpose of training artificial intelligence technologies or systems.

This publication is designed to provide accurate and authoritative information in regard to the subject matter covered. It is sold with the understanding that the publisher is not engaged in rendering legal, accounting, or other professional service. If legal advice or other expert assistance is required, the services of a competent professional person should be sought. —*From a Declaration of Principles Jointly Adopted by a Committee of the American Bar Association and a Committee of Publishers and Associations*

References to internet websites (URLs) were accurate at the time of writing. Neither the author nor Sourcebooks is responsible for URLs that may have expired or changed since the manuscript was prepared.

Published by Sourcebooks
1935 Brookdale RD, Naperville, IL 60563-2773
(630) 961-3900
sourcebooks.com

Cataloging-in-Publication Data is on file with the Library of Congress.

Printed and bound in the United States of America.
MA 10 9 8 7 6 5 4 3 2 1

*To everyone who helps bend the arc toward justice,
then and now*

Contents

Prologue   *xiii*

Chapter 1: Operation Whistle-Stop   1

Chapter 2: Swinging into Action   23
Alexandria, Virginia, October 6, 1964

Chapter 3: Never Stand on the Sidelines   37
Fredericksburg and Ashland, Virginia, October 6, 1964

Chapter 4: The Real Value of It   49
Richmond, Virginia, October 6, 1964

Chapter 5: Time Marches On   59
Petersburg, Virginia, October 6, 1964

Chapter 6: We Know Who's Right   69
Suffolk and Norfolk, Virginia, October 6, 1964

Chapter 7: A Message of Good Will 77
Ahoskie, North Carolina, October 6, 1964

Chapter 8: Lessons of the Past 83
Tarboro, Rocky Mount, Wilson, and Selma, North Carolina, October 6, 1964

Chapter 9: The Great Persuader 91
Raleigh, North Carolina, October 6, 1964

Chapter 10: Not-So-Secret Weapon 107
Durham, North Carolina, October 7, 1964

Chapter 11: With Every Turn of the Wheels 117
Burlington and Greensboro, North Carolina, October 7, 1964

Chapter 12: You Can't Catch Us 123
High Point, Thomasville, Lexington, Salisbury, and Concord, North Carolina, October 7, 1964

Chapter 13: Campaign Right Hand 129
Charlotte, North Carolina, October 7, 1964

Chapter 14: How Did You Get to Be This Way? 135
Rock Hill, South Carolina, October 7, 1964

Chapter 15: A Little Excitement 145
Chester and Winnsboro, South Carolina, October 7, 1964

Chapter 16: Mad and Cool 153
Columbia and Orangeburg, South Carolina, October 7, 1964

Chapter 17: Dividing Line 163
Charleston, South Carolina, October 7, 1964

Chapter 18: We'll Yell a Little Louder   177
Charleston, Yemassee, and Ridgeland, South Carolina, October 8, 1964

Chapter 19: It Takes Women to Have Guts   183
Savannah, Jesup, Blackshear, Waycross, Homerville, Valdosta, and Thomasville, Georgia, October 8, 1964

Chapter 20: Courageous Willingness   199
Drifton and Tallahassee, Florida, October 8, 1964

Chapter 21: I'm Afraid I Bopped Him   209
Chattahoochee, Chipley, Crestview, and Milton, Florida, October 9, 1964

Chapter 22: Hard-Hitting and Down-to-Earth   213
Pensacola, Florida, October 9, 1964

Chapter 23: The New South   219
Flomaton and Mobile, Alabama, October 9, 1964

Chapter 24: Voice Their Convictions   229
Edgewater Park, Biloxi, Mississippi, October 9, 1964

Chapter 25: What a Team They Were   237
New Orleans, Louisiana, October 9, 1964

Epilogue   253

Author's Note and Acknowledgments   257
Source Notes   261
Notes   269
Index   319
About the Author   334

Prologue

September 1964. A chartered plane landed at an airport in Columbia, South Carolina, the only flight scheduled to arrive that afternoon. The tarmac was deserted except for two vehicles, one of which belonged to Donald Russell, the state's governor, who was there to greet White House representative Liz Carpenter and her traveling companions. In the other vehicle, a group of men, silent and sullen, stared as the new arrivals exited the plane.

"What are six men doing in a car just sitting at the airport in midafternoon?" Carpenter asked the governor. She received no response. "I had an eerie feeling," she said, "I was seeing the face of hate."

That evening, Carpenter and a group of supporters of President Lyndon B. Johnson's reelection campaign gathered at the governor's mansion to plan the South Carolina itinerary for an upcoming train tour to be undertaken by First Lady Lady Bird Johnson. The next day, Governor Russell and his family returned home from a dinner outing to find a burlap-wrapped, gasoline-soaked cross burning in the driveway of the executive mansion.

The South was hostile territory for Democrats who supported civil rights. Nearly three months earlier, President Johnson had signed into law the Civil Rights Act of 1964. The act banned employment discrimination based on race, color, religion, sex, or national origin. It also prohibited segregation in public places like parks and libraries and in businesses such as restaurants and hotels, and it mandated the integration of public schools and colleges and universities that received federal funding. The legislation was widely unpopular in the South, made even more unpalatable since a Southern president, who hailed from Texas, had thrown his political heft behind it.

After the signing of the Civil Rights Act, it was reported that compliance in the South was greatest in the "rim states," including Virginia, North Carolina, and Florida, that there was "a lesser degree of obedience" in South Carolina, Georgia, and Louisiana, and the strongest resistance was in Alabama and Mississippi.

These were the eight states through which the First Lady's campaign train would travel. Carpenter, Lady Bird's staff director and press secretary, was on a scouting mission, laying the groundwork for the high-profile, women-led operation. The four-day journey would be made in a nineteen-car train dubbed the "Lady Bird Special," traveling from Washington, DC, to New Orleans. "Much of the Lady Bird Special's route lay through enemy territory," wrote a Southern correspondent for the *New York Times*, rolling through towns on the front lines of the civil rights battle.

At each stop on the scouting mission, Carpenter contacted area newspaper editors for advice. "They had their fingers on the pulse of their town," she said. "They could measure how much goodwill the Democrats had" locally. Fellow scouting members sorted out logistics on where the train would stop and also rallied local politicians and civic leaders. Secret service agents assessed potential security risks and sought information on the Ku Klux Klan (KKK).

Violence had been particularly prevalent that summer, especially in the Deep South. Civil rights workers had stepped up their efforts across the South, including increasing voter registration among Black citizens. In turn, segregationists resorted to terrorism and even murder to try and maintain the status quo. KKK membership soared, and church and cross burnings, like the brazen display at the South Carolina governor's mansion, were commonplace.

The violence took an even darker turn when three voter registration activists—James Chaney, Michael Schwerner, and Andrew Goodman—disappeared in Mississippi. Concern about their fate reached the highest levels of government and made national headlines, partly due to the fact that Schwerner and Goodman were white Northerners. Chaney, who was Black and a Mississippi resident, worked at a community center for the Congress of Racial Equality operated by Schwerner, a former social worker from New York City, and his wife, Rita. Goodman, a college student from Queens, New York, traveled south to participate in the Mississippi Freedom Summer Project. The vast, organized initiative to register Black voters in Mississippi, who had less than seven percent representation, was a bold and dangerous plan.

The first group of Freedom Summer volunteers, Goodman among them, arrived in Mississippi on June 20, just after the Senate passed the Civil Rights Act. The next night, Chaney, Schwerner, and Goodman vanished on a back road after being released from a jail where they were briefly detained. Their alarmed colleagues sought answers about their disappearance and were stonewalled by authorities. The story was dismissed by some as liberal propaganda, including Mississippi Senator James Eastland, who assured President Johnson that it was a publicity stunt.

Two days after the men went missing, President Johnson met with Goodman's and Schwerner's parents in the Oval Office. He delivered to them the devastating news that investigators had found the burned-out hulk of the car in which the young men were traveling, information he learned moments earlier during a call with FBI director J. Edgar Hoover. Johnson ordered Hoover, who was openly hostile to the civil rights movement, to take action in Mississippi and inundate the state with agents.

After a massive, weeks-long search, the bodies of Chaney, Schwerner, and Goodman were found buried in an earthen dam on a farm. The White Knights of the KKK, with the aid of local law enforcement, specifically targeted Schwerner, who they saw as a traitorous white and an interfering Northerner. That summer, in Mississippi alone, another civil rights volunteer was killed. Others involved in the movement were badly beaten, some critically wounded, and more than a thousand people were arrested. Many homes of Black residents and nearly seventy churches were bombed or burned. Similar acts of violence and intimidation were happening throughout the South.

Fanning the flames of animosity was President Johnson's opponent in the 1964 election, Barry Goldwater, an Arizona senator, whose campaign strategy included courting the racist vote. "While not himself a racist, Mr. Goldwater articulates a philosophy which gives aid and comfort to the racists," said the Reverend Dr. Martin Luther King Jr. on the day Goldwater accepted the Republican nomination for president.

Lady Bird frankly admitted that her train trip through the South was "as political as all get-out." Her aim was to attempt to "hold the South for Lyndon." But it was also more than that. A Texan with Alabama roots, she was proud of her Southern heritage and of what her husband had done for civil rights, and she was unwilling to simply write off this swath of the country. She proposed the journey to help bridge the divide, reaching out to voters while at the same time showing the rest of the nation there was much more to the South than a white populace angry about the passage of the Civil Rights Act. As Lady Bird visited town after town, speaking from a podium at the back of the train, she emphasized the importance of economic prosperity and education and overcoming racial prejudices. She appealed to her fellow Southerners to embrace the new South and not to be left "in the slack waters of history."

Shortly after Liz Carpenter's scouting mission, undeterred by the prospect of danger, the First Lady boarded the custom-tailored train and rode headlong into the powder keg of Southern politics.

1

Operation Whistle-Stop

An unexpected sight stopped travelers in their tracks at Union Station in Washington, DC, on October 4, 1964: a brightly bedecked, ninety-foot-long train car. Its exterior sides were adorned with red, white, and blue stripes. There was catchily named "victory blue" on the bottom, a swath of white in the middle, and at the top, "landslide red" with the words LADY BIRD SPECIAL emblazoned in white script. Windows were plastered with matching posters touting LBJ FOR THE USA. A brass platform on the back of the train car featured a blue backdrop and a scalloped, red-and-white aluminum awning. A microphone-equipped podium, a public address system, and four loudspeakers mounted on the roof above the platform further indicated that this was no standard passenger train. A bevy of "Ladies for Lyndon" handed out campaign paraphernalia, and members of the press were given a sneak peek inside the show-stopping parlor-observation car.

Two days later, the First Lady of the United States, Lady Bird

Johnson, boarded what was "probably the most colorful vehicle in whistle-stop history." Using the time-honored whistle-stop tour, a campaign method named for the brief stops made in small towns along the train tracks, she was on a mission to aid her husband's reelection bid—and she was breaking ground to do it. Never before had a First Lady taken to the campaign trail on her own and so ambitiously.

That morning, the nineteen-car Lady Bird Special, with three hundred people aboard, rolled out of Union Station, crossed the Potomac River, and headed south, bound for New Orleans. The four-day journey would cover 1,682 miles through eight states and make forty-seven stops along the way.

The First Lady's "train sortie through the South will be incomparably the most important campaign effort undertaken by the wife of an American president," stated syndicated newspaper columnist William E. White. "This is not to be one of those tea-sipping, all-we-girls-together enterprises, redolent of the spirit of lawn parties and polite discussions among madam chairladies which have so long typified the distaff side of American politics. This is to be a precedent-making and major effort by a President's wife—in a region from which both sprang and which both love—to say for a husband what he cannot in this case so well say for himself."

On July 2, 1964, President Johnson signed into law one of the most significant legislative achievements in United States history. It was also one of the most divisive.

Five days after President John F. Kennedy's assassination in November 1963, Johnson addressed a joint session of Congress and announced his intention to pursue his predecessor's agenda. He emphasized one piece of legislation in particular.

"No memorial oration or eulogy could more eloquently honor President Kennedy's memory than the earliest possible passage of the civil rights bill for which he fought so long," said Johnson.

He had a pointed message for the Southern Democrats with a

history of obstructing civil rights legislation. "We have talked long enough in this country about equal rights. We have talked for one hundred years or more. It is time now to write the next chapter, and to write it in the books of law."

President Johnson told the nation, "John Kennedy's death commands what his life conveyed—that America must move forward. The time has come for Americans of all races and creeds and political beliefs to understand and to respect one another. So let us put an end to the teaching and the preaching of hate and evil and violence."

Johnson drew on his extensive political acumen and experience, garnered over more than two decades serving in the House of Representatives and the Senate, to help pass the legislation. While he was majority leader, he successfully steered the Civil Rights Acts of 1957 and 1960 through the Senate. Although the Acts were significant milestones—the first federal civil rights legislation since Reconstruction—by the time they were passed, the laws had been watered down to limit their impact and make them difficult to enforce.

President Johnson was determined that this time, the Civil Rights Act would not be weakened, saying, "I don't intend to cavil or compromise."

Predictably, resistance to these proposed sweeping changes was fierce. When the bill reached the Senate, it ran up against a group of Democratic Southern senators who filibustered for a record-breaking sixty working days. But such efforts could not withstand the "earnest, dogged work and the legislative expertise of Lyndon," as Lady Bird saw it, and that of other lawmakers.

The events unfolding in the Senate were propelled by the historic winds of change culminating from decades of efforts by civil rights leaders. As Senator Everett Dirksen, an Illinois Republican and one of the leading lawmakers in the battle for a civil rights bill, said in remarks that quoted novelist Victor Hugo, "No army can withstand the strength of an idea whose time has come." And the Southern

Democratic insurgency could not. On June 19, the Senate followed the House and finally passed the Civil Rights Act of 1964.

Lady Bird left the signing ceremony in the East Room at the White House feeling as if she "had seen the beginning of something in this nation's history, fraught with untold good and much pain and trouble."

Johnson, who hailed from Texas, was called a traitor to the South, and animosity toward him ran high. Sixty-six percent of Southern whites disapproved of the passing of the Civil Rights Act. Alabama Governor George Wallace declared it "the most monstrous piece of legislation ever enacted by the United States Congress." When the presidential contest kicked into high gear that fall, civil rights was the dominant domestic matter.

Campaign advisers urged Johnson to "avoid the racial issue," which was not limited to the South. That summer, riots erupted in Philadelphia, Harlem, and elsewhere in the North, a response to occurrences of police brutality and to the systemic socioeconomic suppression of people of color. "I was concerned that the riots foreshadowed trouble and divisiveness in the country, but I knew this issue could not and should not be avoided," said President Johnson. "I made it clear that I considered civil rights in all its aspects an important campaign issue."

The Republican presidential contender, Barry Goldwater, campaigned through the South courting segregationists under the guise of advocating for "states' rights." He touted his vote against the Civil Rights Act of 1964, arguing that it was an overreach by the federal government and that civil rights, desegregation, and voting rights were issues that should be left to the states to decide.

Given the tense political climate and the backlash, a train tour through the South was considered too dangerous for President Johnson to undertake. Nearly two thousand miles of railroad track would be challenging to protect, and the shadow of Kennedy's assassination still loomed over the nation. The recently released Warren Commission Report took the Secret Service to task for inadequate protections on the day of Kennedy's death and recommended specific increased security measures going forward for the president. The day before the Lady Bird Special left Washington, DC, Johnson rode for the first time in the newly reinforced presidential limousine, which had been almost completely rebuilt. Outfitted with armor plating and bulletproof glass, the vehicle could now withstand a direct hit from a .30-caliber rifle.

Plus, it was widely predicted that Johnson would win the election and that even without the South, he was headed for a victory. Polls had him leading over Goldwater by wide margins. Some of President Johnson's advisers and Democratic strategists cautioned against allocating campaign resources in the South, arguing that it was a lost cause, "so why make the effort."

But neither the president nor Lady Bird were willing to simply dismiss the South. "We must go," she said to Liz Carpenter. "We must let them know that we love the South. We respect them. We have not turned our backs on them. I don't think there's much chance of carrying it for Lyndon, judging by the letters I get from my Alabama cousins. But at least we won't lose by default."

Carpenter was tasked with exploring options on how best to campaign in this section of the country. At the Democratic National Convention in Atlantic City that August, she met with a number of Democratic Southern governors. A proposed plan to host receptions for Lady Bird at their statehouses was scrapped due to two concerns. One was the governors' fear that such an overt display of unity with a president despised by many of their constituents would stoke support for Republicans. In addition, the Secret Service feared that the receptions, held in challenging-to-protect circular statehouse rotundas, would increase the susceptibility of the First Lady to a sniper's bullet.

Instead it was decided on a whistle-stop tour, with the Secret Service implementing tightly controlled security measures. Agents would canvas towns ahead of time, coordinate with local law enforcement, ride on the train, and be present at every stop, surveying by helicopter, flanking the platform where Lady Bird spoke, and circulating among the crowds.

"I don't think anybody at the time realized how nervous the Secret Service was about that trip and what kind of challenges [Lady Bird] was taking on in going into the Deep South," said a White House employee.

In early September, India Edwards, a consultant with the Department of Labor, wrote to Carpenter with concern after hearing that Lady Bird was planning a trip into the South. Edwards relayed that a friend of hers, "a Floridian and a very smart woman," had a sense of unease while on a two-week drive along the Gulf Coast, never seeing "anything but Goldwater bumper stickers any place on the trip." Due to that and other observations, Edwards said, "she feels that some very unpleasant incidents are brewing or being brewed."

After Lady Bird's whistle-stop tour was announced in the press in mid-September, a threat was reported to the FBI of a potential plot targeting the train. An informant revealed that a Mississippi barber and gun dealer for the KKK had proposed using dynamite to blow up a bridge over which the Lady Bird Special would travel, but he couldn't get any other Klansmen to go along with him. Even so, as an added precaution, the Secret Service insisted that an extra engine precede the train by fifteen minutes in case the tracks were wired with explosives, a safeguard that weighed heavily on Lady Bird's conscience.

The whistle-stop idea was a callback to the 1960 election when Johnson, the vice-presidential candidate on the ticket with Kennedy, stumped through the South on an eleven-car train called the LBJ Special. Whistle-stops were a long-standing tradition in U.S. presidential contests, and Harry Truman, who campaigned extensively by train in a long shot and ultimately successful bid for the presidency in 1948, suggested it to Johnson. "You may not believe this, Lyndon," he said, "but there are still a hell of a lot of people in this country who don't know where the airport is. But they damn sure know where the depot is. And if you let 'em know you're coming, they'll be down and listen to you." Liz Carpenter concurred, saying, "small Southern towns are made to order" for whistle-stops. Like Lady Bird, she had been on board the 1960 campaign train. The depots tended to be centrally located in highly trafficked downtown areas along with department stores, tractor supply stores, and other retailers.

The Lady Bird Special was the culmination of its namesake's twenty-seven years in politics alongside her husband. In a proposal for the whistle-stop idea, Carpenter noted that, "next to the President, Mrs. Johnson is the ticket's best drawing power in the South." Lady Bird had charm and grace and what one reporter described as a "picturesque" drawl, combined with sincerity and a genuine affection for people and for the South. And she was an experienced traveler, from the days of Johnson's first Senate run when she trekked across Texas to accompanying her vice-president husband on frequent government trips in the United States and around the world.

During her first ten months as First Lady, she logged about 45,000 miles traversing the country, focusing in particular on raising awareness about the Johnson administration's efforts to address poverty and inequality. Lady Bird was often compared by reporters to Eleanor Roosevelt, both for her extensive travels and for her approach to the role of First Lady. Like the peripatetic Eleanor, who was known as being the "eyes and ears" for her president husband, Lady Bird was interested in "learning from people" and not just statistics.

One of her aims as First Lady, she said during a press breakfast at the Democratic National Convention, was to "be a link between the President and the people." In many ways, she viewed herself as a reporter, albeit for "a very private editor." As she said, "I try to report to him, factually, what I see and hear in the places that I visit. I try to pass along to him the opinions, the aspirations, the moods, and the needs of the people I talk to."

The month before the whistle-stop tour, Lady Bird headed out West to visit Native American reservations and national parks with Stewart Udall, the secretary of the interior. Udall was enthusiastic about the idea from the start, telling Carpenter, who suggested the trip, "No First Lady within memory has gone to an Indian reservation to make a survey of conditions." The trip garnered extensive media attention and augmented Lady Bird's place in the national spotlight. Newspapers carried front-page stories written by Helen Thomas of the United Press International and other reporters who accompanied the First Lady. The wide-ranging itinerary included visiting the Crow Reservation in Montana, dedicating Utah's Flaming Gorge Dam, and delivering a commencement speech at the University of Utah. In Wyoming, Lady Bird rafted a twenty-two-mile stretch of the Snake River and met with a group of the state's notable women, among them Nellie Tayloe Ross, the first woman to serve as governor of a U.S. state. Udall deemed the trip a triumphant success. "Mrs. Johnson was extremely effective in her appearances on her 'land and people' tour in the West last week," he told the president. "I am confident [she] could win the West all by herself if we gave her the opportunity."

Although billed as nonpolitical, the Western trip took Lady Bird into Goldwater territory. Just after her return, Douglass Cater, a special assistant to the president, wrote to his boss. "Mrs. Johnson represents a political asset for the campaign which is unique in Presidential history. She is highly appealing and effective on the platform. She comes across as intelligent and knowledgeable and unlike Eleanor Roosevelt thoroughly feminine. She maintains grace under the most hectic conditions," he said. "Politicians and reporters alike felt she would be more sought after than the Vice-Presidential nominee for many occasions. The consensus was that she should make a number of treks apart from you—that she could give the extra push in critical states, visiting communities that lie outside the Presidential circuit."

While Lady Bird was out West, the president was asked at a news conference whether she would be campaigning that fall in his reelection bid. "She is and she will," he confirmed.

When the whistle-stop idea came to fruition shortly after, not everyone in the West Wing was on board. One of the president's advisers, Kenneth O'Donnell, formerly JFK's chief of staff and part of the group known as Kennedy's "Irish Mafia," tried to act as a gatekeeper. He repeatedly refused to meet with Liz Carpenter and Bess Abell, the White House social secretary, to discuss the campaign train.

Carpenter had previously worked for Johnson when he was vice president and still assisted him on projects. Instead of giving in to O'Donnell's gatekeeping, Carpenter went straight to the commander in chief himself. Johnson was "so enthusiastic about what Mrs. Johnson could do on a train trip that we sat there and planned it." O'Donnell learned a hard lesson for underestimating the women on Johnson's political team. "The President yanked him up there on the second floor of the White House" as they were discussing the whistle-stop tour, Carpenter recalled. "I enjoyed watching Kenny O'Donnell being brought around by the President of the United States on the value of women, and he had to suffer three of them—Mrs. Johnson, Bess, and me."

Still, O'Donnell doubled down on his misogyny and "turned up his nose at the whole thing. He sat sphinx-like in meetings with me—half laughing at the whole idea and obviously feeling that neither the South nor women were important in the campaign," said Carpenter. "[He] had no respect for any women in politics whatsoever."

O'Donnell was no match for Liz Carpenter, a veteran of the Washington political scene and a longtime professional associate and friend of Lady Bird and President Johnson. "But I would be less than honest," Carpenter admitted, "if I didn't credit the O'Donnell attitude with whetting my appetite to make that whistle-stop a spectacular political happening like he'd never seen in South Boston."

Carpenter was a former journalist, and she knew how to harness the power of the media. A whistle-stop tour would hold dramatic appeal for the press, "much easier to 'sell' than piecemeal visits here and there," she reasoned. According to Dewey Long of the White House Transportation Office, "the best 'train man in the business'" who had mapped out Truman's whistle-stop tour and joined the Lady Bird Special team, the farther Truman went, the more the train's popularity and momentum snowballed.

Once Johnson was briefed on what Carpenter dubbed "Operation Whistle-stop," she said, "I had LBJ all the way with me," paraphrasing a 1964 campaign slogan. "The President knew that Mrs. Johnson would be loved in the South," added Carpenter. "[He] wanted her to go on the whistle-stop because he knew her value."

Johnson had masterminded much of his own 1960 campaign train, which the press called "a sharp, efficient show." Known as "a master of details," he lent a hand in planning Lady Bird's whistle-stop tour, poring over maps and schedules with his wife. The Lady Bird Special traveled on six different major railroad lines, passing through some 180 communities. Stops were determined by a variety of factors—where the tracks went, where the train could reach by nightfall, which towns were gathering places for the counties, and where the president and his running mate, Minnesota Senator Hubert Humphrey, needed the votes.

The town of Ahoskie, North Carolina, population 4,800, was added to the itinerary after the White House received a telegram:

> Dear Mrs. Johnson, please stop in Ahoskie. No important person has visited here since Buffalo Bill, and no passenger train has stopped in 12 years.

"Stop there!" the president urged. "If they want you that bad, you'll get everyone out from three counties."

Lady Bird's determination to make the most of the trip also helped shape the itinerary. "Don't give me the easy towns," she told Carpenter.

"Anyone can get into Atlanta—it's the new, modern South. Let me take the tough ones." As Carpenter explained, that meant places neither the president nor Senator Humphrey "could get in and out of with their hide on" or ones "they couldn't take the time to visit" because they were considered lost causes for getting votes.

Operation Whistle-stop was organized out of the East Wing, the domain of the First Lady's staff, in a matter of weeks and carefully orchestrated down to the last detail.

Lady Bird wanted to be a working First Lady, and she professionalized the role. She began by hiring the first East Wing staff director, Liz Carpenter, and assembling a team to work on her projects—planning public appearances, writing speeches, maintaining contacts with Congress and other key groups, and coordinating with the media. Lady Bird's decision to hire Carpenter was also notable for another reason: she was the first professional journalist to serve as a First Lady's press secretary.

Carpenter was born in a rural Texas town in 1920, just after the ratification of the Nineteenth Amendment that gave women the right to vote. When her older brother reached college age, her mother "packed us all up" and moved to Austin so that her children could attend "The University." There Carpenter became "involved in everything political and journalistic" and was "the first girl vice president of the student body."

After graduating in 1942, Carpenter headed for Washington, DC, with stars in her eyes and a journalism degree in her suitcase. She landed a job working as a secretary and reporter for Esther Van Wagoner Tufty, nicknamed "the Duchess," who ran a news bureau for twenty-six Michigan newspapers. The press pass that came with the job "took me everywhere," said Carpenter. "I began to meet the city and know its temperaments."

Carpenter's rise through the journalistic ranks included reporting on Texas politics in Washington for the *Austin American-Statesman* when Lyndon Johnson was in Congress. Eventually she cofounded with her husband, Les, a news bureau that covered Capitol Hill and the White House for Southwest newspapers and other publications.

In 1960, Carpenter received a call from Lady Bird, who was one of the first people she had met when she arrived in wartime Washington. "Lyndon and I have been talking," said Lady Bird. She had a question for Carpenter. Would she consider taking off from her newspaper business until after the election? Johnson had just accepted the vice-presidential nomination on the ticket with Kennedy. Lady Bird planned to be on the campaign trail, and she needed someone traveling with her and assisting her with strategy and scheduling. She then added the line that changed Carpenter's future: "We wonder if you will share the great adventure of our lives."

Carpenter nearly turned down the job offer due to a crippling fear of flying, a necessity when campaigning, but she ultimately accepted with encouragement from her husband and children. "It was too great an opportunity to miss," said Carpenter. Some people thought she had taken leave of her senses, but she "enjoyed the change of assignment—answering the questions instead of asking them." By the time the 1960 election was over, Carpenter was "a willing captive of politics" and joined Vice President Johnson's staff as an executive assistant.

Later, after Johnson became president, Carpenter knew what role she wanted, and it wasn't in the West Wing. During a conversation with Lady Bird as they mused about how Johnson's vice-presidential staff could best make the transition to the White House, Carpenter mustered up her courage. "As for me," she told Lady Bird, "I would like to be your press secretary, if you'd let me."

"Liz, I'd love to have you as press secretary," Lady Bird responded. "And my staff director."

During Carpenter's years as a reporter in Washington, she found it disappointing that no First Lady had ever named a professional newswoman as her press secretary, someone who truly knew the requirements of the media—reporters looking for timely and colorful stories, the pressures of operating on deadline, and the need to have questions answered quickly and honestly.

Like Carpenter, Lady Bird had an excellent rapport with the press. Unlike previous First Ladies who resented the invasion of privacy and shunned reporters, Lady Bird once again took inspiration from Eleanor Roosevelt. Eleanor's media savvy included regular briefings with newspaperwomen, who were excluded from ones held by the president. Like Eleanor, Lady Bird knew that as a working First Lady, she could achieve her aims more effectively by including the media and working with them to convey her message to the country.

It helped that Lady Bird "understood a reporter's needs," said Carpenter. Lady Bird too had a journalism degree from the University of Texas at Austin (along with one in history) and for twenty years had owned and run a Texas radio station, which she transformed from a small-time operation into a media conglomerate. "She knew the language of the trade, the difference between an A.M. and P.M. deadline, that it is better to be accessible than evasive," Carpenter said.

For Carpenter, working in the East Wing was "the best of all worlds. I was in a position to serve the President by serving Mrs. Johnson, perhaps to influence him from time to time, to lend a hand to his press relations in an indirect way, and yet not have the responsibility of that grueling daily job of briefing newsmen." The way Carpenter viewed the division of duties between the West and the East Wings was simple. "The West Wing serves the President; the East Wing serves the President and the First Lady." To anyone who needed further clarification about her job, she said, "I help her help him."

Along with Lady Bird and Liz Carpenter, the other primary member of the East Wing team was Bess Abell, who managed the social side of the White House. She orchestrated everything from state dinners, which took weeks of highly detailed preparation, to receptions and teas for thousands of guests to other special events like a Derby Day fete on the White House lawn and a Christmas party for six hundred children of White House staff members. And she did it all with a refined firmness that earned her the Secret Service code name "Iron Butterfly."

Abell "cut her eyeteeth on big-league politics" as the daughter of a former governor and senator, and she held a degree in political science from the University of Kentucky. A Washington insider, she knew the capital's social scene "inside and out." Abell was another longtime friend and associate of the Johnson family. After the 1960 election, Lady Bird hired Abell as her personal secretary. Abell's appointment to "Second the Second Lady" made news, as did her later appointment as the White House social secretary.

"She is well-equipped for the job—by birth, Southern tradition and long friendship with the new President's family," reported the *Washington Post*. "She is expected to be just as resourceful and gracious at the White House when she assists the new First Lady at functions for visiting heads of state."

When the Johnsons entered the White House, it was assumed that Abell would stay on with the First Lady. "What was not assumed was that I would be the social secretary," said Abell. She decided that she wanted the job and talked with Carpenter about it. "I don't know what Mrs. Johnson's and the President's plans are, but this is what I want to do," she said. "Don't let anybody tell them I can't do it because I've got small children and I don't want that extra responsibility. I do."

Lady Bird said of Abell, "She had the right blend of quiet competence and aggressive persistence, and creative talents too—the last in marked degree."

Abell also had an unflappability that served her well, particularly since dealing with last-minute seating changes at state dinners and other crises was part of the job. So was fulfilling the sometimes-challenging requests of the president, such as the evening he decided to host a luncheon for several dignitaries visiting Washington—the next day. (The chef and the head butler turned the air blue when they learned the news.) Abell and her assistants went into action, working the phones until midnight inviting guests, and the event went off as smoothly as if it had been planned for weeks.

The social entertainment office in the East Wing had a refrigerator and a shower (and a clock above the door that was set five minutes ahead). "Social secretaries are expected to work like plowhorses all day and look like butterflies at night. Thus, the shower," said Carpenter.

Abell's combination of political savvy and social skills was forged during her upbringing in Kentucky. She learned about politics from her father, who throughout his career was a state senator, the governor of Kentucky, a U.S. congressman, and a U.S. senator, during which time he was appointed Democratic Party whip working under Lyndon Johnson. From her mother, the local postmaster, Abell learned the art of social etiquette. She helped her plan events for the town's women, even making place cards when her mother's friends came over for bridge.

Abell brought her organizational skills and creative flair to the Lady Bird Special, organizing the physical setup of the train. She outfitted the parlor-observation car, procured hundreds of thousands of campaign giveaways, and worked with the First Lady to create a menu featuring Southern-inspired dishes and favorites served at the Johnson ranch in Texas. In addition, Abell lined up pre-rally entertainment for waiting crowds at various stops, among them the Brothers Four, a popular folk group who volunteered their services to the campaign. As the train's departure date drew near, she received and monitored weather reports to manage any necessary contingency plans.

Operation Whistle-stop primarily recruited the wives of Southern politicians and Johnson administration staff members, most of whom were friends of Lady Bird and had substantial experience in politics.

"I will match the political talents of Southern women against any others, anytime and any place," declared Carpenter. "They have the uncanny ability to look fragile and lovely as a magnolia blossom, and still possess the managerial ability of [a union] organizer."

Signing on as co-chairs of the Lady Bird Special were politically talented Southerners Lindy Boggs and Virginia Russell, each of whom took a lead role in the whistle-stop tour planning and who would ride the train from start to finish.

Lindy Boggs was "a figure in political life from the moment she hit Washington," said Lady Bird. Like Lady Bird, Lindy, a Louisiana native, came to the capital as the young wife of a congressman after her husband, Hale, was elected to the House of Representatives in 1940. She managed his political campaigns and was a presence in his New Orleans and Washington offices.

"Early on, Hale established with politicians at home that I was his direct representative and that they could say anything to me that they could say to him," said Lindy. "Whatever decisions I made, they would be his final decisions."

Lindy was a Democratic strategist and campaigner, a popular public speaker, and a renowned hostess who did the cooking herself at 1,000-person garden parties, and she had managed President John F. Kennedy's inaugural balls. She was widely active in the 1964 campaign on behalf of the Johnson-Humphrey ticket as well as for Hale, who was up for reelection. The Boggs's political partnership continued with the Lady Bird Special. Hale, the House majority whip, served as a master of ceremonies for the duration of the journey.

Lindy was an optimum choice to co-chair the Lady Bird Special. She was so adept at navigating the Washington political and social scene that "Lindy" became a byword in the capitol vocabulary. "When someone has a job to do or a question to be answered or a problem to be solved—'call Lindy' is often to be heard," wrote a reporter. "Behind the soft Southern accent of her native New Orleans, Lindy Boggs can use, in turn, courtesy, persuasion or firmness to make a point or complete a task."

So committed was Virginia Russell to the Lady Bird Special that she relocated from Columbia, South Carolina, to Washington, DC, for several weeks and took up residence in a White House guest room. She and Lindy set up an office in a building two blocks away that by mid-September was bustling with a busy crew of volunteers. "People are afraid to stick their head in here to say hello to us, for fear I'll put them to work," said Lindy.

Washington *Evening Star* reporter Isabelle Shelton, who planned to be on the campaign train, dropped by the office to interview Virginia and Lindy about their roles in the Lady Bird Special. Virginia, a former schoolteacher, was described by associates as brilliant, well read, witty, and charming. Shelton noted, "If you were to sit and listen to the understated comments of this obviously gentle Southern lady, you never would guess that she is one of the best politicians in her part of the country." When Virginia's husband, Governor Donald Russell of South Carolina, ran for office two years earlier, they worked as a team through a grueling campaign. He unequivocally praised her as being "the best politician in the South." The governor planned to board the Lady Bird Special in Charlotte, North Carolina, and ride the train through their home state.

Lady Bird, Lindy, and Liz Carpenter were all involved with the LBJ Special in 1960 and had gleaned some knowledge of how a campaign train operates. But the Lady Bird Special "was a whole new ball game," said Carpenter. It was more elaborate, more organized, and with more spectacle and flair—right down to the themed menu—all of which was designed to maximize the impact and garner widespread publicity. In addition, the pace would be swift, with anywhere between eight and fifteen stops each day.

It was "a fantastic job of engineering" that involved thousands of people from those in the East Wing headquarters to coordinators, committee members, and other volunteers in every local community from Alexandria, Virginia, the first stop, to the end of the line in New Orleans.

Crucial to the tour's success were the advance teams that preceded the train and aided communities in preparing for the event. They did everything from coordinating logistics on where the train would stop to generating publicity to ensure a crowd, which for Operation Whistle-stop included crop duster–style planes flying over stations with a banner announcing the Lady Bird Special was on its way.

When Carpenter briefed the president on the advance teams, he offered some input.

"You've got to have plenty of advance men, and I don't mean just men. They're all right, but use some of the women around here who are can-do women." He continued with suggestions: "Have them hold meetings in each town, send out postcards, put ads in the newspaper inviting people to the depot."

Carpenter said, "This was pure Johnson—cajoling, beating the maximum effort out of you. It always worked. I redoubled my effort."

Some fifty advance men and women covered every city and town on the Lady Bird Special's itinerary. "All of these good-looking women, able women, were very much considered at the head of the ranks by the President," said Carpenter. "He never underestimated their value, and he was the one that insisted on advance women."

A newspaper headline touted, "Advance Women for Lady Bird Are Something New in Politics," but it wasn't an entirely new strategy. Lindy Boggs and several other women had done advance work in the South for the LBJ Special. During that campaign, they flew into an area, "whipped up interest," and then immediately "went flying off." This time, Lindy and Virginia would advance the route a week before the Lady Bird Special, attend a series of regional meetings, and leave behind a White House–designated coordinator in each area to work with local women's committees and others. "Lyndon knew that women would work the phones, spread enthusiasm, and bring out big crowds," said Lindy. After advancing, she and Virginia would then return to Washington to ride the train.

Just before the advance team set out, Carpenter called a meeting at the White House mess, a large room in the West Wing they could use after hours. Lady Bird came by to thank the volunteers for giving their time to her husband's campaign. "I know the Civil Rights Act was right, and I don't mind saying so. But I'm tired of people making the South the whipping boy of the Democratic Party," she told them during a heartfelt pep talk. Said Carpenter, "Advance men are, by nature, a cynical, rollicking group, but there was a long silence, and then—standing applause. There wasn't a man there who wouldn't have gladly gone all the way to Appomattox for her."

While Carpenter rallied the advance team and primed the press, Bess Abell took on a formidable task: locating the parlor-observation car that would anchor the Lady Bird Special. Popular on passenger trains in the late nineteenth and early twentieth centuries, this special type of car had one long, unbroken room with seating designed for socializing. A rear platform with an overhanging roof, emulating a porch, allowed passengers to enjoy views of passing scenery. Unfortunately, parlor-observation cars had waned in popularity. "We were told that there wasn't such a thing; that those cars just went out with bustles [and] were not available," said Abell. She thought it was essential, and so did the president, who helped with the search.

The LBJ Special had featured a rear car with a platform. Not only could it be festively decorated and eye-catching, the setup was also practical for whistle-stopping. To save time, the back platform doubled as a stage, and speeches could be made without ever leaving the train. It was also ideal for adding to the spectacle. A consummate showman, Johnson would exit the parlor car, dramatically drawing back a dark blue curtain as he stepped onto the platform in view of the audience.

After much searching and scouring railyards, a once-grand railway car called the Queen Mary was located and rescued from a junk heap in Pennsylvania. Abell set about transforming the derelict parlor-observation car, which was thirty-four years old and in shambles, into a showpiece. The back platform was designed and equipped by a renowned Washington, DC, architect. Along with lighting and sound equipment and new red, white, and blue decor, a white drumhead was attached to the back brass railing with the words LADY BIRD SPECIAL on it, the handiwork of the White House calligrapher.

Inside, the polished-up hospitality car, "the equivalent of a rolling LBJ Ranch," served as a reception room and waiting area for the guests being introduced on the platform at each stop. The walls and ceiling were painted light blue, seats were covered in bright red and blue cotton fabric by the White House upholsterer, and photos of the Johnson family were displayed on the walls. VIPs could scrawl notes on specially branded postcards—"Sent from the Lady Bird Special"—and post them from the car's mailbox. Added to the advance men's duties was arranging for blocks of ice to be loaded onto the base of the un-air-conditioned train. This method cooled down the hospitality car, which at any one time had about sixty people in it.

Adjacent to the hospitality car were living and working quarters for Lady Bird and her daughters, twenty-year-old Lynda and seventeen-year-old Luci, who each rode along for two days of the trip. There was an office with a television set, an electric typewriter, and a telephone with a direct line to the White House; seating and dining areas; two bedrooms; a bathroom in rose and beige (with the only bathtub on the train); and a galley kitchen where a chef and his assistant prepared meals for the First Lady and her guests.

Next came Car #3, a Pullman six-bedroom lounge car with office space for Carpenter, Abell, and lead advance man Joe Moran. In another chamber, Secret Service personnel and railroad protective agents set up facilities for air and ground communications.

One of the most highly trafficked areas on the train was Car #3's lounge, which was used to receive the rotating roster of people who were invited to ride the train. In what was itself a feat of organization, more than a thousand short-term guests rode the Lady Bird Special and required accommodating. As had been done on the LBJ Special, they typically boarded one stop before reaching their home area and exited at their stop when they were introduced on the back platform.

A reporter noted, "Speech-making was only half the campaign story aboard the 'Lady Bird Special.'" Politicking was done while the train was in motion. Depending on the guest, they were given hard-hitting political talk by Democratic Party leaders or a gentler reminder that the president needed their support. As one local delegation was told in between stops, "President Johnson is willing to give you and the nation four years out of his life. He's asking you only for four weeks of your time to work for him and his election on November 3rd."

Guests were then escorted in small groups to Car #2 to speak with Lady Bird and have a photo taken with her. Finally, it was on to the hospitality car for more socializing and political talk before being introduced at their home stop.

A surefire way to ensure coverage for the whistle-stop tour was to bring the media along for the ride. The next two and a half cars were used by reporters, photographers, and television crews. The rolling press rooms were equipped with typewriters, a Western Union filing desk, a news release desk, and tape recorder outlets for recording the speeches being given on the back platform, and an Air Express representative was on hand to ship film—all of which permitted coverage of events from the train.

Additional cars housed other members of the Lady Bird Special's support team, including fifteen "Ladies for Lyndon" who acted as hostesses on the train and greeted crowds at each stop. An East Wing memo to the hostesses noted that they were asked to participate in the campaign train "not for their looks (though it might appear that way), but because all can double in brass—type, telephone, run errands, be charming and useful, and not be thin-skinned." In addition, all fifteen women were Southern born. "This campaign needed to go into the South, and it needed to go in as gracious a way as it could," said Scooter

Miller, who headed up the hostesses. "That was our country, and we wanted to go."

The Ladies for Lyndon were women who had worked in congressional offices and for the White House and in the State Department. One was Lady Bird's second cousin, a recent college graduate and the sole single woman in the group. Another currently served as secretary to the Democratic National Committee, the first woman to do so. Also among their ranks were women who, before marrying, were a geologist, a high school history and government teacher, and an assistant newspaper editor, and all of whom were active in civic and political endeavors. Barbara Howar had two reasons for signing on for hostess duties: campaigning for Johnson, "the best available bet to save the country from Goldwater conservatism," and being spared from "domestic boredom."

Two dining cars on the Lady Bird Special remained open continuously throughout the trip. Cooks, stewards, and waiters worked in shifts serving up dishes like Luci's Brownies; Whistling Dixie Fried Shrimp; the Photographer's Special "Say Cheese" Plate; Fried Half Spring Chicken, A La Landslide; and the LBJ Steak Platter, which could be ordered "raring-to-go," "middle of the road," or "all-the-way."

Nine cars were used as sleeping quarters for the Lady Bird Special support team, members of the press, the kitchen staff, security operatives, and railroad personnel and to store the campaign items handed out at each stop. The two cars directly behind the engine were occupied by U.S. Army command units to provide an added layer of security for the train and its passengers.

Finally, the groundwork for the trip was laid and the colorful train outfitted, loaded, and ready to leave the depot. That October morning in Union Station, the locomotive engines roared to life. A conductor gave the final call for boarding the Lady Bird Special. The sound of a whistle pierced the air, and the train began moving down the tracks. The "most unusual whistle-stop campaign in political history" had begun.

2

Swinging into Action

Tuesday, October 6, 1964
Alexandria, Virginia, 7:00 a.m.

A carnival-like atmosphere accompanied the Lady Bird Special's arrival in Alexandria. Some 8,000 people, who had waited nearly an hour in the chilly morning air, lined the tracks near the depot in the city's Old Town section, cheering loudly and waving flags and banners. Three area high school bands struck up a robust rendition of "The Yellow Rose of Texas."

The few Goldwater supporters in attendance, some brandishing derogatory Johnson signs or ones lauding their candidate, were vastly outnumbered by the friendly, enthusiastic crowd. Students were given permission to skip school to attend the trackside rally, which was seen as "an exercise in citizenship," said an education official. If Republicans were to plan a similar whistle-stop in Alexandria, he added, "we'll try to do the same for them."

The Ladies for Lyndon hostesses appeared with a flourish on the platform. Attired in matching, festively patriotic garb—blue shirtwaist dresses embroidered with LBJ and accented with a red-and-white belt, white gloves, navy blue shoes, and white roll-brimmed hats with a blue and red ribbon—they fanned out picturesquely before hastening down the steps. Carrying baskets branded with LBJ FOR THE USA, they circulated among the crowd, pressing buttons, matchbooks, peppermint taffy with CHOOSE LYNDON wrappers, and other campaign swag into eager hands.

Spectators waved LADY BIRD and LYNDON pennants and donned paper engineer caps, while the children present energetically tooted yellow plastic train whistles. Throughout the trip, people at each stop volunteered to be "Johnson Girls" and assist the Lady Bird Special crew. Here in Alexandria, 150 local women and teenagers, dressed in dark blue clothing and campaign hats, contributed by handing out political literature and balloons.

Print, television, and radio reporters assembled in a roped-off area in front of the Lady Bird Special's parlor-observation car. Reporters furiously scribbled notes, photographers captured images, bulbs flashing, and cameramen recorded footage of the events. On the platform, a master of ceremonies began amping up the crowd even further.

But beneath all "the hoopla" and excitement of the colorful campaign train "was as serious a motive as ever stirred the most calculating of politicians," noted Arthur Edson, an Associated Press correspondent who rode the Lady Bird Special. "Never before has the wife of a president gone out so unabashedly hunting votes for her husband." The South was threatening to tip over to Goldwater, "and Lady Bird was out to keep it loyally Democratic."

That morning, the First Lady and the president were up before dawn after hosting a state dinner the night before for the visiting Philippine president and his wife. Together they boarded the Lady

Bird Special at Union Station, along with their daughter Lynda, and traveled to Alexandria for the whistle-stop tour's kickoff.

The First Lady stood poised at the podium in front of the microphones with the president beside her, beaming and nodding agreement as she spoke, and Lynda on the platform with them.

"Sunshine and lots of friends, what could be a better way to start the whistle-stop—right here in Alexandria, in view of the monument to one of your first and foremost citizens, George Washington," said Lady Bird.

She implored Northern Virginians to "vote for both Johnsons" appearing on the platform. Sharing the spotlight with the presidential couple was Augustus C. Johnson, the district's underdog Democratic candidate for Congress. (BIND UP THE NATION'S WOUNDS WITH JOHNSON & JOHNSON read some placards.)

State and local Democratic candidates running for office were given a boost at every stop as the Lady Bird Special wended its way to New Orleans. In addition, the campaign train was intended to strengthen party unity and to show support for Democratic politicians weathering the storm of hostility and dissatisfaction about the passage of the Civil Rights Act.

Two days before the whistle-stop tour was announced to the press in mid-September, Lady Bird made courtesy calls to the governors and senators, all of whom were Democrats, in the states where she would travel and invited them to participate. She spent several hours placing and receiving telephone calls as the White House switchboard operators tracked down the men wherever they happened to be at the time.

Lady Bird was unsure of the reactions she would get since all sixteen senators on the calling list had voted against the recent Civil Rights Act, and some of them had done the filibustering. "I don't think I'll have many takers," she confided to Liz Carpenter. "But it's only polite to ask."

The men's varied responses reflected the shift taking place in the Southern political landscape, one that was largely cemented during the 1964 election. Some enthusiastically accepted Lady Bird's invitation to participate in the campaign train some agreed after calculating the political risk, others dodged the invitation, and some outright refused.

"The conversations [went] something like this," Carpenter recalled. Lady Bird led with, "Governor, I'm thinking about coming down and campaigning in your state and I'd love your advice." In fact, plans were already in place, and they didn't need advice, but Lady Bird knew how best to play her hand.

"They loved to give advice," Carpenter added. The First Lady would listen for a long while as they told her "how tough things were for the Democrats. They would have been fine if Lyndon hadn't been so gol-darned hardheaded about the Civil Rights Act."

Lady Bird responded, "Well, I know there is a long education process that is necessary, but I was thinking about coming through on a whistle-stop train. You see, I don't want the South to be overlooked in this campaign. And we have lots of good friends and kinfolks there." Then she would take a deep breath and say, "I was hoping that you and your wife would join us and ride the whistle-stop through your state."

The first governor she called, Virginia's Albertis S. Harrison Jr., accepted the invitation and said that he and his wife would be cochairs for their state. Senator Harry Byrd respectfully declined, citing the recent death of his wife, although in actuality he was a staunch segregationist. (Byrd single-handedly filibustered against the 1964 Civil Rights Act for fourteen hours and thirteen minutes.) Virginia's other senator, A. Willis Robertson, told the First Lady he would be antelope hunting in Montana. "A lovely place, and I'm sure he'll have fun," she noted in her diary.

North Carolina's politicians were more amenable. The governor, Terry Sanford, along with senators Sam Ervin and Everett Jordan, were delighted to join the campaign train and would be accompanied by their spouses. Lady Bird was unable to reach Dan K. Moore, a "somewhat hostile fellow Democratic" and the party's gubernatorial candidate, or his wife, Jeanelle, and she resolved to track them down and issue the invitation.

South Carolina's governor, Donald Russell, was on board and would act as co-chair through the state with his wife, Virginia. The day before Lady Bird's call, he publicly stated his support for the president. At a news conference, he called Johnson the "best qualified and most competent man for the presidency" due to his "breadth of vision."

Calls to South Carolina's senators yielded mixed results. The senior senator, Olin Johnston, enthusiastically accepted the invitation on behalf of himself and his wife and suggested that his daughters, "mighty good hard-working Democrats," take part as well. Johnston was avidly campaigning for the Johnson-Humphrey ticket, telling the media, "I'm all out for President Johnson." He declared that he would be "derelict in my duty" if he did not support the president.

The opposite reaction came from Senator Strom Thurmond. He politely refused the First Lady's invitation due to a difference of opinion on the president's policies. When Thurmond added that he had a basic decision to make soon, Lady Bird replied that she hoped he wouldn't do anything rash. Reflecting on the call in her diary, she astutely surmised, "The decision could be concerned with any one of several things—the old road of Dixiecrat, bolting the party in some fashion, or complete severance with the Democrats and going over to the Republicans." Five days later, Thurmond announced his defection to the Republican Party in a fifteen-minute television broadcast that aired in eight Southern states. He began earnestly campaigning for Goldwater soon after. Capitol Hill sources later leaked to the press details about Thurmond's conversation with Lady Bird in an attempt to portray his refusal of the invitation as a setback for the Lady Bird Special.

After Thurmond's brush-off, Lady Bird proceeded to forge ahead with the courtesy calls. "So here we go, marching through Georgia!" Senator Richard Russell, President Johnson's friend and former mentor, offered some advice on where to go but declined to ride the train. Lady Bird's observation: "His differences with Lyndon on Civil Rights are those of a man ten years older and deeply imbedded in the mores of his state." Russell was the senator who started the filibuster of the Civil Rights Act of 1964, after cautioning Johnson not to press for the legislation. "It's going to cost you the South and cost you the election," said Russell. Johnson replied, "If that's the price I've got to pay, I'll pay it gladly."

Next on Lady Bird's calling list was Georgia's Senator Herman Talmadge, who accepted the invitation with a caveat: he would participate if his schedule permitted. "That is an elastic and dependable phrase," noted Lady Bird. The senator did say that his wife, Betty, however, planned to "ride the train all the way." Talmadge later admitted that he never had any intention of taking part and that he expected the Lady Bird Special would be "booed from one end of the state to the other."

The Georgia calls ended on a high note. Lady Bird received an affirmative answer from Betty Foy Sanders, who would be pleased to ride the train and act as state co-chair with her husband, Governor Carl Sanders. The couple were "among our strongest friends on the whole route," said Lady Bird. Sanders was another governor who actively campaigned for President Johnson.

Next it was on to Florida. Senator Spessard Holland, engaged in a reelection race of his own, half-heartedly committed to meeting the Lady Bird Special in Tallahassee. Senator George Smathers, on the other hand, would travel with the Lady Bird Special through the state, as would his wife, Rosemary. (Although Smathers voted against the Civil Rights Act of 1964, he was a behind-the-scenes operator, privately strategizing with President Johnson and helping pave the way for the bill's passage.)

Lady Bird wasn't the only one in the White House trying to reach Farris Bryant, Florida's governor. She asked to put the call through, to which a switchboard operator responded, "But I'm already trying to get Governor Bryant for the President." When Lady Bird finally got Governor Bryant on the line, she found that he and his wife, Julia, "were among the most available and interested." In the 1960 election, Bryant, who ran as a segregationist but espoused nonviolence, had declined to campaign for Kennedy. When the Civil Rights Act of 1964 became law, he urged Floridians to accept it, and he oversaw the state's integration of schools and other public institutions.

Lady Bird figured there was no use in calling George Wallace, the governor of Alabama, and doubted "it would even be courteous to do so." Wallace was the nation's most infamous segregationist and had unsuccessfully challenged Lyndon for the presidential nomination in the Democratic primaries. In Wallace's 1963 gubernatorial inauguration speech, he declared, "I say segregation now, segregation tomorrow, segregation forever." Painfully for Lady Bird, Alabama was the state with which she had "the most personal bonds," and it was also the one "most adamantly against us." The state was so anti-Johnson that he was not listed on the election ballot.

Lady Bird did call Alabama's senators. John Sparkman, sounding as if he were hedging his bets, said he would be "mighty glad" to join the campaign train unless Congress were in session—in which case his wife would stand in for him. Senator Lister Hill, who was in the hospital, promised to be there if his health permitted.

Next up was Mississippi, another ardently anti-Johnson state. Senator John Stennis, who was involved in a difficult reelection campaign, declined Lady Bird's invitation with the excuse that "he thought he could do more good in a different way." Even the ace White House switchboard operators couldn't reach Senator James Eastland, and as for Governor Paul Johnson, Lady Bird concluded there was no need to call him either. Two days earlier, at the state Democratic convention, the governor urged fellow Mississippians to defeat the Johnson-Humphrey ticket, which he called "the most dangerous political combination in the history of this nation."

Responses from the Louisiana politicians played out along the same lines. Governor John McKeithen did not want to be publicly associated with the campaign train but assured Lady Bird that he was "working for the Democrats, you understand." Lady Bird "hung up with the feeling that he faced a formidable and angry populace and was not about to take them on in the outspoken bulldog way of an Olin Johnston." As for the state's senators, Allen Ellender said he would be happy to board the train and ride into New Orleans. Russell Long, however, was in Tokyo and couldn't be reached.

By the time of the 1964 presidential election, the long-dominant Democratic Party in the South—whose ranks ranged from liberal to conservative—was ready to splinter. Nationally, the Democratic Party had been moving further left of center for decades, spurred by Franklin D. Roosevelt's New Deal legislation in the 1930s, Harry Truman's integration of the military in 1948, and Kennedy's presentation of a civil rights bill in Congress before his death. The final straw for Southerners opposed to integration was the passage of the Civil Rights Act of 1964. After the bill's signing, President Johnson remarked to an aide, "I think we just delivered the South to the Republican party for a long time to come."

That October morning in Alexandria, the First Lady, clad in a red wool dress and matching jacket, addressed head-on the backlash toward her husband and expressed their mutual support for the Civil Rights Act. "The voice was soft, but the words were strong," said Carpenter.

Lady Bird shared with the audience her reasons for making the whistle-stop. "I wanted to make this trip because I am proud of the South, and I am proud that I am part of the South," she told the audience. She shared her love of the South's gentility and courtesy, its old customs and traditions like keeping up with your kinfolk and long Sunday dinners after church.

Lady Bird continued, "I am even more proud of the new South, the glistening new skylines of the cities, the spirit of growth, the signs of prosperity, both in the factory and on the farm. There are so many advances in the South, in its economy, in its interest in the arts, in its progress in education."

She called out those who derided the South and Southerners. Echoing what she had told the advance team, she said, "I share the irritation when unthinking people make snide jokes about the South as if the history and tradition of our region could be dismissed with ridicule. None of this is right. None of this is good for the future of our country. We must search for the ties that bind us together, not settle for the tensions that divide us."

She quoted Robert E. Lee, the Confederate general, who after the Civil War advised a woman angered that her two sons wanted to go north to school: "Abandon all these local animosities and make your sons Americans."

Lady Bird continued, "I wanted to tell you from Alexandria to New Orleans that to this President and his wife the South is a respected and valued and beloved part of this country."

She addressed the divisiveness of the Civil Rights Act and the need for the nation to come together, saying, "We are a nation of laws, not men. And our greatness is our ability to adjust to the national consensus. The law to assure equal rights," which was passed in Congress with bipartisan support, "has been received by the South for the most part in a way that is a great credit to local leadership, to mayors and ministers, to white citizens and Negro leaders, to all the Mr. and Mrs. John Citizens who live in our communities. This convinces me of something I have always believed, that there is in the Southland more love than hate."

Lady Bird again steered her speech to address the thorniest

campaign issue: "I think we all understand that the hard duty of assuring equal rights and constitutional rights to all Americans falls not only on the President of the United States, but upon all who love this land." After the enthusiastic applause died down, she added, "I am sure we will rise to that duty."

The First Lady concluded her remarks by saying, "To me, as to you, the South is not a place of geography but a place of the heart. And so it is with great joy that I undertake what for me is, in every sense, a journey of the heart."

She then yielded the podium to "the speaker in my family, my husband and the President of the United States."

"Ladies and gentlemen, boys and girls," said the president, "Alexandria has been chosen as the first stop for one of the greatest campaigners in America, and I am very proud to announce that I am her husband."

Lady Bird brought to the role of First Lady more experience in national political life than anyone who preceded her. She was introduced to the Washington political scene after marrying Lyndon in 1934, when she had just turned twenty-two. Johnson was then the top aide to Richard Kleberg, a U.S. congressman from Texas. Kleberg left the day-to-day running of his congressional office to Johnson, whose drive and diligence got him noticed on Capitol Hill. One of those Johnson impressed was President Franklin D. Roosevelt, who the next year appointed him the Texas-based director of the National Youth Administration, a New Deal initiative to assist young Americans with finding employment during the Great Depression.

In 1937, Johnson launched his first bid for office after the U.S. congressman in his home district, which included Austin and the rural Hill Country where he grew up, died suddenly of a heart attack. With just two months until the special election to fill the congressional seat, he needed funds immediately to launch a campaign against eight other, more well-known contenders.

SWINGING INTO ACTION

Lady Bird consulted Lyndon's mentor, Alvin J. Wirtz, a veteran Texas politician, and asked what her husband's chances were of winning the seat. The response—slim but viable—was good enough for Lady Bird. She went toe-to-toe with her father to get a $10,000 advance on an inheritance from her late mother, and she staked her twenty-eight-year-old husband's run for Congress.

Even Lyndon Johnson's seasoned opponents were no match for his resolve and powerhouse energy. He grabbed headlines by announcing his candidacy first, strategically campaigned as a steadfast supporter of Roosevelt and the New Deal, and—with Austin largely dominated by one of his rivals—ceaselessly canvassed the small towns in every county in the district. Two days before the election, he collapsed at a campaign event and underwent emergency surgery for acute appendicitis. On election day, from his hospital bed, he asked Lady Bird to work the phones to get out the vote and drive people to the polls, helping him clinch an upset victory.

Back in Washington, Lady Bird later faced what she described as a "year of decision" following the United States' entry into World War II. On December 8, 1941, one day after the attack on Pearl Harbor, Johnson, a member of the Naval Reserve, asked for active duty. In her husband's absence, Lady Bird decided to run his congressional office and "keep the line of contact" with the people of his district. Sometimes those constituents would come by Johnson's Capitol Hill office to meet their hometown representative when they were in Washington. One day, a recent college graduate who had just arrived in the city stopped into the office. Congressman Johnson was in the South Pacific, "but there to meet you and shake hands with you was his wife," recalled Liz Carpenter. "She made you immediately feel welcome."

Lady Bird relished the empowering experience of running the congressional office for several months. "I have a full-time job!" she wrote to a friend. The office was "so stimulating and interesting" that she "graduated" herself from business school, she relayed in another letter. Lady Bird and the staff worked long and hard to "keep up Lyndon's standards." She arrived around eight thirty every morning and stayed "until Lyndon Johnson quitting time—which is when everything is done." The office received between sixty and eighty letters daily, most of which were answered the same day and always within twenty-four hours. She handled everything from dealing with the impact of rationing in the district and imparting war news to congratulating newlyweds and graduates.

Lady Bird recalled, "Out of the cauldron of that war year, I received two powerful gifts." One was the knowledge and reassurance that she could "do a job" and that she could make a living for herself. The next year, to allay the uncertainties of relying on a politician's salary, she used inheritance money to buy a debt-ridden Austin radio station. After six months of relentless effort, the station yielded a profit of $18, and from there she built a multimillion-dollar radio and television enterprise.

The second gift Lady Bird received during the "year of decision" was "a keener understanding of what went to make up my husband's life in Congress." Her role as a congressional wife expanded after Johnson was elected to the U.S. Senate and later when he became minority and then majority leader. "She fell in love with the Senate and became deeply involved with what he was doing," said Carpenter. It was a matter of pride for Johnson that his wife, as he did, knew the Senate "like a book." Lady Bird frequently went to the Senate gallery and observed debates, and at home she listened to Speaker of the House Sam Rayburn and her husband discuss the politics of passing legislation. "She has had the best teacher in the world in government, in really practical government," said Carpenter. "She has probably heard more conversations on close votes and how you get them and the realisms of politics. Now, she has enjoyed this. She has learned by it, and she has become awfully good at it."

When Lyndon first began campaigning for office, Lady Bird

stayed mostly behind the scenes or "just went along and said 'howdy' to the voters." That changed dramatically when Johnson ran for the U.S. Senate in 1948. During a hotly contested primary runoff, Lady Bird "swung into action." She made speeches to women's groups across the state, worked the phones, and participated in strategy sessions. Her involvement in the campaign led a newspaper to declare her an "able vote-getter." Johnson won the primary by eighty-seven votes and went on to secure the Senate seat.

Early in the 1960 election, John Kennedy called the LBJ Ranch in Texas, not for his running mate but for Lady Bird. As Lady Bird and Lyndon listened on separate telephones, Kennedy explained that his wife, Jackie, wanted to limit her campaign involvement since she was pregnant and worried about a miscarriage. Instead, would Lady Bird take the lead in voter outreach to women?

"Certainly," Lady Bird replied. She campaigned extensively, both on her own and with Lyndon, garnering such headlines as "Lady Bird Shows Color and Wit" and "Johnson's Biggest Booster—Lady Bird Brightens Rough Campaign Road." Her speeches, given everywhere from the observation car of the LBJ Special to the steps of Borough Hall in Queens, New York, were lauded as "sheer magic" by the press. "There was a sly, devastating emotional wallop in her voice and sentiments." The Kennedy-Johnson ticket won Texas with a razor-thin margin. On election night, Bobby Kennedy, the new president-elect's brother and campaign manager, shouted, "Lady Bird has carried Texas!"

As the vice president's wife, Lady Bird's goal was "helping Lyndon all that I can, helping Mrs. Kennedy whenever she needs me, and becoming a more alive me." She had a higher profile and more involved role than was typical for a Second Lady, frequently attending functions in place of Jackie Kennedy, who had less of an inclination for politics. Lady Bird earned a reputation as "Washington's No. 1 pinch hitter." When needed, she also stood in for Lyndon, President Kennedy, and other administration members, attending speaking engagements or receiving official guests, sometimes on short notice. Said a White House aide, "Lady Bird is invaluable to us."

By the time Johnson became president, Lady Bird was his most trusted political and personal adviser. And, as she had proven, an extremely effective one. When it came time to campaign for his reelection in 1964, there was no question that she could handle an unprecedented whistle-stop tour into political enemy territory.

"Somebody else can have Madison Avenue. I'll take Bird," Johnson once quipped. Now, the Lady Bird Special was giving him a high-profile platform more valuable than any advertising campaign.

The president took his turn at the podium in Alexandria, imploring the audience to contribute their time, talents, and energy to the Johnson-Humphrey ticket. "From now until election day, we are going to talk about the problems of the future, for this should be a campaign in which we explore the different ways to meet the new challenges of America in the turbulent sixties," he said. Once that victory was secured, the country could "get on with the tangible and difficult work of this fast-moving decade that we live in."

Johnson also told the audience that he and Lady Bird planned to meet up that night in Raleigh, NC, and again three days later at the end of the line—if he could catch up with her, a remark that evoked laughs. "I plan to use the jet Air Force One to try to meet her in New Orleans," he said. "But Lady Bird on her train will probably beat me there. She always does."

In Alexandria, the president saw his wife's train leave the depot. He then strode toward a waiting helicopter, shaking hands with people on both sides of the tracks along the way. By the time he was whisked back to the White House, the Lady Bird Special was well underway on what would be, in the words of a reporter on board, "four astonishing days."

3

Never Stand on the Sidelines

Tuesday, October 6, 1964
Fredericksburg, Virginia, 8:26 a.m.

Around the time the Lady Bird Special was due to arrive at its next stop in Fredericksburg, the waiting crowd spied the lead engine as it came into view across a railroad bridge. "Here she comes," voices roared. But as the engine chugged closer and passed the depot, the enthusiasm quickly deflated when they saw there was only one nondescript car attached to it.

The first-ever visit of a First Lady to Fredericksburg was marked by the heavy security that would be repeated at every stop. All the city's officers were on duty, along with state police, college policemen, and sheriffs and deputies from surrounding communities. Shortly before the train was due to arrive, a Fredericksburg police lieutenant spotted two ladders poking up above the roofline of a house on a street facing the train depot and, as a precaution, had them removed.

A contingent of Secret Service personnel had been in town for several days to give the area a final check and to brief local law enforcement on their duties. At the rally, they kept a close eye on spectators and rigorously checked the credentials of anyone approaching the area where the train would stop. Two helicopters flew overhead, scanning for anything that looked amiss and to keep unauthorized aircraft from approaching the area. A third helicopter, a jungle-green U.S. Marine Corps chopper, hovered above the Lady Bird Special as it chugged down the tracks. All other rail traffic in and out of Fredericksburg was suspended until after the Lady Bird Special departed and the crowds dispersed. The only time security had been tighter was when President Franklin D. Roosevelt's private train passed through during World War II.

When the Lady Bird Special showed up fifteen minutes after the initial excitement and confusion caused by the decoy engine, it was hard to miss. Five miles outside town, music began blaring from the train's elaborate loudspeaker system, alternating between "Happy Days Are Here Again" and "Hello, Lyndon!" The latter song was adapted into a campaign ditty by composer Jerry Herman from the title tune of his Broadway musical *Hello, Dolly!*. The crowd's enthusiasm revived, and even the sign-carrying Goldwater supporters "looked fairly cheerful about the whole thing."

Once the train came to a stop and the Ladies for Lyndon had begun their work, one of the traveling troupe's masters of ceremonies took charge. "I'm Luther Hodges of North Carolina, Democrat all the way through," he boomed into the microphones on the back platform. Hodges was taking time off from his day job as the U.S. secretary of commerce to ride the campaign train.

The cold, windy weather that began the morning in Alexandria had given way to brighter skies. "The sun of the commonwealth shines brightly today on this train," said Lieutenant Governor Mills Godwin, currently the ranking Virginian riding along, before introducing the "First Lady of the Land."

Lady Bird told the audience how familiar she was with Fredericksburg, a town steeped in history. She reminisced about "happy summer weekends driving over the countryside" to get there during the years her husband spent in Congress.

Lady Bird recalled visiting "elegant Kenmore," a Georgian-style brick mansion built in the 1770s by George Washington's sister Betty and her husband, Fielding Lewis. At Kenmore, which opened as a museum in 1925, she sampled its famous gingerbread made from the private recipe of George Washington's mother. She stopped by Mary Washington's home (purchased for her by her son in 1772), "where you feel the presence of America's beginnings," and walked past James Monroe's law office.

Every speech Lady Bird gave during the whistle-stop tour was customized. While she touched on many of the same points throughout the trip and routinely emphasized her husband's vast experience in political office, her speeches were tailored for each stop. She immediately established a rapport with the audience by referencing a local connection or anecdote, a technique that President Johnson, considered a masterful campaigner, used to great effect in his speeches.

More than forty speeches had to be carefully crafted before the Lady Bird Special set out. In early September, a team of six women assembled to help Lady Bird with researching and drafting the speeches, which needed to include the unique details on the towns and areas where the train would stop. During their initial planning meeting, Lady Bird also conveyed her "general beliefs and what I wanted to say, the impression I wanted to leave behind."

To prepare for the tour, Lady Bird culled information from library books and received research compiled by personnel at the National Geographic Society. She read briefing books prepared by the advance teams. She talked to Congress members and their wives to ask advice and to pick their brains about the states, cities, and towns on the whistle-stop route, some of which she had previously visited. She received extensive data on economic gains and conditions in the South since 1960, overall and state by state, concerning per capita personal income, employment, and new industrial development and a summary of the impact that Barry Goldwater's proposal to cut off farm price supports in the South might have.

"Mrs. Johnson is a great one to weigh every word," said Liz Carpenter, "and she doesn't want to say anything that isn't her own belief."

The extensive preparation for the whistle-stop tour was typical of Lady Bird. Before every state visit at the White House, she diligently studied the briefing papers and talking points the State Department compiled for the president. "She wanted to learn, and she wanted to be a more interesting dinner partner for the Prime Minister, King or Shah who would be on her right for three hours or more at a dinner," said Carpenter. Lady Bird studied maps and learned about the visiting dignitary's country—what its neighboring nations were, prominent Americans who had been there, and what topics were conversational taboos. (Once, when Lady Bird and Lyndon were away from Washington, their daughters were invited to the Kennedy White House to attend a state dinner for the president of the Sudan. Her advice to them when they called asking for guidance on deportment: "Read all you can find in the encyclopedia about the Sudan, and don't drink any of the wine at dinner.")

Lady Bird went to great lengths to ensure every guest at the White House had a memorable experience. She always remembered the excitement she felt when she attended a dinner during the Roosevelt administration in February 1941, writing about the experience in her diary:

> *Tonight, I went to my first (will it be the last and only!?!) Dinner at the White House! Everything managed with watchmaker's precision!... The dinner was in honor of the Duchess of Luxembourg and her family... After dinner the ladies and Mrs. R. (Roosevelt) went to one drawing room and*

> *the men somewhere else. We had coffee and visited and Mrs. R. moved from group to group. Then we went upstairs and saw "Philadelphia Story"—big day!!*

As First Lady, she spent long hours preparing so that she could offer more than a perfunctory hello and a handshake in the receiving line. She studied guest lists, often under the hair dryer at the beauty parlor, learning about each visitor to make that personal connection. Author Paul Horgan was delighted when she commented on his latest book, the 1920s-set novel *Everything to Live For*. Another guest, a lumber company secretary, was surprised when she was asked about a forthcoming trip to the Caribbean, which Lady Bird remembered after hearing a staff member mention it in passing.

Lady Bird's efforts to connect with audiences on the whistle-stop tour did not go unnoticed. According to a local Fredericksburg reporter, "Perhaps the most impressive part of [her] appearance was an obvious knack for saying just the right things." Another newspaper's headline acknowledged, "Lady Bird Demonstrates She Did Her Homework for Tour" and cited her fact-laden speeches. A student reporter was "very much impressed" by the First Lady's "friendliness and her calm composure" and the "surprising" local references like Kenmore's gingerbread. "This pleased her audience."

While the whistle-stop tour was still in the planning stages, Carpenter told a reporter that Lady Bird "is already beginning to worry about what she is going to say because she had rather shake hands than make speeches." When Lady Bird graduated from high school at the top of her class, she made sure she ranked third to avoid being valedictorian or salutatorian and having to speak at the commencement ceremony.

Although Lady Bird's anxiety at giving speeches never entirely abated, she worked hard to improve at it. Five years earlier, she had enrolled in a public-speaking course, learning to talk more slowly and to modulate the pitch of her voice. With continued practice and determination, she went from being so nervous at the podium her hands shook to becoming a more relaxed and effective public speaker.

Lady Bird's speaking style differed from that of the president. He was more hard-hitting and gregarious, sometimes even tossing his Stetson hat into the crowd, while she used a lighter touch. Her speech in Fredericksburg combined the laudatory, the folksy, and the erudite, working in quotes by the likes of Ralph Waldo Emerson and Thomas Jefferson while still conveying the political messages she had come to deliver.

"I do not need to tell you, who blend together so well the graciousness of the eighteenth century with the challenge[s] of the twentieth, that history is still happening—and happening to us," she told the crowd. "I admire the way the people of Fredericksburg and nearby counties are looking to future needs—and preparing to meet them in time."

Lady Bird's intent on this trip was to woo the South, beginning with Virginia, which hadn't voted Democratic in a presidential election since 1948. Observed a *Washington Post* reporter, "Democrats are putting on the strongest campaign in years to prevent Mr. Goldwater from getting the State's 12 [electoral] votes."

Lady Bird continued drawing in the Fredericksburg audience, earning the greatest applause when she referenced the Salem Church Dam, a long-sought project and a campaign issue, followed by a mention of Mary Washington College. Several hundred Mary Washington students whooped and cheered the loudest when she shouted out their school, which was founded in 1908 as a women's college. The presence of so many screaming young people led one man to remark, "You'd think the Beatles had come to town." (Beatlemania swept the United States earlier that year when the band made its first American tour.)

"And now, as we go traveling through your beautiful Virginia, I just want to leave you with this thought," said the First Lady. "In his nomination acceptance speech the President said, 'This is a dangerous and a difficult world in which we live. I promise no easy answers. But I do promise this: I pledge the firmness to defend freedom, the strength to support that firmness, and a constant, patient effort to move the world toward peace instead of war.'

"It is our privilege to choose our leader. In doing so, we make a conscious choice in shaping our personal destiny. Your own Thomas Jefferson said, 'Let the people know the facts and they will decide wisely.' History has proven him right.

"I believe in our President. And I believe in your right to choose and in your wisdom to do so wisely."

Lady Bird rounded out the program in Fredericksburg by introducing her eldest daughter, Lynda Bird. Lynda thanked the young people in the crowd "for coming out today" and put in a plug for the reelection of a Democratic Congress, saying the past session "has done more for education than any other Congress. As a college student, I want to have more Congresses like that."

A local arrangements co-chair, Etta Belle Northington, deemed the visit, which turned from the scheduled ten minutes into seventeen, "a great success." While riding on the train, she talked with Lady Bird about the difference between the 1960 campaign, prior to President Kennedy's assassination, and the current one. "I told her every step we made in our arrangements had to be cleared by a security officer," remarked Northington. "She said that was something she had learned to live with."

A ten-minute stop by a visitor doesn't usually require such tight security or so much preparation, noted a local newspaper. Northington and another area resident spearheaded the preparations for Fredericksburg. An advance man, William Durland, spent a week in town. A Washington, DC, attorney, he volunteered his time to the presidential campaign and two weeks earlier had advanced an appearance by Senator Humphrey in Kentucky. One of Lindy and Virginia's White House coordinators,

Bette McClure, also spent a week in Fredericksburg to assist with last-minute details. Of the eleven White House coordinators, she was the only one campaigning for the first time, "leaving home and family" to plunge into politics "because she believes in the responsibility of all citizens to contribute something to the aid of their party."

In addition to write-ups about the Lady Bird Special's upcoming visit, McClure's and Durland's activities generated additional publicity. One newspaper article noted that in between a coffee get-together, a luncheon, and a reception in McClure's honor, she presented to the mayor a biography, *The President's Lady*, which was autographed by Lady Bird and intended for the local library.

Etta Belle Northington deemed the visit a success, and so did the media. "Like Lyndon or not, today's stop here of the Lady Bird Special left little doubt that the President's family represents a potent campaign asset," stated the local paper. "Even hard-core Goldwater supporters were admitting that the LBJ ladies might just swing thousands of Southern votes back into the Democratic column."

As the Lady Bird Special's visit in Fredericksburg wound down, a chime sounded, signaling that it was time for the train to be on its way. "Goodbye!" shouted Lynda, waving a pennant with HELLO on one side and LYNDON on the other. As the train prepared to depart, a band started playing "Dixie." The college students and other spectators started singing the song, and Lynda joined in.

"Aren't they just lovely," said a woman wearing a paper LBJ hat and waving a Lady Bird pennant. A woman standing next to her, also decked out in Johnson campaign gear, concurred.

"Well, that does it," remarked another spectator as the train pulled out of the station. "Barry might as well forget Fredericksburg."

Ashland, Virginia, 9:23 a.m.

"This is a five-minute stop. Get off at your own risk." Liz Carpenter issued the warning to reporters as she walked through the press cars on the approach into Ashland. "If you miss the train, enroll at Randolph-Macon College."

Lady Bird felt at home in Ashland, she told the 1,500-person crowd assembled, because "some of my closest relatives are students." The audience, many of whom were college students, laughed along with her. She then struck a more serious note.

"I wish I was your age because I want to see the 1960s settle into the focus of history. I believe we are standing right on the verge of a period in man's history unsurpassed since the Renaissance as a potential for good and also, desperately enough, a potential for disruption," said the First Lady. She urged them to participate in the affairs of their communities and of the nation. "Never stand on the sidelines. When I look at the hundreds of students like this, I like to recall the words of Virginia own Thomas Jefferson: 'I like the dreams of the future better than the history of the past.'"

The Lady Bird Special's impending arrival in Ashland was front-page news, announced five days earlier in the town's weekly newspaper. The precise location where the train would stop was given, along with a roundup of other notable figures who had previously been to Ashland. Presidents Taft, Wilson, and Roosevelt had all stopped in town, and so had Katharine Hepburn. In 1938, the actress visited the area with her mother and father, whose alma mater was Randolph-Macon College.

After the Lady Bird Special's visit, additional front-page coverage of the event was accompanied by an editorial praising the behavior of the rally's attendees. "The general feeling of the community seems to be that when representatives of the White House, especially members of the First Family, and for whatever reason, travel through and stop for a visit in your community, they should be extended the warmest hospitalities," stated a newspaper editorial. On the day the First Lady was in Ashland, "with a few exceptions, Republicans and Democrats expressed friendly greetings."

The state's ranking politicians riding the train, Lieutenant Governor Godwin and Governor Albertis Harrison, who joined at the next stop in Richmond, emphasized Virginia hospitality and stressed that it should be accorded to the First Lady.

As Helen Thomas reported, "There were politicians who didn't support her husband's policies, but they couldn't ignore the First Lady and still be considered gentlemen." Another journalist agreed, saying, "For local Democratic leaders under pressure from Goldwater rooters, this is a relatively easy train to climb aboard. After all, who can criticize a Southern gentleman for giving gallant escort to a lady?"

A Goldwater-supporting columnist was asked by an acquaintance if Republicans were planning a demonstration while the Lady Bird Special was in town, he wrote in the Ashland *Herald-Progress*. He replied that he hadn't heard of any, "and out of respect for the First Lady we wouldn't approve of any."

Part of the reason a women's advance party had preceded the LBJ Special in 1960 was due to Johnson's concern about the response his representatives would receive. "In the South," Lindy Boggs recalled, "in a year when there were civil rights difficulties, the only way he could send a team out and be sure it was met with politeness was if it had women on it."

When Lady Bird finished her remarks in Ashland, she introduced the college student in her family. Lynda delivered her remarks "with the presence of an experienced campaigner, and held her poise through all the turmoil of the departure," wrote a Randolph-Macon student in the college newspaper.

Lynda had already been out on the campaign trail for weeks, including taking turns with her sister, Luci, as the guest of honor at fundraising barbecues around the country sponsored by the Young Citizens for Johnson. (The events took place on weekends, so they didn't interfere with their schooling.) The month before setting out on the Lady Bird Special, Lynda represented her father in Athens at the wedding of King Constantine of Greece and Princess Anne-Marie of Denmark.

"They were born and raised in this," said Lady Bird. She often told her daughters, "Any job you're doing for your country is entitled to all you can give it."

Lynda and Luci represented their much-in-demand mother whenever they were needed. Over one long weekend, Lynda received three different groups at the White House: nearly five hundred young Democrats of New York, one hundred high school students representing the William Randolph Hearst Foundation, and one hundred college editors from across the country.

"They do it graciously and with great aplomb," said Liz Carpenter. "I'm just sorry the Johnsons didn't have more children. A family of twelve wouldn't satisfy all the needs."

Although the Lady Bird Special was scheduled for only a four-minute stop in Ashland, it remained for ten minutes. As the train prepared to depart, the Ladies for Lyndon hostesses serenaded the crowd by singing "Hello, Lyndon!" Then the Lady Bird Special continued on its way, "leaving the air alive with the electricity of a presidential campaign."

4

The Real Value of It

Tuesday, October 6, 1964
Richmond, Virginia, 9:47 a.m.

While coming into Richmond twenty minutes after leaving Ashland, the Lady Bird Special lurched sharply. Passengers were flung "helter skelter," and others, standing in the aisles waiting to detrain, "fell like dominos." That was when riders discovered that Dr. Janet Travell was on board, as she attended to people who were shaken and bruised. The doctor remained in high demand for the remainder of the trip, with about 50 percent of the train population and some of the short-haul guests requiring medical attention at some point along the way.

Dr. Travell was the White House physician, the first woman to hold the post. She followed in her father's footsteps and became a doctor, as did her younger sister, graduating at the head of her class from Cornell University Medical College and beginning her career at a New York City hospital in the late 1920s. Dr. Travell was a pioneer in the work of charting patterns of pain in the body, and she specialized in the relief of muscle pain.

In 1955, a colleague referred a patient to Dr. Travell for treatment: John F. Kennedy, the junior U.S. senator from Massachusetts, who suffered from chronic pain in his knee and lower back. An already existing back strain was exacerbated by injuries he received as a U.S. Navy officer and PT boat commander in the Pacific during World War II.

When Kennedy appointed Dr. Travell to the top medical position at the White House in 1961, it broke with tradition. And not just because he hired a woman for the job. The appointment ruffled some feathers in Washington, especially among members of the military, from whose ranks White House physicians had been drawn since the 1920s.

President Kennedy referred to Dr. Travell as a "genius," and members of his family believed that he would never have become president if she had not restored his health.

Time magazine expressed what made Dr. Travell special in its article on her precedent-shattering appointment: "A key ingredient in any Travell prescription is her own personality. Forceful but warm, enthusiastic but eminently sane, she gives her patients some of her own confidence and that intangible touch of magic that is often better than any drug or needle."

On the Lady Bird Special, Dr. Travell was "physician, nurse, and pharmacist," on call day and night. Her small sleeping compartment doubled as a storage closet, bursting with neatly labeled boxes of supplies she brought on board. The whirlwind whistle-stop tour was not her first adventurous train ride. In 1926, newly graduated from medical school, she traveled across Europe for three days in a third-class rail car with forty other young doctors she had just met, en route to a conference. They elected her to be their mascot, christened her "Miss America," and gave her the best of the sleeping options: an overhead luggage rack that resembled a feeding trough.

"It was a good thing someone in the White House" made the decision to have Dr. Travell aboard the Lady Bird Special, noted a reporter. She "accustomed herself with ease to the needs of her new clientele." During the four-day journey, Dr. Travell "felt almost like an old time country doctor." She treated everything from high blood pressure and a laryngitis epidemic to headaches, sprained ankles, and cinders in the eyes from the locomotive ash packed onto the tracks. "And newspaper people always have ulcers," said the doctor.

One morning, as Dr. Travell walked through the train, it seemed as if every person stopped her to ask advice or to say thank you. "She's the second most important person on the trip," said Liz Carpenter, joking that the doctor prescribed more medication than she herself issued press releases. By trip's end, Dr. Travell had a new nickname: "the heroine of the Whistle-Stop tour."

After the rough ride into Richmond came what some observers said was the highlight of the Lady Bird Special's foray through Virginia: Governor Albertis Harrison climbed aboard.

Harrison's association with the Lady Bird Special made front-page news in late September after his office announced that he planned to ride the train and would be an honorary chairman. The conservative Democratic governor's overtly public support for President Johnson angered opponents of the Civil Rights Act.

"It is never pleasant to have one's illusions shattered. I am mindful of this because I [have] had such an experience," wrote a disgruntled Virginian in a letter to the *Richmond Times-Dispatch*. The occasion that so disturbed him was reading in the paper that the "supposedly conservative" governor would board the Lady Bird Special. "Incredible!" he lamented. "We were simply not prepared for this."

Harrison's announcement caused a stir since he had previously offered only a lukewarm endorsement for the Johnson-Humphrey ticket. And to the dismay of anti-Johnson Virginians, he made clear that greeting the First Lady in Richmond was more than just a perfunctorily cordial gesture.

"In President Johnson, we have one whom we have known and with whom we have worked for many years in an atmosphere of friendliness and understanding," Governor Harrison told an enthusiastic Richmond crowd while speaking on the back platform of the Lady Bird Special. "His reelection will be our best assurance of continued open lines of communication on problems of mutual concern and matters of national import."

Governor Harrison "endorsed the President flat-out," reported the *Richmond Times-Dispatch*.

Liz Carpenter's media strategy was working.

The paper's coverage of the Lady Bird Special began on September 14, the day after the White House released the announcement of the campaign train, with a front-page headline: "First Lady Starts Tour October 6." Stories continued in the weeks leading up to the train's arrival, from the efforts of local organizers and details on Lady Bird's wardrobe to presidential election poll results indicating that although Virginia was "firmly in the GOP column," the Lady Bird Special "could swing votes to LBJ—no question about it."

Coverage increased significantly as the occasion drew closer. The day before Lady Bird's appearance, the paper reminded readers "'Lady Bird Special' Is on the Way." Included was a hand-drawn map showing where the train would stop, instructions on how best to approach the area, and an outline of the schedule of events.

The day of the train's arrival, there was another front-page mention. "The 'Lady Bird Special,' a 19-car railroad groundling without wings but with a lot of red, white and blue feathers, will make an eight-hour swoop across Virginia today in quest of votes for President Johnson." Governor Harrison received a prominent plug too as the one who would lead the local dignitaries greeting the train in Richmond.

The *Times-Dispatch*'s heaviest coverage came the next day with reports of the Lady Bird Special, the speeches, and the festivities splashed across the front page. A large photograph of the First Lady and Lynda addressing the crowd in Richmond appeared just beneath the masthead, along with four articles about the campaign train and another about a speech President Johnson delivered in Raleigh later that night. Altogether, that day's issue included nine separate articles related to the Lady Bird Special, including a full page devoted to photographs and commentary. (One negative article referred to it as the "train to socialism.")

"Spreading Southern accents and Dixieland music wherever it goes," the Lady Bird Special "is a big rolling symbol of an intense but strictly soft-sell effort to hold the South for a Southern-born President," reported Charles McDowell Jr., one of several *Times-Dispatch* reporters aboard the train. "Nobody misses the point that this is Lyndon B. Johnson's train, and he is aboard in spirit."

McDowell and other male colleagues reported on the political angles associated with the Lady Bird Special. Alongside their front-page coverage the day after the train's arrival was a callout box, "Today in Politics," listing other not-to-miss stories in that day's issue. The second item promised readers "A woman's view of Mrs. Lyndon Johnson as a campaigner." The article, written by Estelle Jackson, appeared in the *Times-Dispatch*'s "women's pages," which was where women journalists were still largely relegated to working. (At the time, only one woman, a theater writer and critic, worked in the *Times-Dispatch*'s newsroom.)

In the late nineteenth century, publishers wanted to attract women readers and profit from the advertising revenue that came with them. They hired women to report on society news and community projects and to write about fashion, recipes, homemaking, child-rearing, and other topics assumed to be of interest to women. Since it was challenging for these journalists to break out beyond the women's pages, some started covering hard news topics and other empowering stories from the "woman's angle." Estelle Jackson reported on the Equal Pay Act; a woman race car driver, a gender-busting sensation in 1964; and two women pioneers in the pharmaceutical industry.

In Jackson's article about the Lady Bird Special, she described in detail the First Lady's hairstyle and wardrobe, down to the jewelry she wore (a triple strand of pearls, a jeweled donkey pin, and a plain gold bangle). She also weaved in political points. Reporting on the Alexandria stop, she relayed that the First Lady "garnered cheers when she called the South 'a respected and valued and beloved part of the country,' when she said the President has 'always felt that problems are there to be solved, not simply deplored,' and when she said that Americans will 'rise to that duty' of assuring 'equal and constitutional rights to all Americans.'" When describing Lady Bird's rolling quarters to readers, she was the one who observed that "speech-making was only half the campaign story aboard" the train.

The press corps on the Lady Bird Special crossed gender lines. When Liz Carpenter announced the trip, she estimated getting fifty or so journalists on board. That assumption was quickly cast aside. "I greatly underestimated the power of a woman and a whistle-stop," said Carpenter. The press list swiftly skyrocketed to 225—the capacity of the train—and she had to "put 'a lid' on it."

Among the press corps were print, radio, and televisions reporters. Some of the women journalists who regularly covered the First Lady and often accompanied her on trips signed up. So did many veteran male political reporters "because they knew it would be a colorful political story," said Carpenter. "Others came along because they are—let's face it—frightened fliers, like me. The train offered them a chance to travel in the style they liked, as well as cover a political story."

Many press members were aboard the train from beginning to end. Others rode for part of the time or for a stop or two through their states. The trip received massive amounts of local coverage along the route, while reporters with the Associated Press and other wire service agencies ensured a steady stream of stories in newspapers nationwide. Newspapers were still talking about the Lady Bird Special and its impact through the election in November and beyond.

The uniqueness of the endeavor, along with some controversy along the tracks, appealed to writers and editors. "The real value of it, if you want to look at it from pure politics, is that for four days you stayed on the big news shows," said Carpenter. "You had five minutes every night—time you can't buy or afford to buy in a campaign."

The Southern-bound whistle-stop tour "was a good idea, masterly executed by Lady Bird," observed NBC correspondent Nancy Dickerson, one of the trailblazing journalists on board the train. A former schoolteacher who studied Spanish and Portuguese at the University of Wisconsin, Dickerson arrived in Washington in 1951. She worked as a registrar at Georgetown University and then as a staff assistant for the Senate Foreign Relations Committee before beginning a broadcasting career in 1954 as a producer on the CBS radio programs *The Leading Question* and *Capitol Cloakroom*. While a male hire was preferred, Dickerson's Capitol Hill connections, key for booking program guests, helped earn her the position. During her six years producing at CBS, which expanded to encompass television as well as radio, her ultimate goal was to be a correspondent. Dickerson's journalistic coups, including orchestrating an interview with camera-shy Sam Rayburn, the Speaker of the House, led to her becoming the first female news correspondent for CBS television.

Dickerson continued to break ground, including in 1960, when she became the first woman to report from the floor of a national political convention. It was an especially impressive feat in a business so entrenched in misogyny that a scathing *New York Times Magazine* article on the television industry concluded, "A woman—no matter how qualified—must be twice as good as a man to succeed." The psychiatrist who made that statement also asserted that women were part of the problem for buying into the idea that they were inferior to men.

Dickerson had no such uncertainties. In 1963, she signed on with NBC, where she was the first woman to have her own daily newscast and one of only three women who appeared regularly on network news.

Dickerson's and other television correspondents' coverage from the Lady Bird Special brought even greater awareness to the campaign train. "Often the people who came down to meet the train had been watching our progress on their home screens," said Dickerson.

In Richmond, a Goldwater stronghold, the *Times-Dispatch* reported that some 5,000 people turned out see the Lady Bird Special and give the train "a noisy, cheerful welcome." Lady Bird returned the crowd's enthusiasm "with deep-drawled flattery and promise of good years ahead—if her husband is elected."

City police and federal agents staged a tight security operation in the area around the train station. Spectators were kept behind closely supervised lines. Atop nearby buildings and bridges spanning the tracks, armed officers scanned the area through high-powered binoculars.

Photographer and high school senior Tom Rook ran up against the security machine, which was "tight as a nail." Since he didn't have a press pass, he jumped over the three-foot-high rope cordoning off the tracks. Police tossed him out, so he went to the other side of the tracks and tried again. Tenacious Tom kept trying until security personnel finally decided to let him stay. When the Lady Bird Special left the station, Tom ran after the train. "I was about nine feet from Lynda Bird and Mrs. Johnson," he said, "and I got about 20 good pictures." Two photographs he took appeared on the front page of the *Commentator*, his high school newspaper.

At the Richmond rally, Goldwater backers couldn't resist making their presence known. As Lady Bird spoke at the Richmond station, they unfurled a seven-foot-long banner, the biggest of the trip, that said FLY AWAY, LADY BIRD. HERE IN RICHMOND BARRY IS THE CAT'S MEOW. It was adorned with a cartoonish, catlike profile of the GOP candidate wearing horn-rimmed spectacles and his mouth full of feathers.

Some in the GOP similarly hoped to make a political feast out of Lady Bird's visit. The campaign manager for the district's Republican House candidate claimed the Lady Bird Special would enhance his party's chances for victory. He believed that the enthusiasm of Democratic officials who welcomed the First Lady, like Governor Harrison, showed they were participating in a "total sellout" of conservative voters. He was also the one who deemed the Lady Bird Special "the train to socialism."

The departure chime signaling the end of the Richmond rally sounded just as Lynda was about to speak. "I think I've already been cut off before I began," she said with good humor. She added a hasty plea for the young people in the audience to join her in volunteering for the Democratic ticket. She added, "Thank you all for coming out here today."

Since the train was on a tight schedule, Lynda, as the closing speaker, was repeatedly interrupted by the departure chime. This might have happened less frequently if the often long-winded men who preceded her on the platform took a page from Lady Bird's playbook. Said reporter Charles McDowell Jr., "She has a brief, direct style that more male politicians ought to emulate."

5

Time Marches On

Tuesday, October 6, 1964
Petersburg, Virginia, 10:55 a.m.

A black limousine with Goldwater-Byrd bumper stickers crept through Virginia two days ahead of the Lady Bird Special. Its occupant was Democrat-turned-Republican Strom Thurmond, who made nine speaking stops in the state, overlapping with some places that were on the Lady Bird Special's itinerary. The South Carolina senator told audiences he switched parties to reflect the wishes of his constituents and didn't see himself ever becoming a Democrat again.

"The Republican party will become the conservative party of the nation," Thurmond declared at a rally, "and I'm a conservative."

After his opening speech, he was asked by newsmen why he didn't mention the Johnson administration's new civil rights law.

"Civil right[s]," said Thurmond, "is just one facet of the big overriding issue of government power."

When Virginia's Democrats for Goldwater-Byrd organizers sought a way to try and counter the Lady Bird Special, Thurmond heeded the call. But the opposition's efforts to derail the Lady Bird Special's impact failed.

The First Lady was met with fanfare in Petersburg, Norfolk, and Suffolk, her last three stops in Virginia and where Thurmond also stumped. In Petersburg, a Goldwater hotbed, 2,500 people turned out for the Lady Bird Special while the highest estimates for the Thurmond crowd were several hundred. The low turnout for the senator was attributed to the last-minute notice of his visit and the incessant rain.

In Petersburg, Lady Bird delivered her message of unity and respect for the South. She continued the pattern of remarking on highlights in the town's past before reminding people of what was at stake in the present and in the future. "I know that Petersburg is one of Virginia's big tobacco and peanut markets and that great improvements in farm income and farm family living have come within our lifetime," she said. "It gets clearer every day what a difference better training and higher skills and the lifting of young people's sights can make in the life of a community. This state is to be congratulated when its legislators see the new opportunities in education and vote their needed support."

Dovetailing with the First Lady's themes of education and economic prosperity, train emcee Luther Hodges used his time on the podium to share his life story with the audience. He was born on a tenant tobacco farm in Virginia in 1898. A year later, after tobacco prices hit rock bottom, his father moved the family across the state line to North Carolina. As soon as Hodges and his siblings reached the age of twelve, they were sent to work in a cotton mill to help the family eke out a living. He later served in World War I, graduated from the University of North Carolina, and forged a successful career as a businessman in textile manufacturing. Hodges went on to become the governor of North Carolina, followed by "the great privilege and honor" of serving in President Johnson's cabinet.

"I think that what the Democratic Party has done for us through the years, what it has done particularly the last three and two-third years, and what it promises for the future, I can with all sincerity recommend it," said Hodges. "And I very much hope that you think along those lines."

In Petersburg, Governor Harrison continued his accolades. "I think we can agree that heaven and earth has conspired to give us this day," he told the crowd. He extended Virginia hospitality to the First Lady, a "very gracious, a very lovely, a very charming person."

Not everyone in the crowd was convinced. A woman holding a baby said she admired the First Lady "for coming down this way but her husband will have to get his votes himself. And he can't do that by trying to change people's way of living."

A Petersburg businessman in attendance at the gathering vowed he'd vote for Goldwater. "I can be a Democrat in state politics but a Republican when it come[s] to voting for the President," he said. "Our governor is on that train, but you don't see old Harry Byrd," he tittered, referring to the state's absent segregationist senator. Emboldened now, he offered an opinion on the First Lady and her whistle-stop tour. "Some of us Southerners think she should be home, like all women."

The foolish fellow uttered that statement to Gloria Negri, who decidedly did not share his outmoded views. Negri was a talented, gutsy reporter at the *Boston Globe* who once offered to sit on a park bench alone at night to lure the Boston Strangler. Negri's byline regularly appeared on the front page, and during her five years at the *Globe*, she had covered a wide range of stories, from murder trials to standing with North Carolina "freedom fighters" while reporting on a memorial for John F. Kennedy at his Massachusetts birthplace.

Unlike many of her colleagues, Negri never worked on the women's pages. She got her big break in the *Globe*'s newsroom one slow

Saturday. When word of a shooting came in, the all-male editors were confounded since the only reporter available to cover the story was Negri. They couldn't possibly subject a woman to the horrors of a grisly crime scene. Negri shut down their doubts, telling them, "Send me." She got the story.

Equally lost on the Petersburg businessman was that the train parked near him on the tracks, riding its way into history, was run by women. Luther Hodges, Hale Boggs, and other men were an important part of the endeavor, but the team's women "were calling the signals," said Liz Carpenter.

The Petersburg businessman must have missed an article published six weeks earlier in the Washington, DC-based newspaper the *Evening Star*, prominently placed with the headline "Johnson, Humphrey Wives Both Top-Notch Campaigners: First Lady Setting Trail Blazing Pace." In August, with Johnson's nomination secured at the Democratic National Convention, "the country is about to see a campaigning First Lady the likes of which it has never seen before," predicted *Star* reporter Isabelle Shelton.

"In Lady Bird Johnson, the President has an extremely capable, seemingly inexhaustible sidekick who can be expected to seek out votes in creeks and hollows, mountains and valleys, farms and city squares across the land," Shelton added.

Shelton, Negri, Nancy Dickerson, and every other woman journalist on the train had to overcome odds to be in her position. Shelton was a teenager when she decided that she would be a newspaper reporter "come hell or high water." At age twenty-five, she applied for a reporter's job at the newly founded *Chicago Sun*, which was launched in 1941 by department store magnate Marshall Field III to rival the *Chicago Tribune*. Shelton was told there were no jobs available for reporters. However, the features editor needed a secretary if she were interested.

Eager to get her foot in the door at a newspaper, Shelton accepted the secretarial job and continued lobbying her bosses for a reporting position. She finally got her chance two years later as more and more male staffers left to serve in World War II. In a letter to her brother, Shelton wrote that she had "attained her heart's desire—I'm a reporter." The manpower shortage also meant that she was given a wider range of assignments than would have been typical, including covering conventions and other political events.

In 1948, Shelton married a fellow journalist and moved to Washington, DC, where her husband worked. By that time, war veterans had returned, newsrooms were overstaffed, and she had difficulty finding a job as a reporter. She began working for the *Cincinnati Enquirer*'s Washington bureau in a position that was part reporting and part secretarial. One of her tasks was to write a weekly society column to keep the hometown apprised of their senators' and representatives' social activities. Like her friend Liz Carpenter had done, Shelton—a self-described "political junkie"—used the opportunity to learns the ways of Capitol Hill. Then, on Carpenter's advice, Shelton applied for a job on the women's pages of the Washington *Evening Star*. Like Estelle Jackson and other reporters, she worked within the confines to address broader topics.

In her "Top-Notch Campaigners" article, Shelton noted that Lady Bird was most often compared to Eleanor Roosevelt for her intrepidness, information gathering, and involvement in government. And yet even trailblazing Eleanor did not participate in the outright campaigning that Lady Bird was doing.

When Eleanor was First Lady in the 1930s and '40s, "the times had not advanced sufficiently...for a President's wife openly to solicit votes for her husband and other candidates." Although Eleanor urged people to register and vote, she avoided making partisan speeches for her husband and tried to remain in the background. "The job of a candidate's wife," Eleanor said, "is to shrink up small and be as inconspicuous as possible."

Traditionally, candidates' wives and other female family members were primarily seen and not heard. Harry Truman once discouraged his sister from attending a political meeting for fear it would give columnists "and the rest of the gossips a chance to say that my family, particularly the women of my family, are courting the limelight." He added, "So please don't go." During Truman's 1948 whistle-stop tour, his wife, Bess, and their daughter, Margaret, remained inside the parlor car while he spoke. He would then wind up the crowd by asking, "How'd ya' like to meet my wife and daughter?" Bess would come out from behind a royal blue curtain, smiling and waving as her husband referred to her as "the boss," followed by Margaret, "the one who bosses the boss." (He never acceded to Bess and Margaret's requests that he stop referring to them this way.)

Although Bess and Margaret did not campaign, their appearance turned out to be a highlight of the whistle-stops, and the sight of his family supporting the long-shot candidate is credited with helping Truman win reelection.

Lady Bird once asked Lucy George, a senator's wife, if she campaigned with her husband. "Yes, I go around with him all the time," Lucy responded. "I don't make any speeches. I just sit up on the platform to show them I don't have a club foot."

But "time marches on," concluded Shelton.

In 1960, leading up to the presidential nominations at the national party conventions, political spouses were "in the spotlight as never before," reported the Associated Press. "It's no secret that a candidate's wife is counted among his political asset[s], or liabilities. The wives are in politics whether they want to be or not."

After Kennedy and Johnson teamed up on the ticket that year, the women in their families worked on their behalf. Other than Johnson's first run for Congress in 1937, when women's campaigning was, according to Lady Bird, largely relegated to packing a husband's bag and washing his socks, she had more actively participated in all his campaigns. Kennedy's mother, Rose, and his sisters had done the same since his first congressional campaign in 1946, when they hosted house parties. During his 1952 bid for a Massachusetts Senate seat, they expanded their outreach with a series of large-scale, enormously popular teas across the state. After making a short talk, Kennedy, then a congressman, would greet guests by the thousands in a receiving line, sometimes propped up on crutches due to his back condition. Kennedy beat his opponent, the incumbent Massachusetts senator, Henry Cabot Lodge Jr., by 70,737 votes. The fact that some 70,000 people attended the teas "is, I daresay, a coincidence. But I also think that the tea parties helped," said Rose Kennedy. Lodge believed it was no coincidence, saying, "It was those damn tea parties that beat me."

In 1960, Lady Bird joined forces with various women in the Kennedy family for joint appearances. A tour she organized through Texas with Eunice Shriver, Kennedy's sister, and Ethel Kennedy, his sister-in-law, was labeled the "Tea Party Task Force" by *Time* magazine. She arranged a second tour of Texas cities later in the campaign with Ethel and Jean Kennedy Smith, another of the presidential candidate's sisters. Lady Bird insisted on greeting each guest and expected the Kennedy women to do the same. Even after spraining her ankle, she worked through the pain at one event to greet the thousands of guests in attendance. Declared a reporter, "If vivacity and vitality of the candidates' wives, sisters, mothers and friends were an issue in this Presidential campaign, the Kennedy-Johnson women would already have the election in their handbags."

When Lyndon Johnson became president in late 1963, he intended to accelerate all the progress women had made on the campaign trail and beyond. Early in his first term, he found Liz Carpenter waiting at a White House elevator and swept her into his office. He wanted her to help him end what he called "stag Government" by finding qualified women to appoint and promote. He suggested she contact Esther Peterson, director of the Women's Bureau at the Department of Labor, "and be prepared with facts and figures worthy of an audience with the Cabinet." When was the meeting taking place? The next morning at 10:00 a.m.

"We were there," said Carpenter. She and Peterson worked all night on their presentation. "We assured the Cabinet that all brains didn't come in male packages."

After Carpenter and Peterson finished presenting, President Johnson took over. He was certain there were "plenty of high-level positions available for qualified women" in their departments, Carpenter recalled him saying. He was also sure there were many women already on their payrolls "who have been waiting for promotions for a long time." The Cabinet members were ordered back to their departments and instructed to see what they could do. They were to report back to the president the next week on their progress.

"Those were the magic words—'report back to me,'" said Carpenter. "The program began to move. All over the government, personnel officers who had been ignoring their women employees for years suddenly had a wolflike gleam in their eyes. The hunt was on."

Carpenter helped lead the search, and within a few months, there were more than 150 new appointees, including ambassadorial and other positions within the State Department, and 800 promotions. Among those elevated at the State Department was Charlotte Moton Hubbard, whose promotion to deputy assistant secretary of state for public affairs made her the top-ranking Black woman in the federal government.

"Our determination to enlist women in this Administration is no sporadic, election-year objective. It will be a continuing aim not because it is politic but because it is sound," said Johnson.

The president's hiring of Geraldine Whittington was both sound and politic.

Just before 10:00 p.m. on December 23, 1963, Whittington received what she initially thought was a prank call at her Washington, DC, apartment. It was President Johnson ringing to ask her to come to the Oval Office right away. By the time she arrived an hour later, he had verified her references and shared the news with civil rights leaders Roy Wilkins and Whitney Young: He was hiring the first Black secretary to a U.S. president.

Whittington was highly qualified for the job. She had a fourteen-year government career in secretarial positions from the State Department to the White House, where she worked for presidential aides Jack Valenti and Bill Moyers. By hiring Whittington, President Johnson was also demonstrating his commitment to racial justice. (His staff later arranged for Whittington to appear on the game show *What's My Line?*, where a celebrity panel quizzed guests to determine their occupations, to make her appointment known to the public.)

President Johnson wasn't done causing a stir.

On New Year's Eve, he took three of his personal secretaries with him to a cocktail reception at the Forty Acres Club, the faculty club at the University of Texas at Austin. A group of professors had been protesting the club's segregation policy for more than a year without success. That evening, Johnson walked into the soiree with Whittington on his arm and integrated the elite institution. A law professor in attendance whispered to Bill Moyers, "Does the president know what he's doing?" Moyers responded, "He always knows what he's doing."

When Johnson vowed to end "stag" government, he "meant business," stated a newspaper headline shortly before the Lady Bird Special got underway. In the accompanying article, Helen Thomas reported on the president's open admiration for what he referred to as women's "stick-to-itiveness, courage and never-say-die attitude that you don't find in a man. They don't ever give up when they believe something deeply." And women had three attributes that he liked and that were key in orchestrating the Lady Bird Special: "imagination, initiative and ingenuity."

6

We Know Who's Right

Tuesday, October 6, 1964
Suffolk, Virginia, 12:18 p.m.

"My God," said the mayor of Suffolk, "she's got out more than the football team."

The Lady Bird Special had briefly ridden out of Goldwater territory and into "the LBJ-all-the-way" cities of Suffolk and Norfolk.

Most estimates pegged the lunchtime turnout in Suffolk, a peanut growing and processing center, at 8,000 (in a town of 10,000). The local paper predicted that arguments about the size of the crowd, which some placed as low as 3,000 and others as high as 12,000, would "still be heard years from now." Regardless of the exact number, it was said to be the largest rally in Suffolk history.

Like other towns along the whistle-stop route, Lady Bird's arrival was a first: never before had an immediate member of a president's family visited Suffolk. The campaign train dominated local news coverage the week before and after its arrival.

Spectators lined the railroad tracks "as far as anyone could see," while others perched on freight cars for a better view. After the Lady Bird Special came to a halt, throngs of people surged around the platform car as homemade signs waved above the crowd.

A reporter noted that on its first day, the Lady Bird Special always attracted a scattering of Goldwater supporters as well as a large number of Black spectators. In Suffolk, people of color made up the majority of attendees.

After the enthusiastic crowd quieted enough, master of ceremonies Hale Boggs got the show going by introducing "one of your famous sons," Lieutenant Governor Mills Godwin.

"This is a great day for Suffolk and the tri-county area," said Godwin. "We are particularly honored that this great train, with the First Lady of our land and her daughter aboard and with many other prominent dignitaries, has found it possible to stop in our city today. This is a great democratic team, and you are here today in support of this great effort."

The Lady Bird Special caused a commotion among Virginia politicians well before it arrived. For decades, conservative Democratic Senator Harry Byrd (who declined Lady Bird's invitation to ride the train) and his cohorts had dominated state politics. An opponent of the Civil Rights Act of 1964, Byrd was working behind the scenes to keep the Virginia Democratic Party from supporting President Johnson's reelection. By agreeing to ride the train, Lieutenant Governor Godwin defied the "Byrd Organization" and outraged segregationists. So did Governor Harrison, who provoked further outrage with the unequivocally pro-Johnson speech he gave aboard the Lady Bird Special in Richmond.

The Byrd Organization maintained its power largely through the imposition of levies on voting intended to discourage the participation of the state's lower-income, Black population, a Jim Crow law in place for more than sixty years. But with the ratification of the Twenty-Fourth Amendment to the U.S. Constitution in January 1964, states could no longer impose a poll tax in federal elections. This contributed to a significant increase in registered Black voters in Virginia.

Riding the Lady Bird Special was a calculated political risk for Godwin. But he planned to run for governor in 1965, and he had a vastly racist reputation to overcome. As a state senator, he and other politicians had advocated massive resistance, a strategy using legislation to make the school desegregation process more difficult.

In 1954, the U.S. Supreme Court ruling on *Brown v. Board of Education* found school segregation to be unconstitutional but did not mandate how or when desegregation was to be achieved. A follow-up decision issued the next year, generally referred to as *Brown II*, ordered states to desegregate public schools "with all deliberate speed." The ambiguous phrase left room for interpretation and allowed politicians at the state and local levels to enact obstructionist legislation. The fight to bring about school desegregation fell mostly to civil rights organizations to pursue through the courts. Massive resistance, a term coined by Byrd, delayed large-scale desegregation of Virginia's public schools for a decade and served as a model for other Southern states.

Now, Godwin was looking to project a moderate image to broaden his appeal to Black voters and others in a state that was becoming more centrist. By aligning himself with the national Democratic ticket and a president lauded for advancing civil rights and for his Great Society agenda, Godwin could help rebrand his image. (Shortly after Johnson became president, he set forth an ambitious legislative agenda, called the Great Society, with the main goal the elimination of poverty and racial injustice.)

Godwin's motives were politically self-serving, but he genuinely supported Johnson over Goldwater, who he viewed as too far to the right. Goldwater's casual attitude about nuclear weapons, his inexperience in foreign affairs, and his hostility toward federal programs like farm subsidies and Social Security concerned voters in Virginia and the rest of the country.

Once Godwin decided to take the political risk of riding the Lady Bird Special, he did it with gusto, boarding in Washington, DC, and riding through Virginia, visible at every stop. Regardless of his reasons, his presence on the train created a stir in Virginia and boosted the Johnson-Humphrey campaign in the state.

When Lady Bird took the podium in Suffolk, she told the crowd, "I don't think there's any secret why I am on this trip. I came here to talk about my husband and his record." Since becoming president on a "dreadful day" ten months earlier, "he has tried with all that is in him to keep our country on a steady course of economic prosperity, to face the world with firm strength, and to seek practical ways to help those Americans still in need."

Conduct of the Suffolk crowds for both Lady Bird's and Strom Thurmond's visits "should make this community proud," stated a newspaper editorial. The emphasis was on polite politics, not vitriol, with "none of the heckling that has become such a big part of political rallies now."

Lynda summed up the program in Suffolk by referencing some of the signs being held aloft.

"I noticed one or two over here for me, and I'm particularly exuberant to see somebody cheering for me, because Mother gets all the lines," she said to cheers and applause.

Then came "the high point of the Lady Bird Special's visit" when Lynda, as she had at previous stops, referenced a sign lettered with a much-used Goldwater slogan: In our hearts, we know who is right. Said Lynda, "I'm glad that we live in a country where even a few people who may not like us can at least put up their signs too. Because in our hearts, *we* know who's right." Noted the paper, "The young lady nicely, and appropriately, put the sign bearer in his place."

Norfolk, Virginia, 1:10 p.m.

During Lady Bird's speeches throughout the day in Virginia, she made mention of the "new South" and the advances taking place.

That the First Lady "truly was in a 'New South' was an especially visible reality in this world port and unsurpassed naval complex," reported the *New Journal and Guide*. The paper had been publishing since 1900 and was the oldest Black-owned business in Norfolk.

Cited as an example of the "New South" were the Johnson Girls who formed an honor guard at the civic center where the ceremonies took place. They were a "markedly integrated" ensemble of young women brought together from area high schools and colleges.

By this time, Norfolk had successfully integrated its public schools after a tumultuous start. Municipal leaders initially adhered to the massive resistance movement engineered by Harry Byrd, Mills Godwin, and other politicians. They shut down six all-white junior high and high schools in what was the state's largest school district to prevent the enrollment of seventeen Black students.

Initially, 151 Black students applied to the all-white schools. Only seventeen were accepted after intense testing that required them to achieve scores at least two grade levels ahead of their current grade. Those seventeen students, as well as thousands of white students, were out of school for months as adherence to school integration was challenged in the courts. The "Norfolk 17," as the students became known, were subject to scare tactics by segregationists who attempted to intimidate them with threatening phone calls and cross burnings.

While public schools were closed, the Norfolk 17 continued their education with classes at a local church. They also received guidance on how to handle the racial conflict they were sure to encounter when they finally integrated schools—and did. When schools reopened in February 1959 after a court ruling, they were subject to verbal and physical abuse from fellow classmates, parents, and teachers. "We had to prove something to the world," said Patricia Turner. She held her younger brother's hand while they walked toward the school entrance as people spat and yelled and threw stones at them.

"It was hard for each one of the 17," said Patricia. "It was not easy at all."

Nearly six years later, the scene in Norfolk had significantly shifted. In addition to the integrated ensemble of Johnson Girls, another example of progressiveness cited by the *New Journal and Guide* was the presence of numerous Black civic leaders on the speakers' platform that day, seated alongside Virginia's highest-ranking politicians, Governor Harrison and Lieutenant Governor Godwin. They included newspaper publisher Thomas W. Young, A. B. Jackson, a prize-winning artist, Mrs. Arthur T. Freeman with the Tidewater Voter Registration Project, and Victor J. Ashe, an attorney and chairman of Democrats for Election of the Johnson-Humphrey Ticket, the last two of whom had ridden on the Lady Bird Special into Norfolk.

The *Journal and Guide* reported that A. B. Jackson was "warmly greeted and thanked in view of thousands by the First Lady and her vivacious daughter, Lynda Bird." Jackson, a Yale University fine arts graduate and head of the art department at Norfolk State College, presented a gift to Lady Bird: a portrait he painted of Lynda as Norfolk's Azalea Queen in 1961.

A third example of the "New South" also involved Lady Bird herself. As her motorcade traveled from the Suffolk railyard to the civic center for the first of several off-train rallies, she requested that the driver stop the car. She and Lynda got out and "grasped outstretched hands—white and colored alike—with a 'Hi, thank you'" for the babies, tots, teens, and adults lining the avenue.

Throughout the day, in speech after speech, Lady Bird "delivered some belts to the political attitudes of Republican candidate Barry Goldwater without calling his name."

At the podium in Norfolk, she told the audience the country required a spirit that believes "the word 'yes' is a richer and fuller and more practical word than 'no' and 'never.' It requires faith that the future really can be bright, not devotion to a kind of past that never was."

As a reporter observed, "These are fairly outspoken words for any politician in the South these days." Coming from the president, they "might not sit too well. From Mrs. Johnson, they don't seem to mind."

Meanwhile, back in Washington, the president was receiving reports on the Lady Bird Special's progress south. At a diplomatic reception, he told guests about the impressive turnout in Norfolk—people gathered at the station, along the motorcade route, and at the civic center ceremonies. He cited crowds at 20,000, a number given by police, although once again estimates varied widely. But even the lowest, 12,000, greatly exceeded his own tally when he campaigned in Norfolk in 1960. He told the audience that he had a mere 2,500.

A reporter noted that based on Johnson's next remark, Republicans "missed the boat" when they declined to make their nominee Maine Senator Margaret Chase Smith, the first woman to actively seek the presidential nomination of a major political party.

"If a woman announces against me between now and November," Johnson said, "I'm withdrawing."

Suffolk, Virginia, 3:11 p.m.

Before crossing into North Carolina, the Lady Bird Special returned to Suffolk to switch engines. As the train came to a stop at a siding outside the city, someone on board spotted a young man standing on a dusty road gazing at the train. What set off alarm bells were the two shotguns he was carrying. Secret Service agents quickly flooded the area. The young man, presumably a hunter, was questioned by plainclothes officers, who confiscated the weapons until the train began moving again.

This wasn't the last time a gun-toting young man would appear near the train. The Lady Bird Special's route traversed areas where both harmless hunters and people harboring strong, sometimes violent attachments to the "old South" were common. Neither the Secret Service nor anyone on the train could distinguish intentions in advance or from a distance. Memories of President Kennedy's assassination were still fresh in people's minds, as were other recent political killings like those of James Chaney, Michael Schwerner, and Andrew Goodman that summer. Encounters such as the one in Suffolk highlighted the underlying sense of foreboding that, although overshadowed by the daily demands and festivities of the whistle-stop campaign, was a constant companion on the train.

7

A Message of Good Will

Tuesday, October 6, 1964
Ahoskie, North Carolina, 4:22 p.m.

By the time the Lady Bird Special trundled into Ahoskie, it was running an hour behind schedule. The late arrival didn't dampen the mood for the waiting spectators, who had begun gathering in the early afternoon.

The weather was crisp and sunny. A brass band played.

A huge welcome banner was draped across the main street near the train depot. Preparations for the First Lady's arrival had continued late into the night as workers decorated the downtown streets with bunting and flags following thirty-one straight hours of rain.

At least 1,000 signs were held high, one of which read Swing along with Lady Bird. Another: Tar Heels love Lady Bird. The throngs were so enormous that police had difficulty clearing the tracks so the train could ease to a stop in the center of town. Adding to the commotion, the Lady Bird Special overshot its appointed stopping place and had to back up about forty feet.

A Secret Service agent attempted to corral an inquisitive terrier who wandered around the tracks, got underfoot in the press section, and almost leaped onto the train.

A woman worked her way through the crowd and grasped Lady Bird's hand. She said, "I got up at 3 o'clock this morning and milked twenty cows so I could get here by train time!"

It was in Ahoskie where Lady Bird "settled down to knowing" she was going to enjoy the whistle-stop tour. "Such an air of excitement and friendliness prevailed that I began to loosen up," she said.

The president's intuition that "you'll get everyone out from three counties" neighboring the small, underserved town of Ahoskie was spot on. The stop was only added to the itinerary after the White House received the telegram requesting a visit. True to prediction, the Lady Bird Special turned out about 10,000 people, more than double the town's population.

An old-timer claimed, "This is the second biggest crowd we've had since Buffalo Bill brought his Wild West show here in 1916." A local congressman, too young to remember the sharp-shooting showman, said, "This is the biggest thing I have ever seen happen here."

Hale Boggs wasted no time finding his rhythm. He emphatically declared that Goldwater's "Southern strategy" was being "dashed under the wheels" of the Lady Bird Special. Traditionally, Black voters had cast their ballots for the Republicans, the party of Abraham Lincoln and emancipation. But Republican strategists made the calculated decision to disenfranchise them in favor of preserving and increasing support among white voters by endorsing discrimination and segregation, a direct play to siphon away from the Democratic Party people angry about the Civil Rights Act.

At the same time, Black voters were further breaking with the tradition of supporting Republican candidates. The same week the Lady

Bird Special went through North Carolina, the state's chapter of the NAACP held a convention. A national director for the organization, Gloster B. Current, warned against Goldwater. "The Negro voter realizes that Goldwater is the greatest threat to America ever posed in the 20th century," he said. "While the polls are running favorably to Lyndon Johnson, make no mistake. There are many more citizens than you would believe who are in agreement with the racist views of the Republican candidate." Current continued, "Who appoints the attorney general? The President of the United States. I ask you this question: Would you want Senator Strom Thurmond as your next attorney general?"

In an unprecedented move, the NAACP had adopted a resolution calling on the Republican party to deny Goldwater the presidential nomination. It was the first time in the organization's fifty-five years that such a resolution was passed identifying an aspirant by name and party. The NAACP opposed Goldwater for three reasons: he sided with Southern segregationists in voting against the Civil Rights Act of 1964; his presidential bid was supported by the Ku Klux Klan, the John Birch Society, and other extremist groups; and he believed that "issues involving equality and justice for Negroes should be left to the states." States like Mississippi, where Chaney, Schwerner, and Goodman were brutally murdered and where, the year before, civil rights activist Medgar Evers was fatally shot in the back in his driveway by a sniper with a high-powered rifle.

In another departure from tradition, the *Saturday Evening Post* urged its readers to elect President Johnson. "Even more strongly," the magazine's editors advocated for Goldwater's defeat. Although Johnson "has many flaws and leaves much to be desired," he was "unquestionably" well qualified to be president. "We are confident that Johnson will make a good President because he already *is* a good President." In his ten months on the job, he had "shown an ability unmatched in this century to bring all the diverse and warring factions of Congress behind the enactment of positive, progressive and needful legislative programs. In his greatest test as Commander-in-Chief—the attack on our Navy in the Gulf of Tonkin—he acted with both the forcefulness and restraint which is required in the man who alone controls the ultimate weapon and bears all the fearful responsibility which that entails."

The scathing editorial, the first to endorse a Democratic presidential candidate in the more than two hundred years of the magazine's history, labeled Goldwater "an unprincipled and ruthless political jujitsu artist" whose "tongue is like quicksilver; his mind is like quicksand." Declared the editors, "We are...confident that Goldwater would not make a good President. He has not even made a good Senator."

The public denunciations of Goldwater continued from members of his own religious denomination.

"We are profoundly disturbed by the transparent exploitation of racism among white citizens by Senator Barry Goldwater and [his running mate] Congressman William Miller," declared a statement signed by 726 Episcopal bishops, clergy, and laymen. "They have sought to frighten citizens by equating the Negro struggle for freedom with crime and violence in the streets while at the same time encouraging disrespect for law and order by their own expressed contempt for the federal judiciary, especially for the United States Supreme Court. They are ambitious to be elected by inheriting the votes of white racists, cultivating and harvesting the white backlash and by importuning the fears and disquiets of white citizens toward social change in both the North and South."

The clergymen's statement concluded by reiterating, "We deplore and rebuke the manipulation of racism among white citizens by Senator Goldwater and Congressman Miller in this election campaign."

In contrast to the Goldwater campaign's sowing discord, Terry Sanford, the governor of North Carolina, welcomed Lady Bird to the state on an optimistic note. "She has for us a message of good will, a message of great hope, and a message that I know will mean so much to all of America," he said. But before Lady Bird delivered her message, Governor Sanford wanted something from the crowd. "I want us to give her a message. I want you to let her know how we are going to support President Johnson in November." The audience obliged the request with a resounding cheer.

"I just can't tell you how happy this makes me and how wonderful it is to be greeted by such a big crowd," said Lady Bird. Since Ahoskie began as a railroad town and hadn't had a passenger train roll through in more than a decade, she was told the best thing she could do when visiting was to bring in a trainload of passengers. "Well, I've done my best," she said.

After the pleasantries, Lady Bird "got down to brass tacks," talking about education and economics. First, she praised the state's prioritization of education. "When I look at the roster of colleges there are in this state, I remember a Texas governor—never known for his willingness to budget money for the state universities—who once warned his legislature, 'You've gone hog wild about education.' Well, I'm glad [North] Carolina has gone hog wild about education. You have been a beacon-light to the rest of the South." Next, she shared that between 1960 and 1963, the per capita income for North Carolinians increased by $245, a sum that was $13 above the national average. "And I would be remiss," she added, "if I didn't remind you that those have been Democratic years."

Lady Bird ended her speech with a call for Democratic votes. "All of us are here to say—what I suspect you have already guessed—that we hope you will place your confidence in the President again." She also encouraged attendees to vote "right on down the line" for gubernatorial candidate Dan Moore and others on the Democratic slate.

As it was intended to do, the prestige and excitement surrounding the Lady Bird Special was too great for some state politicians to ignore, like Dan Moore. Speculation had been raging in the press for days as to how Moore would receive the Johnsons when they campaigned in North Carolina. He had vowed to vote a straight Democratic line in the 1964 elections, but he refused to openly endorse the Johnson-Humphrey ticket or even to mention the president by name out of concern that he would lose votes to his Republican opponent.

The day before, in the Ahoskie *Herald*'s "Lady Bird special issue," the lead editorial encouraged Moore to endorse the Johnson-Humphrey ticket "while he had such a golden opportunity."

"The time for stand-offishness has run out," the *Herald* proclaimed. "When Judge Moore greets Mrs. Johnson in Ahoskie on Tuesday, the moment of truth will have arrived."

Moore was in Ahoskie to meet the Lady Bird Special, but since it was running late, he left before it arrived to be among the official entourage greeting President Johnson at the airport in Raleigh. (There really was no hurry, since the president was timing his arrival with that of the Lady Bird Special, which had several more stops to make before it reached Raleigh.) Unlike her husband, Jeanelle Moore greeted the First Lady in Ahoskie, rode the train throughout the state, and wasn't reticent with her enthusiasm. "This is a thrilling and wonderful experience," she said on the train platform in Ahoskie. "We are so delighted to see all of these wonderful Tar Heels here to greet the First Lady of the United States. We love all of you."

After spending twenty boisterous and memorable minutes in Ahoskie, the Lady Bird Special was on its way to the next depot. A sign on an overpass offered one last message as the train left town: BYE, BYE, BIRDIE—COME BACK AGAIN SOME DAY.

8

Lessons of the Past

Tuesday, October 6, 1964
Tarboro, North Carolina, 5:43 p.m.

As the Lady Bird Special sped south, all along the tracks, clusters of people in villages and hamlets, in fields and in schoolyards, waved and cheered as the campaign train equivalent of a traveling Wild West show sped by. Lady Bird, Lynda, and the hostesses took turns standing on the back platform so that there was always someone waving back. When the train passed through the town of Aulander, the First Lady waved to the more than a thousand people who had gathered. At Hobgood, the train slowed to a crawl so that she could acknowledge another crowd.

The sun was setting as the train pulled into Tarboro, where no time was wasted during the five-minute stop.

Lady Bird swiftly yet sincerely thanked the crowd for a "marvelous welcome" and highlighted the president's years of service.

"I just want to tell y'all, thank you very much for coming," said Lynda Bird.

Hale Boggs had the last word, yelling, "Don't let anybody tell you that President Johnson isn't going to carry the South."

Rocky Mount, North Carolina, 6:14 p.m.

The Lady Bird Special lingered a bit longer in Rocky Mount, where darkness had fallen. Neon signs aglow around the train station beckoned FOOD and EAT. Because it was suppertime, the crowd wasn't as large as it might have been if the train had been punctual. Still, some 5,000 people greeted the Lady Bird Special, among them a contingent of college students who contributed much "whoop and holler." A famous local figure dressed as Uncle Sam in a black top hat and an American flag–inspired suit joined the dignitaries on the train's back platform.

Only a couple of the myriad signs being held aloft were derogatory enough to attract attention. By the time the First Lady was introduced and took her position at the podium, a group of adolescents and other Goldwater supporters had lost steam and were no longer waving placards above their heads. As she gave her speech, "the dissenting spectators seemed more embarrassed by the incident than did the gracious First Lady."

Lady Bird expressed pleasure that her tour was taking her to smaller towns and rural areas. "I was born in such an area, and I am at home here," she said.

"I am a Southerner and proud of it. I am a Democrat and proud of it." For nearly two decades, she told the audience, she had "had a front row seat on what the government and the men and women who play the hard daily role in it do about the problems that come before them. And I know that the Democratic Party tries to solve them, not just deplore them. My husband started his career in Congress in the Depression years, and neither of us can forget the marks of poverty that scarred the South country. Hungry children and men and women with only despair in their eyes who had lost the patch of land where they had worked or lived."

President Johnson grew up in the isolated, impoverished Texas Hill Country, without electricity or running water. "He felt poverty right to the pit of his stomach, and he could make others feel it, too," said Liz Carpenter. She recalled Johnson telling the press, "When I was a boy in Texas, there was so much poverty around us, we didn't know it had a name." (Later, as a congressman, he achieved one of his proudest accomplishments: navigating the legislative hurdles to bring electrical power to the Hill Country.)

Johnson's first job after graduating from high school was with a road-building crew, and he later worked as a janitor and at other odd jobs to pay his way through Southwest Texas State Teachers College. When money for tuition ran out, he took a hiatus and spent a year teaching at a predominantly Mexican American elementary school where students were so grindingly poor, they often showed up hungry. Nor did they receive much attention or incentive to learn. As Johnson endeavored to improve school conditions, including using his first paycheck to purchase equipment for extracurricular activities, he realized a harsh truth. "College was closed to practically every one of those children because they were too poor."

President Johnson "brought many lessons of the past" with him into his years of political service, Lady Bird told the Rocky Mount crowd, culminating with his ten months in the Oval Office. In his first State of the Union address in January 1964, Johnson declared an "unconditional war on poverty," a cornerstone of his Great Society agenda.

These lessons, Lady Bird believed, "equip him to go on working as your President, and I know that he will work hard along with your own Dan Moore to make a more prosperous future for North Carolina and for our country."

Democratic leaders aboard the train believed that economic considerations would keep some voters in their column who might otherwise have been swayed by racial concerns. One recalled a remark made by a white textile worker who was asked about the hiring of Black people and how that would influence his decision in the presidential election. "I'd rather work by one than stand by one in a soup line," said the man.

With the speeches in Rocky Mount concluded and the departure chime sounded, the Lady Bird Special began to move. As the spectators waved, reporters scrambled up the tracks to reboard the train. In the press cars, the furious clacking of typewriter keys continued until the next stop in Wilson, where they stopped writing long enough to hear the First Lady address another crowd.

Wilson, North Carolina, 6:45 p.m.

The nighttime rallies in Wilson and Selma, the next stop down the track, were the most boisterous of the day.

While Lady Bird was speaking in Wilson, the crowd, which included a large number of teenagers, launched into a chanting contest. A small group started yelling, "We want Barry." A roar of "We want Lyndon" drowned out the opposition.

Lady Bird smiled and thanked "all you young people" for the enthusiasm. "No one has more faith in the young generation than the President and I do," she said. After all, they had "two lively examples" of youth at the White House.

In speech after speech, Lady Bird wrapped her political points in a softer sell. Meanwhile, masters of ceremonies Luther Hodges and Hale Boggs delivered the fiery political rhetoric. "An urbane man in Washington," Boggs transformed into a "shouting spellbinder" on the campaign trail.

"Don't let anybody tell you that Lyndon Johnson isn't going to carry the South," boomed Boggs. "He is a Southerner. He is the first

Southern President in a hundred years. We in the South are not about ready to turn our backs on him and his lovely lady."

By the time the Lady Bird Special reached Wilson, Boggs "had perfected a tag line that evoked roars from the crowd," reported Nan Robertson in the *New York Times*.

Said Boggs, "He and his wife are as much a part of the South as tobacco and cotton and peanuts and grits and red-eye gravy, and you name it, we got it."

The route that brought Nan Robertson aboard the Lady Bird Special began when she was eleven years old. She announced to her best friend, "You know what I want to be when I grow up? A reporter." In addition to a fascination with the power of words, their meanings and nuances, she thought "newspaper work seemed like a lot of fun, and you got to meet all sorts of interesting people." She also thought the profession would fit her personality: friendly, unafraid, curious, and competitive, year after year beating "every boy on my block in wrestling, running, swimming, and tree-climbing."

Robertson earned a bachelor's degree in journalism from Northwestern University, where a professor told her, "You are good enough. You will be a writer." At each class session, he would read aloud students' articles without saying who wrote it. One day, he shared Robertson's piece depicting the blood and violent death in a Chicago meat-processing plant. In vivid prose, she described the assembly line where pigs, dangling head down and squealing, were slaughtered by the slash of a knife to the throat. As the professor read the article in a deliberate monotone, students from time to time would gasp or make sounds of disgust. When the professor finished reading, he paused. "It will come as a surprise to you, perhaps, that the reporter is a *girl*," he told the class to exclamations of amazement. (Robertson received an A-minus on the assignment.)

After graduating in 1948, Robertson sailed for Europe, where she lived in Paris and Berlin and reported for the *New York Herald Tribune*, the *Milwaukee Journal*, and other newspapers. When she returned stateside seven years later, she set her sights on the *New York Times*, which was, "quite simply, in a class by itself." Despite Robertson being an experienced general assignment reporter, the *Times* placed her on the women's pages. This was, after all, where women were typically relegated under the assumption that they, as another *Times* reporter put it, "should not be subject to the danger, the degradation" of covering the news.

Unhappy with the sexist restrictions, Robertson wrote and scrapped her way to the paper's metropolitan staff, where she covered "courts, crime, storms, parades, fires, air crashes, many features and human interest stories, and two national political conventions." In 1963, after her husband accepted a job in Washington, DC, she was hired at the *Times*' bureau there. She was one of only three women in a newsroom that was run "like a men's club."

Shortly after President Johnson took office, Robertson penned a profile of the new First Lady for the popular *Saturday Evening Post*. In what was the magazine's cover story, she surmised that Lady Bird would be "the most political First Lady since Eleanor Roosevelt. She is more than an elected official's wife—she has become herself a consummate politician."

Nowhere was Robertson's assessment more evident than on the Lady Bird Special's first day rolling down the tracks. When the train left Wilson, eleven stops were behind Lady Bird. There was one more to go before she teamed up with the president for a high-stakes rally in Raleigh, the state capital.

Selma, North Carolina, 7:38 p.m.
The boisterous crowd in Selma, some 6,000 strong, welcomed the Lady Bird Special with chants of "LBJ...all the way."

The president, Lady Bird told them, had chuckled over a telegram sent to the White House by the town's mayor, Hayden Wiggs. As an enticement for the train to stop there, Wiggs relayed that the last two presidential candidates to visit Selma had carried the state.

Jeanelle Moore continued to boost the Democratic ticket and entreated attendees for their support. "May I exact a promise from you tonight," she asked. "On November the third, will you keep North Carolina in the Democratic column?"

Spectators in Selma got an added thrill when the First Lady left the train to mingle and shake hands while an issue with the train's brakes was resolved.

Once underway, as the Lady Bird Special continued toward Raleigh, everyone on board agreed and the First Lady most of all: "It had been quite a day."

9

The Great Persuader

Tuesday, October 6, 1964
Raleigh, North Carolina, 8:52 p.m.

Windows in the buildings facing Reynolds Coliseum at the University of North Carolina in Raleigh were ordered by the Secret Service to be kept closed while President Johnson was on campus to headline a campaign rally at the auditorium.

Ten months earlier, Lee Harvey Oswald positioned himself in a sixth-floor window at the Texas School Book Depository in Dallas and took aim at President Kennedy as he traveled in a motorcade through Dealey Plaza. Vice President Johnson and Lady Bird were riding in a convertible two cars behind Kennedy's open limousine. After a rainy morning, the sky had cleared, and the sun was shining brightly. People lined the streets, "the children all smiling, placards, confetti, people waving from windows," Lady Bird recalled. There was such "a gala air" that when she heard a sharp, loud sound, she initially thought someone in the crowd got carried away celebrating and set off firecrackers.

A Secret Service agent riding with the vice president and Lady Bird yelled, "Get down!" as he vaulted into the car's back seat and used his body to shield Johnson. Two more shots rang out. Over the agent's radio, a voice said, "He's hit! Hurry, he's hit!" The car sped along, accelerating faster and faster, until they reached a hospital, where Kennedy's death was pronounced about thirty minutes after the shooting.

Presidents typically take office after a triumphant campaign victory and celebrate with festive inaugural balls. Lyndon Johnson became president amid bloodshed, chaos, and confusion. He took the oath of office aboard Air Force One at Love Field in Dallas with Lady Bird standing on one side of him and Jackie Kennedy on the other. Johnson asked that Sarah T. Hughes, a U.S. district judge in Texas, be the one to swear him in, and she became the first (and to date the only) woman ever to perform the historic task.

"Lyndon's a good man to have in an emergency," Lady Bird once told Liz Carpenter. Those words kept coming back to Carpenter as Air Force One flew from Dallas to Washington with President Kennedy's coffin on board. In the plane's cabin, shades were drawn, voices were in whispers, and the occasional sob was heard. And yet "even on that tragic day," said Carpenter, "the country was never without a president."

The tragic circumstances under which President Johnson and Lady Bird entered the White House were for them made immeasurably worse by the fact that the assassination happened in their home state. On the day Kennedy's body lay in state at the Capitol, Lady Bird contrasted in her diary his death with that of Franklin Roosevelt, the last president to pass away in office and who died of natural causes. "There is that sense of shame over the violence and hatred that has spread through our land. Shame for America! Shame for Texas! But also a determination to help wipe it out!" Referring to Harry Truman ascending to the presidency after Roosevelt's death, Johnson said, "At least his man wasn't murdered."

Three years earlier, Johnson and Kennedy had vied for the 1960 presidential nomination. Kennedy was declared the victor at the Democratic National Convention, and the next day, he asked Johnson to be his running mate. Kennedy surprised the convention by selecting Johnson, who until hours before was his bitter rival in the quest for the presidency. "In these days of great challenge Americans must have a Vice President capable of dealing with the grave problems confronting this nation and the free world," said Kennedy. "Lyndon Johnson has demonstrated on many occasions his brilliant qualifications for the leadership we require today."

"Equally surprising" was Johnson's acceptance of the number two spot. Despite his stinging pride and against the wishes of political allies angered that he would be relinquishing his powerful position of Senate majority leader, he signed on to the ticket. "Bird and I talked it out and agreed that a party which had done so much for us, and people who had worked so hard for us, deserved our help," said Johnson. With a Southern Democrat on the ticket, a Northern Catholic liberal like Kennedy had a better chance of winning the election. Johnson appeared before the convention and said that the party must unite to win in November. He "pledged warm and friendly cooperation with 'the next President,'" John F. Kennedy.

After Johnson formally accepted the VP nomination at the convention, he stood onstage with his arm around Lady Bird. Observed James Reston, a respected veteran journalist, "Lyndon would never have made it this far without the help of that woman. She is magnificent."

After Kennedy's death, Johnson moved swiftly and decisively to lead a stunned and grieving nation. Carpenter drafted the first words the new president spoke to the nation when the plane touched down at Andrews Air Force Base outside Washington, DC: "This is a sad time for all people. We have suffered a loss that cannot be weighed.

For me, it is a deep personal tragedy. I know that the world shares the sorrow that Mrs. Kennedy and her family bear. I will do my best. That is all I can do. I ask for your help—and God's."

Lady Bird felt as though she were "suddenly on stage for a part I never rehearsed; but, like Lyndon," she vowed, "I will do my best."

Along with the president, the country looked to its new First Lady for guidance. "As the shock of past weeks recedes a bit, we are seeing how singularly prepared she is, by nature and by experience, to step into this demanding role," stated a newspaper editorial. "Like her husband, Mrs. Johnson has come into the White House under tragic circumstances that have left the American people shaken and grasping not only for shreds of reassurance in our leadership, but also for some calm and perspective. And here it is that Mrs. Johnson has already walked as First Lady with sure foot."

Lady Bird resolved to continue what she had been doing for years—creating for her husband "an island of peace and serenity," as she said during his Senate days. "I know he can then be free for his work—and I have great respect for that work." That work was now the presidency.

On the day Lady Bird and her family moved into the White House, she recorded in her diary, "The whole country is still numb from the tragedy and it is hard to sort out the days and encompass all that has happened, but I keep reminding myself of Lyndon, for whom it is hardest of all to carry on." She repeated to herself a phrase from Johnson's address to Congress after President Kennedy's death. "Our challenge, he said, is 'not to hesitate, not to pause, not to turn about and linger over this evil moment but to continue on our course so that we may fulfill the destiny that history has set for us.'"

Lady Bird was the serene influence in her relationship with Lyndon. She had been since she "committed matrimony" with a man who said only half jokingly that he thought about politics eighteen hours a day. They met in Austin through a mutual friend and the next day had their first date, during which he proposed. Throughout their ten-week courtship, conducted mostly by letter and the occasional phone call, Lyndon repeatedly asked Lady Bird to marry him. She was more cautious by nature and hesitant about rushing into marriage so quickly. Then Lyndon drove to Lady Bird's family home in Karnack, Texas, showing up unannounced and insisting they marry right away. She packed a bag and left with him, and that night in San Antonio, they tied the knot.

Lady Bird was intelligent and independent-minded, and she admired her high-energy husband's ambition and can-do spirit. She managed with equanimity his mercurial moods, the chaos he often left in his wake, and the demands he made (like having his suits always pressed and ready and the freezers full of food). Johnson was described as "a notoriously unpredictable person who often moves on impulse." Most people who knew Lady Bird saw her as calm and unruffled, a strong, firm woman. He expected her to handle anything and everything and believed that she could, even if it was accommodating twenty weekend guests who would be arriving in an hour.

"He was marvelous, contradictory, with a great natural intelligence...sometimes hurtful, but also sweet and caring and giving," Lady Bird said of Lyndon. "I know we were better together than apart."

He said, "She has made my career possible."

As a "wife, confidante, and active working partner," Lady Bird offered assessments and critiques when warranted. "I never saw her slice a corner on anything," Johnson said. "She is the first to tell me about any mistakes, whether they are financial extravagances or a political boner, and to me that is the test of real character." When asked about her husband's announcement in 1960 that he was seeking the presidential nomination, she said, "I thought it was fine, strong and thrilling." She added, "There are a few minor things I'd like to discuss with him though." And when she thought he spoke too long at political rallies, she would slip him a note that said, "That's enough."

Lady Bird was often compared to Eleanor Roosevelt, but the two First Ladies differed in a significant way. Eleanor had a political life of her own, while Lady Bird only ever worked politically for her husband. Politics had become the focus of Lady Bird's life because of Lyndon, but she also enjoyed it and was good at it. Said Lindy Boggs, "Bird would be just half alive if she divorced herself from politics."

During the 1964 election, Senator John Tower, the Texas Republican who succeeded Johnson in the Senate, stumped for Goldwater. At a rally in Virginia, he sought to score points with the audience by deriding the Lady Bird Special. "That's just like Lyndon," said Tower. "He hides behind a woman's skirt."

Far from hiding behind Lady Bird's skirt, the president took pride in their partnership. "Throughout my political career, Mrs. Johnson has been my principal and equal partner, both in politics and Government service," he said in a message to Democratic National Committeewomen earlier in the year. When the president met his whistle-stopping wife in Raleigh, they stamped "the LBJ brand" on North Carolina, proving they were a political powerhouse.

Cheers and shouts of welcome turned into laughter as the one-car decoy train preceding the Lady Bird Special reached the Southern Railway Station in Raleigh and rolled past, with the engineer and another man bowing and smiling. When the actual Lady Bird Special arrived, the crowd was still buoyant after a cold wait that was so long some children went without dinner.

The First Lady appeared on the back platform, smiling brightly. "It has been a wonderful and dramatic day," she told the 3,000 people gathered at the station. She declared she "was fresh out of speeches," although she briefly lauded North Carolina's emphasis on education. Jeanelle Moore took the microphone and said enthusiastically, "I'm sure we will keep North Carolina in the Democratic column November 3rd."

With that, the train's entourage debarked and, guided by a police escort to speed the motorcade along, headed for the rally at the Reynolds Coliseum. (Dr. Travell always made sure to have an outside seat in the motorcades so she could quickly exit the vehicle and help out in an emergency.)

While the Lady Bird Special was making its way to Raleigh, the president departed the White House. As the campaign train rolled into North Carolina's capital amid fanfare and with momentum running high, Air Force One landed at the airport outside town. Despite authorities urging people to stay away because of parking problems, more than 2,000 spectators showed up to welcome the president. Johnson greeted the official party of dignitaries waiting on the tarmac, including Dan Moore, who sported an LBJ-USA button on his lapel. They exchanged a few words and a brief handshake. The president patted Moore on the back, and both men smiled.

President Johnson then strode toward the shouting crowd gathered near the guard rail bordering the runway for a brisk round of handshaking—something he did routinely and what his staff referred to as "working the fences."

"Welcome to North Carolina, Mr. President," said some spectators as they clasped his hand at the Raleigh airport.

"We're for you all the way, Mr. Johnson," others shouted.

A small cluster of pro-Goldwater sign carriers briefly booed and catcalled from the rear of the crowd, startling other onlookers, but the president paid no attention to them. With Secret Service agents following close behind, he kept up a steady pace along the fence, smiling, shaking hands, and speaking with everyone from high school and college students to cops, mothers, fathers, and children. He stopped only once to pick up an LBJ campaign hat that toppled from a college student's head.

The president worked the entire length of the fence, and when he reached the end, a spectator yelled: "That's what I like about a Democrat. They said you wouldn't come all around—but you did."

Back at the presidential limousine, Johnson paused momentarily with Governor Sanford.

"It's good to be in North Carolina," said Johnson. "The people are warm-hearted."

The Warren Commission Report had pointed out that absolute security for a president was "impossible" unless they were "completely isolated from all contact with the people." Isolating himself was not something President Johnson was going to do. He would often order his car to be stopped and leap from the vehicle to "press the flesh" with street crowds. He explained to anyone "concerned about this habit" that he was far safer making an impromptu foray in the middle of a crowd than he was standing alone at a podium before tens of thousands of people. The Secret Service, he said, considered a spontaneous stop as "in itself a deterrent to risk." He added, "None of the Secret Service boys or the FBI are worried about a fellow shaking hands."

So many spectators lined the ten-mile route into Raleigh that the motorcade was slow going and, at one point, almost completely halted. The president didn't make any impromptu stops during the ride, but he did address the crowd along the way through a public address system in the limousine.

"Hello, there," he said through a bullhorn. "Thanks for coming out. Come on down to the Coliseum."

Elsewhere in the state that day, Republicans were doing their utmost to keep their vice-presidential candidate, William Miller, from being upstaged by the Lady Bird Special and the president's visit. "This is Bill Miller Day [in] North Carolina," said Robert L. Gavin, the Republican candidate for governor. "We've forgotten about that little episode going on down in Raleigh tonight. It's not going to amount to much anyway." (Team Goldwater had no luck stealing the spotlight from Lady Bird and the president, and Miller's visit barely made a blip in the news.)

At the Reynolds Coliseum, where Lady Bird and the president simultaneously made their entrance, they were greeted by yet more thousands of people who couldn't get inside the already-full auditorium. They made their way through the thickest parts of the crowd, shaking eagerly thrust-out hands. Many of the schoolchildren present had been determined to wait no matter how late the guests of honor arrived. Explained one, "Our teacher said we wouldn't have any homework if we would come and see the President." A few Goldwater supporters in the crowd held up signs, while photographers yelled to the president, "Kiss her!" Lady Bird, smiling, shook her head. Her husband bent down and gave her a bear hug instead.

The presidential party entered the coliseum to the sounds of "Hail to the Chief" played by a 170-piece university band.

The crowd, standing, screaming, stomping their feet, and vigorously waving banners, began chanting "We want Johnson" in an ovation that lasted five minutes.

On the stage, the president beamed, Lady Bird smiled, and Lynda did the twist. Jeanelle Moore embraced the president, gave him a kiss on the cheek, and announced her support for the Johnson-Humphrey ticket as her taciturn husband looked on. Later she was heard urging him in a whisper, "Smile, Dan, smile."

Confetti swirled in the huge hall. Red, white, and blue balloons floated to the ceiling, where LBJ-themed posters dangled. Signs and placards held up among the 13,000-person crowd identified everyone from Boy Scout Troop 87 to the International Ladies' Garment Workers' Union.

At 1:00 a.m. the day before, advance man Larry Lloyd received a call in his Raleigh hotel room. "How many bands are we going to have there?" a voice asked.

"Twenty-six, Mr. President," said Lloyd.

"And how about the balloons?"

"There will be as many as you ever saw in one place, Mr. President."

Lloyd delivered on his promise, and 5,000 balloons adorned the auditorium.

As the lead advance man for the president's appearance in Raleigh, Lloyd had "everybody in Washington calling to ask me if I knew what I was doing."

A lot was riding on a successful performance here by the president. In addition to having him give the Lady Bird Special a top-level send-off in Alexandria and meet the train in New Orleans, Liz Carpenter knew that having him appear somewhere along the line would be vital to keep the story sustained in the media. She told Johnson they would "need beefing up" by the time the train reached Raleigh. He replied, "I'll be there."

The other reason Carpenter was keen on Raleigh for the midpoint meetup was due to the state political situation and in particular because Dan Moore "had brought into power a new array of very conservative Democrats who were flirting with the Republican organization." During her scouting mission, Carpenter concluded that Democratic Party campaign coordination was severely lacking in North Carolina. "If we lose North Carolina, it is going to be by *Default* on the part of the State Organization," she reported to the president. While the Republicans were bringing high-profile speakers into the state to campaign, the Democratic organization, seemingly at the behest of Moore's team, was "keeping Democrats *out*."

So contentious was the situation that when Carpenter and her party visited Raleigh on the scouting mission, they had to confer with Governor Sanford, a Johnson supporter, separately from Moore's aides. Moore's staffers kept telling Carpenter that if the Lady Bird Special came to town, they would arrange an event "befitting a lady," perhaps a "tea with petit fours." Said Carpenter, "I seethed as I listened to this kind of outmoded thinking."

Instead of a dainty ladies' tea, the Johnsons' joint event at the coliseum was the largest political rally in the history of the capital and of the state, announced Governor Sanford from the stage. Veteran politicians, policemen, and newsmen swore "they had never seen anything like it in the heart of tobacco land."

Lady Bird told the audience about her journey through Virginia and North Carolina, describing it as "an unforgettable, dramatic, colorful day," before turning over the spotlight to her husband.

"This is about the most beautiful hall I have ever seen," said the president. "I like the decorations. I like the Democratic enthusiasm."

He was there that night for two reasons. "I knew that Mrs. Johnson was going to have a pretty full day...and I wanted to be here to join you in giving her a warm, Southern welcome," he said. The second reason was "political business."

Johnson's presence on the coliseum stage, campaigning as the Democratic Party's presidential nominee, wasn't always a certainty. Earlier in the year, he contemplated whether to seek a four-year term of his own. Despite a zest for the job and confidence in his ability to work with Congress to continue passing meaningful legislation, he was beset by dread and doubt. He turned for counsel to Lady Bird, who he knew would be candid with him. He valued her opinion of his "virtues and flaws" and found her judgment to be "generally excellent." Johnson asked Lady Bird to put down on paper the pros and cons of his staying in the race for president. She responded with a multipoint memo, given to him on May 14, in which she concluded: "Stay in." It was signed "Your loving Wife."

Johnson continued to wrestle with his decision and was still unsure on the day he was supposed to appear at the Democratic National Convention in August. Casting a shadow over accomplishments like passing the Civil Rights Act and launching the war on poverty were anxieties about racial tensions in the United States, from the seething South to rioting in the North, the escalating conflict in Vietnam, responsibility for nuclear weapons in the Cold War era, the attacks on him and his family by the press, and his own physical health (he had a near-fatal heart attack nine years earlier). In the aftermath of Kennedy's assassination, Johnson worked twenty-hour days coordinating with various sections and groups to bring the country together. But he wondered, as he always had, whether "the nation would unite indefinitely behind any Southerner."

That morning, Johnson drafted a proposed statement of resignation. Numerous advisers cautioned against it, including his press secretary, George Reedy, who said that the "decision had come too late" and that his "refusal to run would 'just give the country to Goldwater.'" Johnson also asked Lady Bird for her response to the draft statement. She once again put her thoughts on paper and sent him the following note:

Beloved—

You are as brave a man as Harry Truman—or FDR—or Lincoln. You can go on to find some peace, some achievement amidst all the pain. You have been strong, patient, determined beyond any words of mine to express.

I honor you for it. So does most of the country.

To step out now would be wrong for your country, and I can see nothing but a lonely wasteland for your future. Your friends would be frozen in embarrassed silence and your enemies jeering.

I am not afraid of Time [which had just run an unflattering article about her] *or lies or losing money or defeat.*

In the final analysis I can't carry any of the burdens you talked of—so I know it's only your choice. But I know you are as brave as any of the thirty-five.

I love you always
Bird

Said Johnson, "In a few words she hit me on two most sensitive and compelling points, telling me that what I planned to do would be wrong for my country and that it would show a lack of courage on my part. The message I read most clearly in her note to me was that my announcement to the 1964 convention that I would not run would be taking the easy way out."

Johnson accepted the party's nomination and set an ambitious goal for himself: to win the election with a landslide victory, proving that he had earned the presidency and not just inherited it. His extensive campaigning was fueled by a belief that he owed it to the American populace "to woo them, to state his case, and to win their approval on his own." Should he lose, he didn't want anybody to say he made the same mistake as Tom Dewey in 1948. Dewey, the GOP candidate, took it for granted that the election was a forgone conclusion in his favor—until Harry Truman whistle-stopped to a landslide victory. Plus, Johnson enjoyed being on the campaign trail. "He needed contact with people, and you don't get that in the White House. This rejuvenated him, and it was kind of like recharging batteries," said Marie Fehmer Chiarodo, the president's personal secretary. "It was almost like adrenaline; it was like a B-12 shot."

The rousing rally in Raleigh was a big boost as Johnson campaigned in the South for the first time outside his home state. Political observers and Democratic strategists all agreed: his appearance in Raleigh was "crucial to his overall success in Dixie."

And he delivered.

First the president gave a prepared speech in his strong, showman style. He pointed out his North Carolina ties with a mention that his great-grandfather was born near Raleigh in 1809.

"Politics is the people's business, and that means it has to be the politics of responsibility," he declared. The next morning, he was leaving on a four-day trek through the Midwest. "This campaign trip will be a report on how we have been building a better and a stronger America, and it will make clear the basic choices that all Americans are going to have to make come November. Most important of all, this trip is going to be a report on where we go from here, on which way is up."

He went on to offer unequivocal support for the farm subsidy program, an important issue in the tobacco heartland, and he criticized opponents of it.

He emphasized a tax cut passed that year as part of the Democratic program and lauded the level of education enrollment in North Carolina, which in fifteen years had doubled the number of students in its colleges and universities. "I believe that every boy and girl in this great State and in this great country has a right to all the education they can use," he said, "and as long as I am your President, I intend to work with your State and local governments to make this right a reality."

He proclaimed that "peace on earth" was the most important goal, "a painfully slow progress" that required courage. "We have that courage," he declared.

Finished with the scripted text, Johnson had more to say. Without ever mentioning his opponent by name, he dismantled Goldwater's campaign talking points, including the assertion that personal freedoms were being eroded.

"Don't let anyone tell you that there is not more freedom in all the countries of the world tonight than there has been in any time in your lifetime," said Johnson. "I haven't lost my freedom, not a bit of it. I am freer tonight than I was a year ago because of the [nuclear] test ban treaty, because the air I breathe tonight is not as polluted as it was a year ago. I am freer tonight than I was when I was a boy...because we didn't have groceries on the table and we were chasing rabbits for food," he thundered.

The fiery rhetoric and "evangelistic fervor" were traits that characterized Johnson's speeches more before he became president than they had since, noted a journalist. "The arts of the Great Persuader of the Senate were on display," said another newsman. "Senator Goldwater is outclassed in this kind of combat, and President Johnson gave every indication of knowing it."

The president wound down his speech with a message of unity. "We must all learn somehow to submerge our individual differences to the common good," he said. "There are so many more things that unite us than divide us. There are so many more people in the world that love instead of hate. And we ought to be a nation of lovers, not of haters." Ultimately, he concluded, "This state is going to move forward, as all America is going to move forward."

After the president's speech, he headed to the airport, where he "worked the fences" one more time before boarding Air Force One and flying back to Washington.

Lady Bird and Lynda returned to the Lady Bird Special, which sat guarded on the tracks outside Raleigh, to spend the night.

Dr. Travell amiably tended train passengers well after midnight in a VIP lounge, putting drops in a hostess's eye and with three more patients awaiting their turns for medical attention.

Reporter Louisa Craig and a photographer colleague, Barbara Peterson, got a few hours of shut-eye on rollaway beds in a hotel's meeting room, the only accommodation available in the booked-up city. The thunderous ovation given to the President and the First Lady at the coliseum was still ringing in her ears.

An anonymous tipster rang the *Durham Morning Herald* with news that a group of Goldwater backers were threatening to block the Lady Bird Special from entering Durham the next morning with a "sit down" on the tracks. "If other people can do it, then we can, too," said the caller.

And as an added layer of precaution, railroad workers that night secured every switch along the next several-hundred-mile stretch of the tracks to ensure no one could divert the train from its scheduled course.

10

Not-So-Secret Weapon

Wednesday, October 7, 1964
Durham, North Carolina, 7:04 a.m.

As the Lady Bird Special rolled out of Raleigh the next morning before dawn, newspapers hit stands with a deluge of headlining coverage that confirmed what Lady Bird told reporters the prior evening: the trip was "snowballing remarkably."

The first day on the tracks, the Lady Bird Special covered 300 miles, made thirteen stops, and was a resounding success (and even for veteran reporters felt as if it were "three weeks long").

Most notably, Virginia Governor Albertis Harrison and North Carolina gubernatorial candidate Dan Moore "were both lassoed and pulled closer to the Democratic presidential ticket, with probably beneficial effects for Mr. Johnson in each state."

Similarly to what took place in Virginia, the Lady Bird Special shook up North Carolina state politics by winning Moore's public support for the presidential ticket. "Dan Moore Greets Presidential Plane" blared one headline. The day after the rally in Raleigh, Moore acknowledged Johnson's run for president and said his name for the first time in the campaign, albeit in a backhanded way. "If there is anybody in North Carolina," he said, "as there seems to be some indication, who does not know the name of the nominee, he is Lyndon Baines Johnson."

Governor Harrison shared with the press an altered and more enthusiastic opinion since riding the Lady Bird Special through Virginia the day before. Two months earlier, he predicted that the state would go for Goldwater. Although he still declined to publicly forecast the outcome of the presidential contest, he told reporters that in terms of winning Virginia, Democrats "could take great hope in the size of the crowds that turned out for the 'Lady Bird Special.'" Privately, he now predicted that President Johnson would win Virginia.

An estimated 70,000 people turned out in Virginia and North Carolina on day one of the whistle-stop tour. A news editor concurred with Governor Harrison, declaring the size of the crowds "the surprise" of the campaign train's first day. They were "considerably larger than expected and including almost as many men as women."

Lady Bird was dubbed the Democratic Party's "not-so-secret weapon." Another reporter said, "It would appear from the turnouts at the stops that Mrs. Johnson perhaps would have been an ideal running mate for her husband."

More evidence of the Lady Bird Special's momentum came with the announcement that morning that South Carolina representative John L. McMillan would board the train later in the day. It was "the first hint of backing for the Democratic ticket" from any of the state's congressmen, two of whom had already defected to the Goldwater camp.

Another editorial supposed that President Johnson's campaign was now "really on the road in North Carolina after a slow start."

The rousing, inspiring, hard-hitting political speech he delivered in Raleigh "is a part of today's campaign discussions across the nation." The state Democratic Party chairman, one of the officials who had urged Johnson to delay his visit, believed that "the President's stock rose sharply as the result of the Raleigh appearance."

Not all coverage of the Lady Bird Special was favorable. A longtime political reporter for a local Virginia paper wrote condescendingly of the train's "rather special Texas flavor." (He couldn't take the heat on the Pedernales River Chili, a favorite of the president, or the pickled okra, which he moaned was "hot enough to take the bark off a tree.") He wrote that the First Lady's "Southern accent seemed to thicken with each mile" and falsely claimed that all her jokes fell flat. (He also poked fun at other journalists who, he said, "never knew this part of the country existed.") And yet he ultimately concluded about the First Lady, "Republicans should not take this woman lightly."

As day two of the whistle-stop tour dawned, there was every indication the momentum would keep pace with the wheels rolling on the tracks.

The Lady Bird Special sped through the North Carolina countryside, passing by russet woods and fields dotted with goldenrod and Queen Anne's lace. Even at such an early hour, crowds had already gathered at crossroads and in towns to see the train. From a table in one of the Lady Bird Special's dining cars, a reporter watched schoolchildren waving from a red-clay bank beside the railroad and women in their nightgowns waving from their screen doors.

People from three counties began amassing in Durham, the first stop of the day. They shivered in forty-degree weather, some huddling around coffee urns set up in a parking lot at the train station.

A motorcade of University of North Carolina students left nearby Chapel Hill to meet the train in Durham. Organizers of the auto caravan promised free rides to the rally, entertainment, refreshments, and a return in time for eight o'clock classes.

Governor Sanford and his wife, who were running late in Raleigh and missed the train, raced by car to catch up with the Lady Bird Special.

The group of Goldwater backers who threatened to block the train from entering Durham never materialized.

On newsstands, that day's issue of the *Durham Morning Herald* underscored the historic significance of the First Lady coming to town. "The political nature of her visit lessens in no [way] the warmth and intensity of the welcome Durham and its people and their neighbors who come this morning have for her."

The city had been preparing for weeks for the Lady Bird Special's arrival. City leaders rolled out the red carpet, from a red, white, and blue welcome sign with three-foot-high letters to the unmissable LBJ atop the Central Carolina Bank building, the tallest structure in Durham.

"We want to make the First Lady remember her visit to Durham for the cordiality of our welcome, even as we of Durham will remember it for the honor it brings to the city."

As the 7:00 a.m. arrival time drew near, people moved from the parking lots and began to line both sides of the tracks.

The train pulled in to waving and cheering throngs estimated by the police chief at 12,500. Bands played and students from three area universities and colleges chanted "We want Lyndon" and "We want Johnson."

The size of the crowd at such an early-morning hour was "probably more newsworthy" than the one that greeted President Johnson at Reynolds Coliseum, noted a newspaper publisher and former speaker of the North Carolina House of Representatives. He also pointed out that Black attendees constituted a significant percentage of the crowd along the Lady Bird Special's route, and in Durham, they were a majority.

The overnight mist was still rising from the tobacco fields when the speeches got started on the Lady Bird Special's back platform.

"I don't know when I've ever been so flattered to see so many people getting up this early in the morning," remarked the First Lady.

"I saw a sign back there that said, 'We may be sleepy, but we're good Democrats.'"

Echoing language used by reporters to describe President Johnson during his speech in Raleigh, Lady Bird "warmed to the fray," wrote a journalist, and "fought for votes with the hatchet stroke of the old pros." As was her custom, she established a connection with the audience by recalling an anecdote of how Washington Duke, a local university's namesake, "turned two blind mules and 50 cents (or so the story goes)" into a fortune and "eventually became one of America's great philanthropists." Lady Bird then made her points about prosperity, economic growth, and education.

The only indication of discord was the by now common "battle of the placards." Johnson supporters brandished signs bearing messages like BURY GOLDWATER over a picture of Hitler and RIP 'EM UP, TEAR 'EM UP, GIVE 'EM HELL LYNDON. People labeled "Old Goldwater fools" by a woman in the crowd, as they had at every stop, also had their say with signage.

A Duke University delegation, members of the sorority Zeta Tau Alpha, hoped their sign would be noticed: ZETAS WELCOME LYNDA BIRD. It did catch her eye, and Carol Southmayd, who led the welcome group, was invited on the train for a chat with Lynda and the First Lady. Lynda had been a member of the sorority during her freshman year at the University of Texas at Austin. "She told me she missed the girls in the Zeta chapter at Texas," said Carol. (Lynda transferred to a university in Washington, DC, after her family moved into the White House, in part so that she could lend a hand to her mother.)

Lynda was "first in the hearts of the teenage set" at the Durham rally. Her introduction on the platform brought ear-splitting cheers from the Zetas and other young people gathered around the train. Two junior high school girls were impressed that she was so "proud of her father." They were also impressed by the First Lady campaigning and "going to all that trouble" for President Johnson. The reporter who interviewed the pair concluded that they "saw an example of enthusiasm, self-discipline, and graciousness set for them this morning by two older members of the 'weaker sex' who are proving strong in stamina and in support-getting as they follow the campaign trail for their husband and father."

Such examples were rare at a time when women and girls were encouraged to embrace the role of "housewife" as their highest purpose. The previous year, Betty Friedan identified in *The Feminine Mystique* "the problem that has no name," a widespread unhappiness fomenting among suburban women in the postwar years. Friedan's groundbreaking book, based on five years of research, upended the prevailing belief that women's fulfillment came solely from being wives and mothers, a belief reinforced by nearly every aspect of society. Women were conditioned to believe that if they were truly feminine, they would not want careers, higher education, or political or legal rights.

At stake was more than the abstract issues of equality and justice. Friedan documented how the "feminine mystique" stultified personal growth to such an unhealthy degree that it resulted in conditions like depression, alcoholism, and self-harm. When these conditions "burst like a boil through the image of the happy American housewife," media outlets and "experts" were quick to cast blame on superficial reasons (inept appliance repairmen or too much time at the PTA) or on education as the root cause. They concluded that being exposed to the world of ideas was not the proper preparation for domestic life. Some educators proposed that women no longer be admitted to four-year colleges and universities. Others suggested seeking religion to cure "this toothache of the spirit" or reminded the housewife how lucky she was to be her own boss. A columnist in *Harper's Bazaar* "joked" about taking away women's right to vote. "In the pre-19th Amendment era, the American woman was placid, sheltered and sure of her role in American society. She left all the political decisions to her husband and he, in turn, left all the family decisions to her," he wrote. "Today a woman has to make both the family *and* the political decisions, and it's too much for her."

Lady Bird clearly negated these notions. As she whistle-stopped down the tracks, she proved "that a woman can be a forceful politician and still remain a gracious lady," said Lindy Boggs.

She bridged the divide between the traditional and the progressive at a time when women still had limited legal rights and even wardrobe decisions like wearing pants were controversial. Lady Bird proudly and confidently identified herself as "a wife, mother, businesswoman and politician" and considered being First Lady "a daily working job."

Columnist Richard Wilson and others concurred. "We now have a working woman in the White House and an executive type, at that," wrote Wilson in April 1964.

The First Lady was a highly visible, headline-making role model for women seeking fulfillment beyond waxing the kitchen floor to a sheen. "In an age when the question of a 'dual role' has presented problems for so many women, Mrs. Johnson has successfully woven together the several strands of a complicated life," wrote *Redbook* columnist Margaret Mead. "Mrs. Johnson is giving us a model of what other American women can do and be in the mid-20th century."

Two decades earlier, Betty Friedan and other recent college graduates faced a void when they searched for identity and contemplated their futures. The absence of a variety of role models reinforced the idea that all roads led to domesticity. Now, the nation had a First Lady who helped fill that void.

Life magazine lauded the "zest and sanity" of Lady Bird's address at Radcliffe College in June 1964, deeming it the best commencement speech of the year. "Don't Fear [Says] Lady Bird: Femininity, Brains Mix" and "Radcliffe Seniors Hear Lady Bird Describe the Modern U.S. Woman" declared newspaper headlines.

"Time has brought the emergence of the woman with the dual role," Lady Bird told the Radcliffe graduates. She then pointed out that this wasn't a new concept but rather a resurgent one first born out of necessity. In the pioneering days of the West, women kept house and took leadership in political and social movements. "The Pony Express brought no magazines to ask her complicated questions about whether she liked the dual responsibilities."

Radcliffe seniors were pioneers of a new age, and they need not "fear that your intelligence is a threat to your femininity—that whatever you may achieve in your chosen work outside the home competes dangerously with your desirability as wife and mother. It can, but it needn't," said Lady Bird. "Ultimately, it comes back to the spirit in which you can direct your own life—how happily you can marry both man and job; or how happily you can marry one of them."

Lady Bird issued a political plea and reminded the graduates to use the power of their vote. "When you consider that the majority of potential voters are female and the majority of actual voters male, you can see there is a vast job to be done simply in stirring up the civic interest of women voters."

Lady Bird took this message of women's equal participation in politics and public life to the nation. During a speech on her Western "land and people" tour, she called out laws prohibiting women from serving on juries. Throughout 1964, she spoke forthrightly to her audiences.

"Don't hold back. Don't be shy. Step forward in every way you can to plan boldly, to speak clearly, to offer the leadership which the world needs," Lady Bird said to the American Home Economics Association in Michigan in a speech titled "New Horizons for Women." Women's "potential of strength for good" is exerted each time "we mark a ballot, teach our children, or work for a better community."

The nation's chief executive got the memo. "There are no cabinet officers or agency administrators who don't understand that my husband has a respect and affection for the abilities of women," Lady Bird told the Kentucky Federation of Women's Clubs. "Finding jobs for competent women is Lyndon's daily delight."

While campaigning in Ohio to support Frances McGovern's run for the U.S. House of Representatives, Lady Bird avowed, "The women of this country have a place in public life... In the annals of the Great Society, it will be recorded that women took on their responsibilities alongside men."

In Durham, the two junior high school girls who admired Lady Bird and Lynda witnessed and responded to a goal of the East Wing agenda, "to make the distaff White House a showcase for women in action."

When the train's engines started up, Lynda lifted two LYNDON pennants over her head. The crowd began chanting, "We want Lyndon," and the banners waved in rhythm to the cheers. The train started moving, growing smaller on the horizon, the pennants still fluttering.

The Lady Bird Special arrived early (by modern standards) and tarried briefly. But its stop in Durham would indeed be remembered "as one of the highlights of the city's history."

11

With Every Turn of the Wheels

Wednesday, October 7, 1964
Burlington, North Carolina, 8:10 a.m.

"Why can't Lady Bird Johnson pause for a short while in Burlington when she moves through the state aboard her 'Lady Bird Special'?"

An editorial in the local paper in late September laid out the reasons why Burlington should be added to the whistle-stop tour itinerary. Lady Bird had acquaintances in the area; nearby Elon College bestowed an honorary degree on her husband when he was vice president; it was conveniently situated on the rail line between two already determined stops, Raleigh and Greensboro, so stopping there wouldn't "tear up" the schedule; and the town promised "a warm and gracious reception."

The editorial acknowledged there were people who might not want the First Lady's train to stop in Burlington because they didn't like her husband's political views. "But so far as we know there is no reason to dislike Lady Bird. She's a charming lady, one highly dedicated to being a wife and mother and one who graces the White House as our First Lady before not only the nation but the world," continued the editorial. "Political differences aren't enough to keep us from paying our respects."

Two days later, an update in the newspaper announced that the request had been heard and heeded by the White House. The Lady Bird Special would stop in Burlington.

The promised "warm and gracious" reception came to pass with another robust 6,000-person crowd turning out for the train.

Mayor John Alley awaited the Lady Bird Special's arrival at the station. In his arms, he held seventeen brightly colored boxes of hosiery made by area manufacturers. The boxes were stacked and tied together with a red ribbon and topped with a bow, but they were not individually wrapped. All packages had to be inspected by the Secret Service before they were presented to members of the First Family.

Lady Bird appreciated the mayor's practical gift. "With every turn of the wheels, I have loved our trip through Virginia, through North Carolina, better and better. But it is hard on hosiery," she said. "Thank you, thank you, thank you." She promised to share the bounty with the other women on the train.

Security precautions in Burlington were extensive and involved no less than eight different agencies. Policemen guarded every railroad crossing in the city. State troopers patrolled the roads running parallel to the train, cruising both sides of the track. Officers stood at each overpass and on the roofs of six buildings near the depot. All boxcars were removed from the vicinity. Traffic was routed away from the station, and parking was prohibited in the immediate area. Only emergency vehicles, police cars, and radio and television vans were allowed within one block of the depot.

"We did everything humanly possible to guarantee the safety of the wife of our president," said Alfred Garner, the Burlington police chief. A Secret Service agent who arrived in town the day before praised the security efforts as among the most thorough along the Lady Bird Special's route.

Chief Garner described the sizable crowd as "one of the most orderly I have ever seen." Even the small cluster of people, mostly college students, holding GOLDWATER FOR PRESIDENT signs near the train's back platform were polite. "The Goldwater camp showed no signs of trying to take over the morning from the Democrats. There were no boos, no movements that could have embarrassed those who were wanting the morning to be a tribute to Mrs. Johnson," noted reporters on the scene. "Goldwater supporters, in other words, wanted everyone to know of their feelings, but they also showed their respect for the occasion and for the opposition."

What did the Lady Bird Special carry away from Burlington? The only thing known for sure was the supply of hosiery. Said a spectator, "I don't know what she carried away, except that she might feel pretty good to see so many people out so early." He added, "I'd say, however, that she left a lot."

Once the festivities concluded, the crowd dispersed and the depot area was cleared. Chief Garner breathed a sigh of relief. "I'm glad it's over," he said, "and it looks like everybody is pleased with the result."

Greensboro, North Carolina, 8:53 a.m.

Two station wagons filled with campaign paraphernalia—ribbons, hats, flags, and hundreds of signs—were the first vehicles to arrive at the athletic field on the University of North Carolina campus at Greensboro, one of the oldest colleges for women in the South. A cold wind whipped around as students and other spectators began gathering on the still-damp field near where the train would stop. By 7:30 a.m., the area was teeming with people.

When the Lady Bird Special arrived, an attorney in attendance counted the number of cars that formed the train. "Nineteen cars!" he exclaimed. "Who the h… they got with them?"

Dancing in the air were banners, signs, and pennants announcing, UNION WOMEN WELCOME LADY BIRD, LOCAL 3807, COMMUNICATIONS WORKERS OF AMERICA, LET'S KEEP LADY BIRD OUR FIRST LADY, LBJ IS OUR MAN, and BURY BARRY. The lone man who toted a dissenting sign—L.B. J. AIN'T O.K.—was ignored by the partisan crowd.

Cheers, screams, whistles, and band music filled the air as the campaign train dignitaries walked across a specially built, eighty-five-foot ramp extending from the railroad tracks to a speaker's platform on the athletic field. The loudest cheers erupted when Lady Bird and Lynda, smiling and waving, appeared on the ramp.

Emcee Hale Boggs revisited a point he had touched on the day before. "We hear about Senator Goldwater's so-called Southern strategy," he said. "That strategy supposes that we're going to be pushed back into the past."

He continued to hammer at Barry Goldwater, who was infamous for flip-flopping on campaign issues. "When they say Goldwater, which Goldwater do they mean?" he asked. "The pro- or the anti-civil rights Goldwater? The drop-the-bomb Goldwater or the don't-drop-the-bomb Goldwater? The vote-against-tobacco-and-textiles Goldwater or the vote-for-tobacco-and-textiles Goldwater? The tax-bill or the anti-tax-bill Goldwater? The against-Social-Security Goldwater or the for-Social-Security Goldwater?"

Boggs declared, "I've got news for Senator Goldwater. We Southerners have built a lot of universities. We have learned how to read and write...we aren't being fooled."

Fired up, the congressman proclaimed that Lyndon Johnson would not lead the nation back to an "era of closed textile mills, five-cent wages, depressed towns, people without jobs, without hope."

He asked the crowd, "Is the President going to carry North Carolina?" The crowd responded, "Y-E-E-S."

Before the university chancellor introduced the First Lady, he earned a rousing cheer when he said he had taken Lynda's advice, given the day before during several stops, and "turned out" classes for the occasion.

Lady Bird highlighted North Carolina as a leader in education for opening the first state university in the country. "Your Greensboro had the first tax-supported public school system in the state, and shortly before the turn of the twentieth century it had a larger proportion of its young people enrolled in school than any other Southern city," she continued. Nor had Greensboro slackened its pace since then, with its numerous area colleges totaling the largest student enrollment in North Carolina "and perhaps in the whole Southeast." She recalled with pride that the first major bill Johnson signed as president increased assistance for higher education and broadened the vocational education program.

"I would remind all of you who are enjoying the privilege of good education that with knowledge comes power and with power comes responsibility for whatever community you choose to live in after your graduation," she told the students present.

While the world's problems "are your inheritance and your challenge, there are the problems right next door to overcome." She quoted Edmund Burke, the Anglo-Irish statesman and philosopher, who once said, "The only thing necessary for the triumph of evil is for good men to do nothing." She then offered her own words of wisdom, encouraging all students to make their voices heard and to offer their leadership. "Your country and our world need you."

When the train's departure chime sounded, spectators called out their goodbyes. Some rushed up to the edge of the ramp to shake the First Lady's hand, among them a woman who claimed kinship. Lady Bird replied, "Yes, I'm going to meet a lot of cousins on this trip, I imagine."

12

You Can't Catch Us

Wednesday, October 7, 1964
High Point, North Carolina, 9:50 a.m.

I f it were up to the train crew and the security staff, the Lady Bird Special would have rolled right by the crowd gathered at the station in High Point. But a group of local Democrats on board took their case directly to the First Lady, who recalled stopping there while campaigning on the LBJ Special. She instructed the crew to halt the train in High Point for a brief visit.

The scene greeting the Lady Bird Special contrasted with the one that played out in 1960, when a disappointingly small crowd of several hundred showed up to see the vice-presidential campaign train. An advance man who spent a week in town trying to drum up turnout quietly boarded the LBJ Special and remarked, "This is a rough one."

Despite the still-strong Republican strength in the area, this time, some 2,000 people amassed on the passenger platform at the station and lined the walkways and streets overlooking the tracks. As the train pulled in, high school band members chanted "LBJ for the USA," another band played "Hello, Lyndon!" and the crowd cheered.

Twenty-six Black high school students in High Point made headlines nearly five years earlier for their part in the civil rights movement. They were the first high schoolers to stage a lunch-counter sit-in, a movement started by college students in Greensboro and that subsequently spread throughout the South. After the initial sit-in at a Woolworth lunch counter, the High Point students continued to peacefully protest at various locations in town. In retaliation, they were subject to abuses by white mobs, whose tactics included pelting them with snowballs packed with broken glass and coal.

Greensboro was the third city in North Carolina to desegregate its lunch counters, following Winston-Salem and Charlotte, in July 1960. In High Point, it took another three years of continued effort before lunch counters were desegregated.

As the Lady Bird Special slowed into High Point, Lynda commanded the platform. She called out a greeting, introduced herself and Lady Bird, and mentioned her parents' previous visit. The train barely stopped before it was on the move again. As it began to pull out of the station, several teenage boys ran behind it, carrying placards reading GOLDWATER FOR PRESIDENT and adorned with a large picture of the senator. Lynda flipped on the loudspeaker again and cheerfully reproached the boys and the Southern strategy. "You're running after the twentieth century," she told them. "You can't catch us."

Thomasville, North Carolina, 10:02 a.m.

The Lady Bird Special continued hustling through North Carolina.

"They call this a whistle-stop campaign, but don't kid yourself," joked a reporter. "What it was, in football terms, was a Lady Bird blitz."

During a stop in Thomasville, Lady Bird told the crowd, "I remember how wonderful you all were to Lyndon and me when we were here in 1960."

Her husband made a memorable impression when he accepted the mayor's invitation to take a seat in the "Big Chair" near the tracks. Firemen provided a ladder for him to scale the thirty-foot-tall sculpture, which was crafted from concrete and steel and painted to look like an armchair, a symbol of the city's role in the furniture industry. Once atop the chair, Johnson waved his Stetson hat in the air before tossing it into the crowd.

Secret Service agents warned against Lady Bird leaving the train to perch in the Big Chair, although she was presented with a replica of the famous landmark along with a key to the city.

After the train left Thomasville, reporter Louisa Craig was finally able to have a quick word with Lady Bird Special co-chair Virginia Russell. "I am overwhelmed with the number of persons who have welcomed us at the stops," Virginia said. "Mrs. Johnson is getting very little rest on the trip, and her stamina just amazes me."

For the Lady Bird Special team, each day on the campaign train required an enormous amount of endurance. With so many stops close together, there was "hardly time to work the local VIPs through the train before they were off and another group was boarding," observed a correspondent. And for each stop, there was homework to be done. Bess Abell kept Lady Bird apprised of and prepared with facts about the people she would be meeting, from town mayors and city council members right on down to a fourth cousin once removed and a grade schooler who had written a paper about the First Lady. As if Abell were "conducting a school play," she would exit the train to coordinate the new passengers and the order in which they boarded.

Lexington, North Carolina, 10:22 a.m.

After Thomasville, it was on to Lexington, where security was laxer than it had been in other places. Not only were some of the estimated 5,500 attendees standing on top of freight cars and railroad siding sheds, they congregated on the train station's roof. At street level, they were lined three and four deep.

There were cheers and screams, the high school band played on, the helicopters whirred overhead, and spectators surged as close to the rear platform as the security men allowed. Amid all the commotion, Lady Bird remained serene as she spoke on the platform.

"My only wish is that I could get down there in the crowd and meet every one of you," she said. "As we go further on this whistle-stop, I want to leave you with this thought." Her husband's quarter century of experience included the past ten months as president, during which time they had seen him in action leading the country and so knew what kind of a man and a leader they were getting. "I'm proud of his record," she told the crowd. "I believe you all approve of it, and I hope you will be with us in November."

Salisbury, North Carolina, 10:50 a.m.
In Salisbury, the First Lady began her brief remarks with a jovial "Nothing could be finer than to be in Carolina in the morning." She "bragged on her husband" to the approval of the cheering, sign-waving spectators (and a left-leaning canine wearing a blanket saying, "If I could vote, I'd vote for LBJ").

There were thousands of Johnson fans, four high school bands, scores of policemen, two K-9 police dogs, and a handful of Goldwater supporters in attendance. But only one person received a headline in a major newspaper's full-page coverage of the day's events: "Old Prof. Came on Special Request to Greet 1st Lady." As far as the press could determine, J. Mason Brewer, a sixty-eight-year-old humanities professor at a nearby college, was the only nonofficial there who received a personal invitation from the White House. Brewer was originally from Texas and a friend of the Johnson family. He was a renowned scholar on African American folklore with an impressive résumé—the first Black member of the Texas Folklore Society and the Texas Institute of Letters and the first Black officer in the American Folklore Society, in which he served as vice president. Professor Brewer was escorted onto the train's back platform for a reunion with Lady Bird. "I asked her to give my best to the President," he said, "and tell him when the people go to the polls next month they are not going to let him and the country down."

Lynda called out the opposition at this stop. "I see all these wonderful signs," she said. "I see one or two over here I don't necessarily agree with, but I'm glad that we live in a country where we *can* disagree." Two members of a teenage Republican club lowered slightly the sign they were carrying. Part of the lettering on the sign, which read Now, MORE THAN EVER WE NEED GOLDWATER, fell off before the rally was over.

As the Lady Bird Special prepared to leave Salisbury, Governor Sanford cracked what was reported to be the best joke of the day. Spying a costumed clown in the crowd, he asked, "Who invited Bill Miller here?"

When the departure chime sounded, reporter Barbara McAden was so engrossed in conversation with a local Democrat and the three young children with him that she didn't hear the don't-get-left-behind signal. When she saw the train moving away, she "fled down the tracks" and leaped onto the observation car platform.

Concord, North Carolina, 11:23 a.m.
The Lady Bird Special entered the home stretch in North Carolina with a quick pass in Concord.

The decoy engine continued to confound the crowds. A diesel horn sounded in the distance, and a cheer erupted until the single car rolled past Concord's weathered brick station.

"Oh, darn. That wasn't even it," said a teenaged girl wearing an LBJ hat.

When the real train arrived a few minutes later, Lady Bird gave the crowd a characteristically sincere greeting. "With every stop, it gets better, more colorful, more wonderful. I just can't tell you how much this trip warms my heart and how happy it makes me," she said. She brought greetings from the president, who would like to have been along on the whistle-stop tour and remembered fondly their previous train trip. She continued, "In these last ten, long months that began on such a tragic day, he's tried mighty hard for the people that he works for. That is all of you." He poured into the presidency "all of the intellect and all of the heart and all the steadiness and stability that's in him to keep this country on a prosperous path and to keep us at peace."

As the Lady Bird Special pulled out of the Concord station, a flock of youngsters, given a half-day holiday from school, ran behind the train until it picked up speed and disappeared from view.

13

Campaign Right Hand

Wednesday, October 7, 1964
Charlotte, North Carolina, 11:50 a.m.

"Is there gonna be a football game?" six-year-old Dave Connelly asked his mother.

Amid the festivities at Independence Square in Charlotte, where some 25,000 people packed the area, Dave was most impressed with the band. He held a blue LBJ balloon in one hand and an ice cream cone in the other as his mother explained as best she could why they were there. When she finished, her inquisitive youngster had another question.

"Who's Lady Bird?"

Elsewhere in the crowd, ten-year-old Nancy Lloyd held a sign that said Use Your Head Instead of Your Heart. Vote LBJ. Nancy and about one hundred other students from three fifth-grade classes were studying politics and elections, and they came to Independence Square on a school field trip.

A man with a walkie-talkie, seemingly posing as a Secret Service agent, was spreading the rumor that President Johnson would be in Charlotte.

Sounds of amusement rippled through the crowd when someone hung a GOLDWATER FOR PRESIDENT banner out the window of a building bordering Independence Square.

Across town, the Lady Bird Special arrived at the railway terminal. The mayor and other bigwigs were on hand to greet the train, three bands played, a vendor loudly hawked LBJ and Goldwater buttons, and Lady Bird was presented with a bouquet of yellow roses. Several high school girls ran up to Lynda, wished her well, and asked for her autograph.

Acknowledging the large, enthusiastic crowd, Lady Bird said to those on the train platform with her, "I think Charlotte likes my LBJ."

She then exited the train and greeted a long line of local Democratic Party dignitaries. After that, Lady Bird worked the fences, shaking hands with the spectators who had convened. They included uniformed postmen holding a banner: WELCOME LADY BIRD BRANCH 545 NATIONAL ASSOCIATION OF LETTER CARRIERS. Some of the high school band members were so mesmerized by the First Lady, they stopped playing and tried to get a handshake along with the rest of the crowd.

Lynda, who followed right behind her mother shaking hands, approached a group of teenage girls. Cameras in the group clicked, pennants waved, and their excited sounds rose to a higher pitch. (Another schoolgirl named Lynda, who was in attendance at the rally, planned to make a report on her namesake at school the next day.)

Lynda and Luci both received fan mail daily "from all parts of the world" asking for advice and wanting information. The interest from fellow young people wasn't primarily political, concluded a reporter on the whistle-stop tour, but more like the admiration "heaped upon entertainers like the Beatles or young actresses like Tuesday Weld."

More cheering spectators lined the streets as an eight-vehicle motorcade left the Charlotte train station and headed for Independence Square. Lady Bird waved from the back seat of a convertible, Lynda did the same two cars back, and buses loaded with the press brought up the rear.

Once in Independence Square, Hale Boggs, flashing a "hush-puppy grin," got things rolling by adding a kick to his culinary references. "We had grits for breakfast this morning," he said, "and tonight we might have a mint julep with a little mountain moonshine in it."

Suddenly, the speech giving on the platform was interrupted when five fire trucks came roaring down the street, sirens blaring, and ground to a halt in front of a building on the Square—a building that had three GOLDWATER FOR PRESIDENT banners and a large photo of the senator hanging from some windows. The fire trucks were dispatched after an anonymous male caller claimed there was a fire in the building's elevator shaft, an especially brazen act considering city detectives were staked out on the roof. Within minutes, crews inspected the building from the basement to the penthouse and determined there was no fire.

"It was an unlawful alarm," said the police chief. "I don't know whether it had anything to do with [the] nature of the crowd assembled at the Square, but I rather suspect that it did." The overt effort to "pour cold water" on the Lady Bird Special's rally failed, and the program went on without pause.

"We're running so strong that the Republicans figure they had best call out the fire department to help them with their problems," ribbed Luther Hodges.

Lady Bird, "wearing a red wool suit and a big Texas smile," earned thunderous applause with the first sentence she uttered. "I am pleased to be here in the Queen City of Charlotte—the crown jewel of the Piedmont Crescent."

She referenced points of pride in the city's history, like its nickname, coined during the Revolutionary War by General Charles

Cornwallis when he marched the British army into Charlotte and encountered a fierce "hornet's nest" of resistance. She even gave a sincere shout-out to the local legend claiming Charlotte County leaders signed their own "Mecklenburg Declaration of Independence" denouncing British rule a year before the Continental Congress inked the official one in Philadelphia. One local newspaper credited Lady Bird with "wisely" steering clear of the controversy surrounding the unverified existence of the document.

After Lady Bird noted North Carolina's educational emphasis and economic growth and said she found an aliveness and a spark while traveling through the state, she switched the focus of her speech to a different topic: peace.

"Your goals here in North Carolina do not end with economic development," she said. "You are striving to create an environment in which people may live happily and raise their children soundly. But you know and I know that we cannot breathe easily or raise our children unafraid unless we are sure that all possible steps are being taken to build a stable and lasting peace. To every mother in this crowd, that is the most important thing before us today."

Lady Bird continued, "Building for peace is a day-by-day work. It takes patience and a steady hand at many levels of government. But finally, you get to the ultimate responsibility which rests with the President. My husband has said: 'The true courage in this nuclear age lies in the quest for peace.' I like the way he just summed it up in one sentence like this: 'Our guard is up, but our hand is out.'"

Lady Bird's emphasis on peace underscored a Democratic campaign strategy reminding voters that Goldwater's extremism made him unfit for the presidency. Goldwater characterized the nuclear bomb as "merely another weapon" and indicated that he would give the North Atlantic Treaty Organization's military commanders the authority to use tactical nuclear weapons without consulting the president. "Make no mistake. There is no such thing as a conventional nuclear weapon,"

Johnson responded. "No president of the United States can give up responsibility for deciding when or if to use nuclear weapons."

The possibility of having Goldwater in charge of nuclear weapons was a concern shared by large swaths of voters and led the *Kansas City Star* to "unhesitatingly" endorse President Johnson. The moderately conservative newspaper had not supported a Democratic presidential candidate since backing Grover Cleveland for reelection in 1892. "We are convinced that the cause of world peace would be better served by Mr. Johnson and his foreign policy, with its roots deep in both Democratic and Republican administrations." They feared the Goldwater philosophy "might plunge the world deeper into the uncertainty of greater international tensions" and believed "that to entrust the peace to a Goldwater administration would be an unnecessary and undesirable gamble for the nation to take."

Goldwater's opponent in the 1964 Republican primary, Nelson Rockefeller, asked in campaign literature, "Who do you want in the room with the H-bomb button?" Democrats continued this line of attack, producing a TV commercial that depicted a young girl standing in a field and picking petals off a flower. As she counts upward, her words are replaced by a mission-control countdown that concludes with a mushroom cloud. The "Daisy ad" did not mention Goldwater by name but nonetheless had the desired effect. The ad, which aired only once, on the evening of September 7, 1964, was revolutionary for veering from the tradition of stodgy, fact-filled campaign ads to instead play on viewers' emotions. (The Daisy ad is still one of the most talked-about and controversial political ads.)

In Charlotte, as Lady Bird had done along the line since Alexandria, she "gave a lesson in history—and politicking."

Addressing "politicking," Joe Doster, a reporter for the *Charlotte Observer*, cheekily and cynically assessed the speakers' platform. "Lady Bird was the star, of course," he wrote. The platform is "a stage," and the people on it were "actors playing their parts." One of the "generally understood rules" when deciding who to include is that "the more people on the platform the better." The mayor was there to welcome the First Lady to Charlotte, tell her "what a great town it is," and present her with "a key to the city, a hornets' nest and other things she has no real use for whatsoever." Others were there to convey to various groups that President Johnson was good for them: businessmen, progressives, conservatives, Black people, young people, and women. Jeanelle Moore's presence indicated unity in the party, and that of Democratic officials signified strong backing for the Johnson-Humphrey ticket. State and local candidates were at the rally in force. "Their presence there is supposed to make their supporters like President Johnson better and make President Johnson's supporters like them better," concluded Doster. "That way everybody gains."

In other words, the well-orchestrated, detail-oriented design of the Lady Bird Special was achieving its aims of vote getting and conveying a message of party unity and inclusivity.

An editorial in a rival Charlotte publication summed up the impact of Lady Bird's visit. "The President's chief emissary of good will and strong campaign right hand was all that she might have been," stated the paper. "When she boarded her train afterwards to continue her southern tour, she left behind many new admirers. She is at home among southern people, the President's wife, because she is one herself. In the South, she may help her husband more than he can help himself between now and November 3."

14

How Did You Get to Be This Way?

Wednesday, October 7, 1964
Rock Hill, South Carolina, 1:37 p.m.

When it was remarked that the Lady Bird Special's route rolled across ground on the front lines of the civil rights battle, Rock Hill was one of those places.

On January 31, 1961, a group of nine Black students from Friendship Junior College, along with a civil rights adviser, ordered hamburgers, soft drinks, and coffee at a five-and-dime's lunch counter and were refused service. The group was arrested after declining to leave, jailed for the night, and the next day convicted of trespassing and breach of peace.

The young men employed the "jail, no bail" method of resistance, with nine of them refusing to pay a $100 fine (the one who did pay risked jeopardizing a football scholarship if he was incarcerated). The "Friendship Nine," as they became known, were sentenced to thirty days of hard labor and sent to a county prison farm to work on a road gang.

The extreme tactic of jail, no bail was born partly out of necessity. Activists arrested during the sit-in movement would usually be bailed out of jail by paying a hefty fine, usually around $100 per person (an amount roughly equal to $1,050 today). But as the protests continued, it became a costly endeavor for civil rights groups. The jail, no bail method alleviated the financial burden, while at the same time, it delivered a double whammy to law enforcement: denying funds to continue suppressing the freedom struggle and forcing them to foot the bill for incarceration. In addition, the Friendship Nine's brave act garnered widespread publicity for the civil rights cause.

A week later, Diane Nash, Charles Sherrod, and other members of the Student Nonviolent Coordinating Committee staged a sit-in at the same lunch counter in Rock Hill to support the Friendship Nine. They too were arrested, refused to pay a fine, and jailed. Dr. Martin Luther King Jr. praised their efforts and willingness to endure grievous hardships for the cause. In a letter sent to Nash and Sherrod, he wrote,

TO THE FREEDOM FIGHTERS:

I do want you to know that you have my prayers for your sustained Christian witness in this dark hour in Rock Hill. You have inspired all of us by such demonstrative courage and faith. It is good to know that there still remains a creative minority who would rather lose in a cause that will ultimately win than to win in a cause that will ultimately lose.

Your actions are moral, democratic, Christian and nonviolent. You transcend the judgments of evil men who decry the powerful weapon you are using. Every day that you remain behind bars sears the conscience of that immoral city. You are shaming them into decency.

Great numbers of us will be with you on Sunday—giving thanks for your courageous spirit and asking God's special presence in your lives.

*Faithfully yours,
Martin Luther King, Jr.*

Three months later, Rock Hill was a stop on the first journey of the Freedom Riders. Two integrated groups of Black and white civil rights activists, traveling on separate buses, set out from Washington, DC, and rode through the South to challenge Supreme Court rulings that made segregation in interstate travel illegal—on public buses as well as in restaurants and waiting rooms in terminals that served interstate bus lines.

Passage of the Civil Rights Act was still three years in the future when the Greyhound bus carrying the Freedom Riders pulled into Rock Hill in May 1961. Twenty-one-year-old John Lewis debarked along with fellow riders Al Bigelow and Genevieve Hughes, both of whom were white. "I could tell we were in real trouble as soon as I stepped off the bus," said Lewis. In the terminal, when they went to enter the "Whites" waiting room, they were confronted by a group of young white men.

"I have a right to go in here," said Lewis, "on the grounds of the Supreme Court decision in the *Boynton* case." A fist smashed into the side of his head, the first of the many blows he took even after he fell to the ground. Bigelow stepped in between Lewis and the men, "standing square, with his arms at his sides." The mob then attacked Bigelow, who did not fight back either. It wasn't until Genevieve Hughes blocked the path of several more men heading over and was knocked to the floor that a police officer, who had stood by and watched, finally intervened and stopped the brutality.

None of the original Freedom Riders made it by bus to New Orleans, their final destination. As they traveled through Alabama and

Mississippi, there were more mob attacks, firebombing of a bus, three weeks of incarceration for Lewis and others in the Mississippi state penitentiary, and other heinous acts, some carried out by the KKK and by law enforcement and with the knowledge of the states' governors. Not even direct orders from the White House quelled the violence against the Freedom Riders.

Black motorists were routinely denied service in motels and restaurants along the interstate. Even using gas station restrooms was denied to them, making long journeys even more difficult. Lady Bird witnessed this racial disparity while commuting on the twice-yearly car trips she made between Washington, DC, and Texas when her husband was in Congress. Motel operators would readily cater to her and in the next breath deny her request to book rooms for the Black household members traveling with her. On one trip, a request for a room for the young Lynda's nurse, Otha Ree, was refused with a racial slur. "That was offensive, and I bridled," said Lady Bird. "I was hurt for Otha Ree, and angry, too." Another time, Zephyr Wright, the Johnsons' cook, was refused lodging at one place where a desk clerk said, "We work 'em but we don't sleep 'em." Lady Bird replied, "That's a nasty way to be," and she and her companions drove on.

Zephyr Wright, who studied home economics at Wiley College in Marshall, Texas, was recommended to Lady Bird by the school's president. She began working for the Johnsons in 1942, and she remained the family's personal chef throughout their years in the White House. Wright was instrumental in President Johnson's coming to fully embrace and support civil rights, which by his own admission was a gradual process. James Farmer of the Congress of Racial Equality once asked Johnson why he was pressing so hard to pass the 1964 Civil Rights Act. "Mr. President, how did you get to be this way?" he asked. "You're a southerner, and your congressional record on civil rights was not very good. What changed you?"

Johnson had two answers. One was that becoming president

freed him from accountability primarily to a Southern constituency. The other was how Zephyr Wright's experiences, and those of others in the Johnsons' household, made the issue more personal. One day, when Johnson requested that Wright and her husband, Sammy, drive his vice-presidential car to Texas, she gave him the unvarnished truth about why they would no longer make the trek. She and Sammy ate food out of brown bags, slept in the car, and couldn't even use restrooms.

Johnson spoke of Wright's experiences to persuade reluctant lawmakers to reconsider their stance on civil rights, using them to humanize the abstractness of the legislation. One of those lawmakers was John Stennis, the segregationist Mississippi senator. Johnson gave it to him straight. "They drove through your state," he said. "When they had to go to the bathroom, they would stop, pull off on a side road, and Zephyr Wright, the cook of the Vice President of the United States, would squat in the road to pee." Johnson kept hammering away. "You know, John, that's just bad. That's wrong. And there ought to be something to change that. And it seems to me that if people in Mississippi don't change it voluntarily, that it's just going to be necessary to change it by law."

Zephyr Wright was in the East Room at the White House when President Johnson signed the Civil Rights Act of 1964. Afterward, he handed her one of the many pens he used, saying, "You deserve this more than anybody else."

Other than crossing the state line into South Carolina, there was no indication in Rock Hill that the Lady Bird Special had left the "rim states" of Virginia and North Carolina and entered one with "a lesser degree of obedience" in complying with the Civil Rights Act. Some trouble lay ahead for the Lady Bird Special in South Carolina and elsewhere in the South, but in Rock Hill, the reception for the campaign train was as tremendous as any along the route so far.

The crowd was solidly integrated, largely youthful, and one of the most jovial of the entire trip. The first spectators to arrive at the train station were children excused from school, followed by college students. Then came businessmen and clerks who showed up after the usual Wednesday afternoon store closing, housewives, and others.

"They've never had anything like this, a First Lady visiting Rock Hill," a man said as he shifted a child in his arms. "It's something for kids down here to see. When I was growing up, we never saw anything like this."

A woman with a carload of children stopped her station wagon at a light and shouted to him, "Are those Johnson balloons? I want some for my kids."

Both sides of the railroad track were lined with balloons strung from power poles. Volunteers appeared with a plethora of campaign supplies, and banners and hats were handed out. A bus arrived and unloaded a high school band, one of four that would perform. A bank of telephones was set up where the press could dictate timely stories to their newsrooms. An American flag and a Confederate flag waved in the cool breeze. National guardsmen, city, county, and state police officers, and Secret Service agents moved quietly among the crowd. (The plainclothesmen were identified to each other by tiny colored hatpins in their lapels.)

Signs proclaimed WELCOME LYNDA, WELCOME LADY BIRD, DIXIE IS STILL DEMOCRATIC, ALL THE WAY WITH LBJ, WELCOME TO SOUTH CAROLINA, and many more. Banners with HI, LYNDA on one side and HI, LUCI on the other were held high. A young woman waved to a friend across the tracks. A Winthrop College student intently studied a book. She paused to tell a reporter, "I've got a chemistry test at three."

The tempo picked up as the crowd swelled. The bands launched into musical battles to see which one could play with more vigor. A loudspeaker announced that the Lady Bird Special was running fifteen minutes behind schedule. The crowd groaned, except for a group of grinning teenagers who broke out Goldwater bumper stickers and placards. The dignitaries inside a roped-off area scowled as the renegades unveiled a large GOP sign.

The advance engine rumbled by and drew a vigorous cheer. Cries of "Lady Bird!" could be heard.

There was another lull before the public address system announced that the Lady Bird Special was almost there. The crowd cheered the announcement. The bands began playing again, and a small red-haired boy danced around.

The crowd cheered the helicopters that appeared, buzzing overhead.

Finally, the campaign train rounded a curve and came into view. Some 8,000 people continuously cheered as car after car passed the platform. A porter looked out of a doorway, waved, and received a louder shout.

Joining the platform program were Governor Donald Russell, who was introduced as "a Democrat—without prefix or suffix," and Senator Olin Johnston, "the lone loyal Democratic Senator from the state of South Carolina." In a booming voice, "which always sounds as though he is talking to left field," Senator Johnston assured the crowd, "I know what South Carolina is going to do on November the third when that election comes. They're going to vote Democratic like they've always voted. And I would be derelict in my duty if I didn't stick to my party too."

As the governor, the senator, and a parade of other people were introduced, there was a restless murmuring from the crowd, which at that point had been gathering for five hours. But when Lady Bird stepped up to the podium, they gave her their undivided attention. Even a group of young people carrying Goldwater signs and chanting, "We want Barry," quieted while she spoke.

"My grandmother, Emma Bates, was born in this state," Lady Bird told the crowd. The resounding roar of approval "left no doubt that the thousands gathered here were glad to claim the First Lady as a kissin' cousin." She relayed the president's affinity with and concern for the South, and "there was thunderous applause" for that too. When she referenced the dark November day that brought him to the presidency, the crowd fell silent and "some eyes turned to the nearby rooftops where uniformed police kept a constant vigil."

The Lady Bird Special's visit was well covered by the local paper, the *Herald*, with reporters and photographers on the ground, a reporter in an airplane, and Louisa Craig and Barbara Peterson riding the train from Raleigh. Newspaper publisher Wayne C. Sellers confided in Kara Burney of the White House advance team that he was "getting reckless" by allowing two of his staff members to travel on the Lady Bird Special. Donald and Virginia Russell "had given the whistle-stop workers no illusions that South Carolina would be an easy state," said Burney. "Their predictions proved true."

In Rock Hill, the First Lady, in a "flowing, soft-toned Southern accent, won the regard—if not the votes—of many in the crowd as she delivered her soft-sell political message from-Lyndon-with-love," noted a reporter. "It was, perhaps, less of a crowd than might be expected if her visit had been non-political, but big enough." As at other stops, attendees had a mix of motivations for attending the rally: to support their political party, to voice their opposition, or simply to see the president's wife.

"No matter their reason, they were there and saw and heard a woman making political history," wrote Louisa Craig.

How many votes Lady Bird swayed was questionable since the crowd contained a significant number of spectators not yet old enough to cast ballots. These young people readily shared their reasons for being there. A teenage Goldwater supporter with a sign told a reporter, "I just want to let them know I think he's a better man. I'm not old enough to vote, but I'll be old enough to re-elect him."

Johnson supporters were there in droves, from college students to eleven-year-old Johnnie Mae Avery, who asked her mother's permission to get out of school so that she could see the First Lady.

"I wanted to hear [Mrs. Johnson's] speech and see what her husband's main points are if he's elected President. I'd like very much to see how he's going to help poverty. To me, Johnson's the best for the Presidency," said JoAnne McMullen, a student at Emmett Scott, a Black high school. (South Carolina public schools did not fully desegregate until 1970 when mandated by federal court order.)

High schooler Henry Massy said he would vote for President Johnson because "I don't like Goldwater's views on nuclear weapons." Another said he felt it was important to see the First Lady. "I've seen state and local political figures, but never a national political celebrity." In addition, he disapproved of Goldwater's actions and disliked the way he "twists words."

Some split the difference, like a teenage married couple—he was for Goldwater and she for Johnson.

Nine-year-old Billy Finch's parents thought it was important for him to witness the Lady Bird Special and hear the First Lady speak, but he, thirteen-year-old Rhoda McAteer, and numerous other children came to the rally of their own volition.

Among the littlest attendees was five-year-old Terry Stewart, who accompanied his mother. He declared himself a Democrat, and his mother added that he was a working one, helping her at the party's county headquarters.

Lynda Bird fans were there too.

"I like that daughter," a high school girl said to a friend.

As the train departed, only Lynda remained on the observation platform, tossing candy kisses from a white basket into the crowd.

A small girl received one of the chocolates. "Don't you dare eat that. Save it, save it," her mother said as the Lady Bird Special slowly pulled away, heading even deeper into Goldwater territory.

15

A Little Excitement

Wednesday, October 7, 1964
Chester, South Carolina, 2:16 p.m. and
Winnsboro, South Carolina, 3:05 p.m.

With Governor and Virginia Russell aboard, the atmosphere on the Lady Bird Special "became as southern as gingerbread" as it continued traveling through South Carolina.

In Chester, the train's next stop, banners fluttered, a photographer climbed halfway up a utility pole for an optimum shot, and a little tyke in the front row of the waiting crowd hollered, "We want Lady Bug." A radio broadcast announced game one of the World Series as the underdog St. Louis Cardinals battled the New York Yankees, but the crowd didn't care about the sporting event. A signal light had turned red, indicating the campaign train was coming, and cheers resounded.

"I'm very happy to be here and to welcome to my hometown the

First Lady of the Land," said Governor Russell. "I'm proud of Chester, and I'm proud of what Chester is going to do on November third."

The first speech Russell gave as governor in 1963 was hailed as part of a "New Note in Dixie" by *Time* magazine. "In a pleasant departure from the past," the governor wasn't "just whistling Dixie." Russell promised to give all South Carolinians "the opportunity they truly deserve" and pledged, "We shall work out our problems peaceably, according to our standards of justice and decency." In an even more dramatic break from the past, he and Virginia forewent the traditional inaugural festivities and instead hosted a barbecue on the executive mansion grounds to which everyone in the state was invited. The gathering was attended by Blacks and whites, the first integrated state function since Reconstruction. Virginia loved to entertain, and the size of a crowd never worried her. "It's as easy to plan for one hundred as for ten, and I enjoy people so much," she said. The Russells continued to have an open-house policy at the executive mansion, where groups and individuals were welcome at all hours and the governor personally answered his phone.

In Chester, Lady Bird was honest with the audience. "I don't mind telling you I started out on this trip with a mixture of anxiety and anticipation," she said. "Anxiety because I'm not used to whistle-stopping without my husband and trying to make the speeches." And yet there was also anticipation at returning to "a part of the country that is home to me." She recalled some of the cherished memories from her childhood that she had evoked at previous stops, along with her hope that Chester, "while remaining a stronghold of that type of the South," would embrace the progressive years ahead.

"I think that what every mother and father out there want for their children is freedom from the problems of poverty which cripple in body and spirit, opportunity for education, and a promise of national stability and world peace. And that's what you have on your minds when you're looking for a man to vote for for president.

"I just want to say about the man that I know best, that I have watched him serve the people of this country for the last quarter of a century," Lady Bird continued. "He has brought stability and progress to this country and kept his eyes always looking upward toward things that can bring to America a greater future. I thank you for welcoming us here. It'll be one of the happy memories of these great days traveling through the South."

Even after eleven stops so far that day addressing the crowds, "you could still detect the note of enthusiasm in Mrs. Johnson's and Lynda's voices as they left Chester for Columbia," reported Louisa Craig.

After boarding the train that morning in Raleigh, Craig quickly realized that "whistle-stopping" involved "rail hopping." At each station, sometimes before the train came to a complete stop, reporters and photographers grabbed their equipment and hustled to the platform area.

Nan Robertson recalled the gauntlet of having to "jump off the train, run down the cinder track, get down Lady Bird's remarks, interview people in the crowd, note down a few signs, and sprint back to the central part of the train and the press car to start typing." Even the four to five car lengths reporters had to scramble was arduous along the cinder tracks. Dr. Travell treated the bumps, bruises, and sprained ankles they sustained, especially while attempting to quickly reboard the train, often as it was pulling away from a station.

"It was physically the most grueling of all campaign trips," said Robertson. "If you could survive it and turn out good copy, you could survive anything."

With so many stops made each day, reporters were always pressed for time with barely a moment to rest or to eat. Each reporter had a "roomette," but since Robertson's was six cars away from the press facilities, she seldom used it except to sleep. She had a meal in the dining car once during the four-day trip because "there was too much happening, and it was too crowded and far away." Reporters and news crews primarily subsisted on the offerings at a snack bar adjacent to one of the press cars and the food served at the daily happy hour, like ham biscuits in Virginia and other bites themed to each state.

The timeliness of their stories was critical. NBC correspondent Nancy Dickerson recalled how her television news crew would locate a runner sent to a predetermined stop to pick up film and have it flown to a major city to be processed, all to try and beat the competition on air. ABC had a six-person team aboard the Lady Bird Special to navigate the logistics of getting stories completed in time for the evening news. They took turns leaving the train to "feed the story," while others remained onboard to continue coverage and because someone had to be on the scene "protectively." As ABC News correspondent Marlene Sanders explained, "protectively" was a euphemism for "in case of violence, or in case the candidate is shot." (Sanders was another industry pathbreaker and later that year became the first woman to anchor a network evening newscast when she filled in last minute for the regular host, who had lost his voice.)

Similarly, print reporters for the wire services had a method for quickly turning around their own stories. They would toss copy out a train window to bureau representatives waiting along the route. And those weren't the only challenges, and some mishaps, along the way.

At one stop, a dismayed TV cameraman let loose with "rather colorful language" when he discovered, just as the festivities were concluding, that the film had jammed and he had no usable footage. In Raleigh, a skirmish took place between two photographers jockeying for space in a press pool car on the way to the coliseum. One ended up with a broken tooth after the other smacked him in the face with a camera. Once Liz Carpenter finally located Dr. Travell among the throngs at the rally, novocaine was administered to the patient behind the bleachers and a dental visit arranged for the next overnight stop.

The most serious medical emergency occurred in Charlotte. Journalist Doris Fleeson, the first woman in the country to have a nationally syndicated political column, suffered an attack of high blood pressure. Liz Carpenter's husband, Les, volunteered to fly with Fleeson back to Washington where she would be hospitalized. As they waited at the train station for an ambulance, with Fleeson lying on a stretcher, Carpenter "tried to think of something cheerful to say." She came up with: "You're the only woman in the world, Doris, whom I could trust flat on her back with my husband." Doris lifted her head from the stretcher, glared at Liz, and shouted, "Dammit! I'll never be that sick!"

Despite the hardships, veteran reporters agreed that the Lady Bird Special was an unforgettable journey. Nan Robertson called it "the classic trip of all time."

Legendary White House correspondent Helen Thomas later looked back on the "grueling, grimy journey" as "the most incredible trip" of her career. Like Robertson, she rode all the way from Washington, DC, to New Orleans.

Thomas was a twenty-one-year-old recent college graduate when she went to Washington, DC, in 1942, the same year as Liz Carpenter. The future reporter was born in Kentucky and raised in Detroit, where her father, a Lebanese immigrant, owned and operated a grocery store. Thomas decided to make journalism her vocation when, as a high school sophomore, she garnered her first byline in the school newspaper.

In Washington, Thomas initially took a gig as a restaurant hostess, a position that didn't last long. The reason: she didn't smile enough. Thomas got her break working for the *Washington Daily News* as a "copy girl," which included "fetching coffee for the editors" along with a baptism by fire into the profession.

"Being in a newsroom was like having my every dream as a student come true," said Thomas. "Watching great newsmen and newswomen perform under deadline pressure with the presses rolling was a heady experience. Listening to the headline writers argue over the right word was bracing."

Within months, Thomas was writing local news stories. After a year in Washington, she was hired as a radio writer for the United Press (which later merged with the International News Service and became UPI) and then became a print journalist. She referred to her beat as the "kitchen sink," covering the Justice Department and other federal agencies. After John F. Kennedy's 1960 presidential victory, she became the first woman reporter assigned to the White House by a wire service.

Even for experienced reporters like Thomas, the Lady Bird Special—particularly for those who rode the train the entire way—was what Liz Carpenter described as "a brutal physical endurance test." The reporters, though, seemingly thrived on the hectic pace. "Their stories were making page one," said Carpenter, "and the messages from the editors—'More on Lady Bird train'—were tonic to them."

A greater concern for reporters than meeting deadlines was the fear of being left behind at a whistle-stop, as Barbara McAden almost found out in Salisbury. Before the trip began, Carpenter alerted the press that there would be a "hectic time ahead" and issued a warning memo:

> A whistle will blow two minutes before the train starts moving. We hope we won't be scattering you over the countryside but the train does not wait. In case you get left, look for the advance man. He can easily be identified as the happiest man at the depot because all of his problems have just left. See if he can work out your transportation to a nearby town. If he can't, just take out residence, register and VOTE!

The fear of being left behind came true for Gloria Negri.

Usually when the Lady Bird Special's departure chime sounded, "Mrs. Johnson was still talking," Negri told *Boston Globe* readers. But in Chester, "it was the shortest two minutes in history." By the time Negri reached the entrance to the press car, the train was already moving. Just ahead of her, two colleagues, a man and a woman, were scrambling to get on the train. "He stuffed the girl topside and climbed aboard himself." Negri placed one foot on the bottom step, only to have it shoot out from beneath her as the train picked up speed. "You never forget the looks on the faces of other reporters on the train helplessly reaching out to try to help you aboard," said Negri. "You run alongside, feeling like a complete fool."

Negri was left standing on the tracks as the Lady Bird Special, "gaily emitting the sounds of 'Happy Days Are Here Again,'" disappeared from view.

Being left behind "was not only an embarrassing but a shattering experience," said Negri. Recalling Liz Carpenter's advice, she rushed back to the Chester station to ask for the advance man who "would be waiting for just such emergencies, to take stranded reporters to the next stop." Nobody she spoke with knew the advance man.

Negri explained her plight to deputy sheriff William L. Nunnery and other officials who looked confused at first. Was she perhaps a phony reporter or a Republican spy?

"But chivalry is not dead in the South," Negri declared. "Deputy Nunnery, wearing civilian clothes, put me in a station wagon, got behind the wheel, and we were off like a flash."

The deputy sheriff turned on the siren and hit the gas. It was twenty-six miles to Winnsboro, where the Lady Bird Special was scheduled for only a five-minute stop. "Deputy Nunnery certainly knew how to handle a car," said Negri. "We sailed along narrow, winding roads. He kept saying how he didn't like to live dangerously. We passed other cars and police cars."

If it weren't for Nunnery, Negri likely would not have caught up with the Lady Bird Special in Winnsboro, where the train was pulling to a stop as they arrived. In parting, Nunnery said to Negri, "It's good to have a little excitement around here once in a while."

Negri's next hurdle was getting back on the train. If a stop was only a few minutes long, reporters stayed in the press cars, where the platform speeches were piped in for them to hear.

Since the Secret Service were told that no reporters had debarked at Winnsboro, they were suspicious of Negri's claims.

The town of Winnsboro had little time to make arrangements for the Lady Bird Special's arrival, having been added to the schedule several days earlier. And yet 2,500 people turned out for the train in a town with a population of less than 4,000. Lady Bird briefly greeted the crowd, and then Lynda "turned politician" and had the last word. "Vote Democratic from the court house to the White House," she exclaimed.

Then the Lady Bird Special was off again with Gloria Negri on board.

16

Mad and Cool

Wednesday, October 7, 1964
Columbia, South Carolina, 3:58 p.m.

The Lady Bird Special rocked along, cars and passengers "jostling together as the coach hits rough spots" along rails more often suited to freight. "Everybody gets the large hello" as they're greeted by the train's high-spirited entourage and supplied with souvenirs.

"It's something like putting the Carolina-Clemson game on wheels and speeding it through the South Carolina countryside," wrote a reporter on board.

The merriment and the momentum were still running high as the Lady Bird Special came into Columbia. The station was spruced up for the occasion with a fresh coat of paint and decked in red, white, and blue bunting. An enthusiastic crowd of some 8,000 cheering, banner-waving people greeted the train.

Then the tenor changed. Here in Columbia, the Lady Bird Special encountered its first serious signs of trouble. Said Liz Carpenter, "It was so surprisingly ugly, it left all of us aghast."

Almost as soon as the train came to a halt, chants of "We want Barry" rang out from a relatively small band of protesters who proved exceedingly disruptive. When the mayor started to address the crowd, the chanting grew louder. His admonishments did nothing to dissuade the two dozen young people in their teens and early twenties clustered near the speakers' platform. (Some of the hecklers identified themselves to reporters as University of South Carolina students but refused to give their names.)

The group quieted while a minister led a prayer, but immediately after he uttered "Amen," someone yelled "Goldwater," leading his cohorts to loudly cheer and shout.

Chants of "We want Barry" erupted again as Governor Russell was introduced. "I am proud to be governor of South Carolina because South Carolinians are men and women of good manners and hospitality. And I trust there will be no misguided souls in this audience today who by their conduct will reflect discredit upon the name of this great state."

As the governor, who seemed embarrassed, introduced some of the dignitaries, the chanting began again. "I would give an appeal to those of you who are conducting yourselves in a way that does not reflect credit upon our state to permit us to proceed with this meeting," said Governor Russell, a former university president. This time, the admonishment worked briefly and prompted one of the girls in the group, her eyes reddening, to drop the banner she was holding and leave the crowd. But the lull from the Goldwater group was short-lived, and the chanting and booing renewed.

When Senator Olin Johnston was introduced and rose to speak, a spectator shouted, "We want Strom." The booing increased, but the senator, a fiery orator, was undeterred. "I'm proud to have the privilege to come into South Carolina and tell the people here what I believe is for the best interest of all the people," he declared amid boos and cheers. "I am for Lyndon Johnson all the way." The overwhelmingly supportive audience responded with even louder cheers.

Soon enough, the Goldwater group reignited their refrain of "We want Barry."

A state official in the crowd tried to quiet the cluster. So did Wilma Smith, one of Governor Russell's secretaries, and Elizabeth Johnston, the senator's daughter, who told them, "You need manners."

On the platform, Governor Russell introduced Lady Bird as "a beloved daughter of the South, a woman of rare charm, a woman of deep compassion, the helpmate to the distinguished and able President of the United States." He directed another pointed remark to the disrupters, saying, "I know no one more incapable of a boo than Mrs. Lyndon Johnson."

But the Goldwater group was there to be disruptive. When the governor declared during his introduction of Lady Bird, "I believe with Senator Johnston that President Johnson should be reelected president," a surge of boos erupted.

Even as the crowd gave a resounding cheer when Lady Bird stepped up to the podium, some of the boos and the chanting were still audible. She turned toward the small, contentious cluster, looked directly at them, and held up her hand. The group ceased their chanting, and Lady Bird began to speak. She praised the state's First Lady, Virginia Russell, who, she informed the audience, had been in Washington working on the whistle-stop tour. "I have learned something about her," said Lady Bird. "She reminds me of a combination of two well-known southern heroines from *Gone with the Wind*. She has all the grace and beauty of Melanie, but she has the efficiency and the businesslike capacity of Scarlett O'Hara." The crowd clapped and laughed along with Lady Bird.

There were loud cheers as Lady Bird said, "I am here on behalf of the Democratic Party, the party of your ancestors and mine." She touched on her talking points about peace, "a mosaic of many stones," and how the "ultimate responsibility" for the country's nuclear power "rests on the president." There were more claps and cheers and some booing. "He has said the true courage of this nuclear age lies in the quest for peace, and that is the way I feel. Peace and strength are two sides of the same coin." The boos increased in volume. Lady Bird continued, extolling her husband's years of experience in politics and highlighting his success with the test ban treaty.

Suddenly, a man raised a crutch in the air. Seeing the signal, the heckling youths surged forward toward the platform, chanting, taunting, and waving their placards, one of which said LADY BIRD GO HOME TO YOUR ROOST and another FLY HOME LADY BIRD, YOU OLD BUZZARD. The sound of drum beats and the refrain of "We want Barry" reached a crescendo. Then came a bellow of "South Carolina wants Goldwater."

"Shocked, the crowd looked to see how the First Lady would handle this startling discourtesy," said Liz Carpenter. Added Lindy Boggs, "She was a formidable foe, and the sympathy of the crowd was overwhelmingly in her favor."

Lady Bird took in stride what she later described as "the real cold hostility" and the "continuous heckling." She recalled being "rather proud of the way I'd handled it. I was mad and cool."

Pausing midsentence, she again faced the hecklers and held up her right hand. "My friends," she said without raising her voice. "This is a country of many viewpoints, and I respect your right to express your own. Now it's my turn to express mine. Thank you."

There were thunderous claps and cheers. Lady Bird continued speaking, and the chastened hecklers stayed silent as she finished her speech. She characterized her husband as "a man who works for peace as well as talks of peace." She concluded by saying, "I know that the South is the home of our party. And with the head of the house a man from among us, I do not believe that South Carolina will be leaving home in November. I thank you. I thank you, thank you."

After the rally, a woman holding a Johnson banner said in response to the discourtesy displayed, "We could weep."

University of South Carolina president Dr. Thomas F. Jones sent his "deepest apologies" via telegram to Lady Bird. "The entire University community has been shocked and embarrassed at the misconduct which marred your visit to Columbia." Dr. Jones said the behavior of the hecklers "does not represent nor express the attitude and behavior of 8,482 University students."

The next day's newspaper headlines commended Lady Bird for how she handled the situation. "GOP's Youthful Hecklers Get It" said one, reporting that she "squelched a Goldwater Youth Demonstration in Columbia Wednesday afternoon as effective as a paddle."

Back on the Lady Bird Special, headed for Orangeburg, the heckling was the talk of the train.

"Booing the First Lady is no way to win votes," said Luther Hodges, who had scowled on the platform in Columbia as the demonstrations went on. The Goldwaterites, he declared, "were only helping the Democratic cause."

"The Republican movement in South Carolina is vocal," replied Virginia Russell when asked about the heckling. "And I don't mean that in a complimentary manner." She had warned the advance team that South Carolina would not be an easy state, and yet she was still understandably upset at witnessing the reception the First Lady received in Columbia.

"They were rude young people" who "do not live up to our traditions," Virginia said with tears in her eyes. Overall, she added, "I think the crowds have been wonderful. Mrs. Johnson has been delighted with them too."

Orangeburg, South Carolina, 5:48 p.m.
The Lady Bird Special chugged onward toward Orangeburg, with those on board unsure what they would encounter.

During the campaign train's planning phase, "we had been advised not to stop in Orangeburg because of recent racial incidents," said Liz Carpenter. "But we stopped anyway."

Considered "the most racially troubled place in the state," Orangeburg exemplified why the Civil Rights Act was needed legislation. The white community was determined to hold the color line in a town with two Black higher education institutions, Claflin University and South Carolina State College, and a well-educated, middle-class Black population.

Civil rights activists had been attempting desegregation through peaceful demonstrations and lawsuits for years with incremental success and significant backlash. After the *Brown v. Board of Education* decision, the NAACP branch in Orangeburg petitioned the school board to admit Black children into the town's white schools. Not only was the petition denied, but the state's first "white citizens council" was formed in response. The council went on a vendetta against the petitioners—publishing their names, which opened them up to harassment, firing them from jobs, refusing credit, calling in loans, and halting home deliveries of products like ice and milk. A successful counterboycott against white-owned stores continued for months and led the council to capitulate and back off the tactics they were employing against Black residents.

Subsequently, other civil rights movements, marches, and sit-ins occurred in Orangeburg. Authorities sometimes responded with violence, using tear gas and full-pressure water hoses on demonstrators and making arrests in the hundreds. In 1963, a list of demands was presented to the city council, asking for the desegregation of public accommodations, compliance with *Brown v. Board of Education*, and expanded job opportunities for the Black community. "If put into effect," stated the *Times and Democrat*, the local newspaper, the demands "would do away with all forms of segregation in the city." Town officials and authorities continued pushing back, making more than 1,500 arrests at demonstrations that summer and fall, including activists who were arrested more than once.

Three weeks after President Johnson signed the Civil Rights Act in July 1964, an integrated group of college students spent time in Orangeburg on a civil rights learning tour of the South. The group encountered hostility in restaurants and other venues, sometimes grudgingly served with muttered threats and other times turned away. One afternoon, they were confronted by knife-wielding white teenagers at a swimming area. Another disturbing encounter took place with the town's mayor, S. Clyde Fair. While meeting with the student group in his office, the mayor, who was "reputed to be a tool of the Klan," declared his bitter opposition to integration, saying, "Animal life is supposed to be separated."

Mayor Fair, an avowed Goldwater supporter, did not ride the Lady Bird Special into Orangeburg with other local dignitaries, nor was he invited onto the speakers' platform. Whether by oversight or design isn't known, but when he attempted to approach the platform to present the First Lady with a key to the city, the Secret Service denied him access.

A handful of white Democrats were at the rally in Orangeburg, along with "a sprinkling of white Republicans expressing their disdain." The crowd was made up almost entirely of Black spectators, most of whom were school and college age.

Students like these continued leading the movement for racial equality in Orangeburg long after the Lady Bird Special rode through town. (In February 1968, police opened fire on some two hundred unarmed students demonstrating on the South Carolina State College campus. Three young men were shot and killed, and more than twenty-five others were wounded in what became known as the Orangeburg Massacre.)

During the Lady Bird Special's stop, enthusiasm ran high. Noted a reporter, "It all had the aura of a gigantic pep rally between rival teams." Groups of white youths made themselves known with shouts of "We want Barry," but their voices could barely be heard over the Johnson hubbub.

A group of young women wearing Johnson hats wildly cheered and chanted, "We want Goldwater."

When asked about the hats, one said, "We want them for square dances. I just came to see history."

An editorial in the local paper called for courtesy during the First Lady's visit "whether one has Democratic or Republican leanings." A reverend objected to some of the wording. In a letter to the editor, he took the paper to task for implying that if there were "incidents" at the rally it would be due to the large number of Black attendees expected, "particularly the student bodies of South Carolina State College and Claflin University."

Beneath the pep rally atmosphere was an undercurrent of menace. "Keeping at a distance, a few white men eyed us suspiciously," recalled Liz Carpenter.

The only disturbance came from Goldwater supporters, who brandished signs like ORANGEBURG FOR GOLDWATER and BLACK BIRD SPECIAL. Earlier in the day, they erected a billboard and—taking care to know exactly where the last car on the train would stop—deliberately placed it to align with the speakers' platform. The billboard bore the familiar line, "In your heart you know he's right." (The Goldwater camp came to regret its much-loved slogan, which on some signs was altered to read, "In your heart you know he's far right.")

Clusters of Goldwater supporters chanted periodically during the speaker presentations. Lady Bird ignored the hecklers. "I wanted to come here because I heard there are a lot of good, faithful Democrats," she said. "The Democratic Party has always been concerned with the problems of South Carolina, and I know South Carolina will remember that this fall. I thank you for this wonderful reception."

The Goldwater chants that accompanied Lynda, who followed next, to the podium were counteracted by the enthusiastic reception she received. She thanked the students from Claflin and South Carolina State for being there, and the crowd gave the most robust response of the rally. "We're glad we have all these wonderful people from South Carolina here cheering for us," said Lynda, "because we know those other people are just from the state of confusion."

Despite the opposition's efforts, they could not diminish what was for many a celebratory occasion. The *Times and Democrat* grudgingly admitted, "For the Negroes and a few white Democrats, Wednesday was a historic day. The Republicans left with their own private impressions."

17

Dividing Line

Wednesday, October 7, 1964
Charleston, South Carolina, 7:29 p.m.

> **You will work for three things:**
> 1st [for] Lady Bird to make her Whistle-Stop Tour a success.
> 2nd for the President to assure his election on November 3rd.
> 3rd to meet the new challenge of the organized Republican campaign.
> The success of the Whistle-Stop is going to depend upon the number of [people] at the station stops. This is your first responsibility.

Achieving the number one objective set forth in an instructional memo to the advance women was an uphill battle in Charleston, a city heavily for Goldwater. When Kara Burney, the White House coordinator, arrived on the night of September 30, there was one week until the Lady Bird Special rolled into town, and almost nothing had been done to prepare for the occasion. She didn't even have a typewriter to use.

The day before, Burney had left Washington, DC, with Lindy, Virginia, and the rest of their advance team to head south. Bette McClure and four other women took up their posts in Virginia and North Carolina. When the advance team reached Columbia, South Carolina, they "primarily heard reports of what had *already been done*" by local committees, said Burney. Later that night in Charleston, however, "we did the reporting of what *needed* to be done." The original plan to have Burney divide her time between the two cities was altered on the spot. Given the concerning situation in Charleston, she would remain there for the week and coordinate by telephone with the whistle-stop organizers in Columbia.

When Lady Bird advised Liz Carpenter not to give her the "easy towns" on the campaign train's route, Charleston was one of those places. During an earlier check-in call with Jack Hight, a regional advance man in the South, Carpenter asked him, "Are we going to have a successful stop in Charleston?"

"Frankly, Liz, it's a little lonely," replied Hight. Just one person had shown up to a meeting for local Democrats the evening before.

"Good grief, Jack, do something!" said Carpenter. "I can't believe those people feel closer to Barry Goldwater than they do to Lady Bird Johnson."

"Down here, Liz, they feel closer to George the Third than they do to anyone," Hight said. "You see, there are two Charlestons—old Charleston along the Battery, and suburban Charleston out by the shipyards where the population is. To get a crowd, we'll have to have the stop in a suburban shopping center."

The situation improved slightly by the time Kara Burney, Lindy, and Virginia arrived in Charleston. A group of fifty women, who waited nearly two hours for them after a rainstorm delayed their flight from Columbia, greeted them in a council room at the city hall at 8:00 p.m. The coalition was brought together by Ruth Williams, the Charleston County coordinator for the whistle-stop and the only woman elected to the state House of Representatives.

Every minute counted in Charleston, especially since this stop was more complicated than any other on the Lady Bird Special's route. At fourteen hours, it was the longest, and it involved a train station welcome, a motorcade from the station to the rally site seven miles away and back, a nighttime rally in North Charleston, and another motorcade and a tour of the historic district the next morning.

When advance men Jim Konduros and Pete Sommer arrived a few days before Burney, the Democratic Party didn't even have election headquarters for Charleston County. "Local Democrats were discouraged with what they believed to be an impossible situation, campaign-wise," explained Burney. "Factions needed to be brought together and inspired to make an effort." Konduros and Sommer helped set up a campaign headquarters that would continue to operate through the election.

The day after the headquarters opened in a two-room suite in an apartment building, it was vandalized. Campaign posters and stickers were peeled off the ground-floor windows. The vandals returned the next night for an encore. This time, they painted large red hammers and sickles on the windows and on a car with a Johnson bumper sticker that was parked in front of the building. Although no physical damage was done and nothing was broken, Cecil D. Clay, a co-chair for the Democratic campaign, said, "We are disturbed that there has been such quick reaction."

Along with Konduros and Sommer, Burney got right down to business working on the whistle-stop. "The three of us lived with it, literally, night and day," she said. They met each evening, usually from midnight to 2:00 a.m., to go over their notes and organize for the next day. Jack Hight checked on other whistle-stop cities and then, since it was "obvious that we had more problems than anyone, he came back to help us see it through," said Burney.

Burney was one of the "can-do" women liked and lauded by the president and Lady Bird. After graduating from Texas Technical College, she worked as the women's editor at the *Caller-Times* in Corpus Christi until she married five years later. Burney had been an active volunteer in Democratic politics for sixteen years in her home state of Texas, including organizing campaign events for Lady Bird and the Kennedy women on the "Texas Tea Circuit" in 1960.

Part of the challenge in Charleston was navigating the divided landscape. Situated on a peninsula between two rivers, historic Old Charleston was an entity unto itself, steeped in the past and "strongly Goldwater conservative, even militantly so. But underneath is an ancient tradition of courtesy and hospitality," said Burney. North of the historic district, "one encounters a decidedly different Charleston." This was an area of new growth and development with private industries and businesses and government installations, including a U.S. naval base and an air force base. Here too, Goldwater sentiment ran deep.

Altogether, more than two hundred people in Charleston came together to organize and participate in the whistle-stop preparations.

An insurance company executive who owned several buildings offered Burney the use of a two-room office-bedroom space in a Holiday Inn. He provided the much-needed typewriter, a telephone, office supplies, secretarial services, a station wagon, three additional vehicles and drivers to assist in motorcades, and a list of his business connections.

A lawyer persuaded Charleston's mayor, J. Palmer Gaillard Jr., to show up for the First Lady's visit and also secured a spot to hold the rally. He convinced the president of the company that owned the Pinehaven Shopping Center to host the event in the parking lot. Merchants were called into a meeting and told "in a most decisive manner" that the rally was taking place, and anyone who objected would have his lease bought out.

A rumor was spreading that musicians with a "hot beat" had been invited to play at the rally. The music would supposedly incite Black attendees to riot and destroy the stores in the shopping center. All but one of the twenty-five merchants planned to seek an injunction against staging the event there. "Jim Konduros lived with this tedious problem," reported Burney, "handling it with patience and diplomacy."

Once the rally site was secured, it had to be readied. Volunteers brought in floodlights, a power supply, chairs and tables, microphones, decorations, first aid equipment, and flatbed trailers and lumber to construct the speakers' platform. Special sound equipment was flown in from Cincinnati, Ohio, along with backup speakers to ensure the First Lady's speech could be heard all across the sprawling Pinehaven parking lot.

Committees galvanized by Ruth Williams decorated the freight station outside the city where the train arrived, giving it a new coat of paint, tying palm fronds to all the posts in the railyard, and banking the roadway with magnolia. The rally platform was bedecked with red, white, and blue bunting and magnolia leaves; motorcade buses were arranged and adorned; and Johnson Girls were recruited to greet the train and assist at the rally. At first, it was thought that perhaps ten to fifteen young women could be recruited for the task, but more than one hundred volunteered.

Others contributed to publicity and marketing endeavors like mailing three thousand Lady Bird Special postcards, participating in a telephone campaign, writing radio spots, lining up TV shows, and devising creative methods to get the word out. One local supporter affixed an LBJ FOR THE USA poster and a sign promoting the rally to her white convertible and drove the car around the Charleston area. Along for the ride were her young sons and two beagles, Snoopie and Dixie. Snoopie and Dixie did their parts by wearing signs around their necks, one of which read I LIKE HER and the other I LIKE HIM, in reference to the Johnson family's beagles, Him and Her.

Local volunteers in Charleston aided the whistle-stop efforts despite concerns about reprisal. Dr. Kathleen Riley was an Old Charleston resident who arranged gifts for the First Lady reflective of local customs and traditions. She confided in Burney that she was being given "a hard time" by colleagues due to her public involvement with the whistle-stop. (Burney was so impressed with Dr. Riley, a dermatologist who worked her way through school and "built a respectable practice in a man's world," she recommended her as a guest at the "women doers" luncheons Lady Bird held to highlight women of achievement.)

A Charleston advertising agency owner who did a majority of the work in setting up the rally site and helping to promote the event "will probably receive repercussions from local clients such as banks and other investment accounts," said Burney. A high school honor student was suspended partly for his association with adult Democratic activity. Two bands from white high schools that committed to playing at the rally canceled at the last minute due to the administrators' fear of backlash from Goldwater-supporting parents.

According to the instructions given to the advance team, they were there to assist as needed in whistle-stop preparations while locals took the lead. "This is to be their show," said Burney. She focused heavily on the primary objective: getting people to the train's various stopping points in the state to see the First Lady, including the rally at the Pinehaven Shopping Center. She worked every lead and avenue to reach various groups of people in Charleston and in the surrounding area.

As part of their public relations efforts, the advance women also connected with the media and generated newsworthy stories. Even that was challenging in Charleston, where the newspaper was a monopoly institution and ultraconservative. In the instructional memo to the advance women, Liz Carpenter stated, "Don't buy the line that *these* papers are against us. They are in a lot of places, but they are going to cover Mrs. Johnson. Assume they are our friends." That proved true in Charleston. The paper ran articles on preparations for the Lady Bird Special, even as editorials both deplored the First Lady coming to the city for political purposes and asked for courtesy during her visit.

Carpenter also warned the advance women, "Another thing you are going to have to fight is the lack of imagination in men."

The day before the campaign train's arrival, the Charleston *News and Courier*'s male editors flaunted their misogyny and their belief that they were entitled to define the role of First Lady. "She cannot expect the same kind of reception she would receive on a non-political visit," they stated in what seemed to be tacit condoning of any discourteous behavior that should occur.

"First Ladies have scrupulously refrained from the kind of political activity in which Mrs. Johnson is now engaged. We recall with admiration the ladylike attitude of Mrs. Bess Truman. Though her husband was fighting for his political life in 1948, Mr. Truman never asked his wife to do his politicking for him. And Mrs. Truman had too much respect for her position as First Lady to take part in a traveling political circus.

"Unfortunately, Mr. Johnson has decided to employ his wife as a political worker. He has, therefore, reduced the status of the First Lady in the eyes of the nation. In making a whistle-stop tour, which draws members of the Officeholding Industry who have a stake in keeping their heads in the Democratic trough, Mrs. Johnson must be expected to be regarded as just another political worker. It is deplorable that Mr. and Mrs. Johnson have created this situation."

When dealing with the press, a tougher assignment in some places than others, the advance women were instructed "not to 'be bashful,'" noted Burney. She was no stranger to the spotlight. After the Soviets launched Sputnik, the first artificial satellite to orbit the earth, in 1957, she and her husband gave some two hundred talks in South Texas about their visit to Russia just after a ban on tourists was lifted. And yet during political endeavors, she had always been "most content to work in the background." This time, as a White House coordinator, she was part of the story. Instructed to get "out front" of the train, she gave interviews for television and print. "I am sure I had my picture taken more times in that one week than during the fortysomething years of my life," she said.

Given the challenges in Charleston, local Democratic leaders would have been happy with a turnout of 4,000 at the rally. "We've got 4,000 balloons to give away," said John M. Bleecker Jr., chairman of the county's Young Democrats, "and we hope there'll be more people there than balloons." Some 12,000 people turned out from Charleston and the surrounding Lowcountry, and a robust and enthusiastic crowd greeted the First Lady at the Pinehaven Shopping Center.

Charleston was the third stop in a row where Goldwater supporters were decidedly in the minority but determined to try and tarnish the event. The opposition took it up a notch from Columbia with a larger, seemingly more organized group of about fifty young people standing near the speakers' platform.

"The hecklers came again, some of the same group who had been in Columbia," said Liz Carpenter. "They had their drum and ugly chants: 'Johnson is a Communist. Johnson is a n----- lover.'"

Local Republican Party officials earlier in the week issued a statement about the First Lady's visit. "We question the propriety of her action," said Paul Belknap, the county GOP chairman. "While we deplore her visiting here for political reasons, we still feel respect should be shown for her position as First Lady. We feel the Republican Party should in no way have anything to do with demonstrations against the administration or for Goldwater." Belknap asked that nothing be done to antagonize or embarrass Lady Bird. "If such demonstrations occur they will not have the sanction of the Republican Party but will be the acts of individuals and we discourage such acts."

The appeal for civility went unheeded at the Charleston rally. Attempts by the Lady Bird Special's emcees and others on the speakers' platform to quiet the hecklers failed, and booing and chanting continued during their speeches.

Speaking on the floodlit platform, Hale Boggs paused numerous times amid chants and counter chants as he got the program going. Incensed at the continued, openly hostile display by the Goldwater supporters, he rebuked the youngsters' behavior as "more reminiscent of Hitler than anything in America."

What Kara Burney referred to as a "'blackmail' editorial" in that morning's issue of the *News and Courier* dared state politicians to appear at the rally and publicly avow their support for the Johnson-Humphrey ticket. "We say to the national Democrats in this area, 'Come out, come out, wherever you are.'"

The public, they stated, would be keenly interested to see who was on the platform and that those politicians would have to face the consequences. "The occasion may turn out to be a dividing line in South Carolina politics."

Senator Olin Johnston and Congressman Mendel Rivers, whose district included Charleston, were not afraid to appear on the platform. They delivered rousing rhetoric over the noise of the Goldwaterites. "I don't know where this gang came from," said Rivers. "Whoever is responsible for bringing" them to the rally "ought to be ashamed." He told the audience he planned to remain a Democrat and reminded them that Charleston owed its military facilities to Democratic administrations.

The state's "political spotlight" had focused on the party switch of Strom Thurmond, noted an editorial in the *Index-Journal* of Greenwood, South Carolina. But having Rivers, who was supporting a Democratic presidential ticket for the first time in two decades, on the platform was a coup for the Lady Bird Special. He delivered a "tough love" talk, informing the audience that it was no secret Charleston's principal economy was the $175 million a year federal payroll. "I'm going to tell you this," Rivers said. Charleston was "in the military picture" because Democrats put it there. "And it's going to be the Democrats who are going to keep it here, if indeed you keep it," asserted the congressman.

"However much this type of political approach might be deplored, it will have effect," admitted the *Index-Journal*. "It was made by a conservative Congressman, an advocate of state rights, and was made right in the heart of Goldwater territory in this state."

Senator Johnston was even more blunt than Congressman Rivers. Fired up, eyes flashing, he declared himself a proud Democrat and yelled, "Just holler on. I don't mind hearing you holler, but you're going to have to squeal after November the third."

Gladys Johnston, the senator's wife, took the hecklers to task as well. "Folks, I want to say this: That crowd over there is scared to death, or they wouldn't be acting like such idiots."

Although the severe harassment died down some by the time Lady Bird was introduced, the heckling continued. She paused as she approached the podium. Then a group of the Johnson Girls, who were handing out campaign literature, began chanting "LBJ for the USA." Lady Bird smiled broadly and blew them a kiss.

Lady Bird didn't address the hecklers directly, but she did wave her hand in an appeal for quiet. The noise abated somewhat while she spoke, but the hecklers determinedly continued in the largely quiet crowd. At one point, they chanted over and over, "Lady Bird, fly away; Lady Bird, fly away." Adult men standing near the youth group got into the act too. One cupped his hands around his mouth and screamed, "What's the matter? Daddy can't make his own speeches?" Another yelled, "Oh, shut up," not at the hecklers but at Lady Bird.

At one point, Lady Bird paused amid the frenzied "We want Barry" chanting. A group of young Johnson supporters responded with a counter chant. At times, the din drowned out her words. Still, the "bread and butter message got through," said Liz Carpenter.

"Mrs. Johnson should have gotten an Academy Award," said Ashton Gonella, the First Lady's personal secretary. Even as the crowd booed and catcalled, "she maintained her composure…and handled herself beautifully."

Lady Bird remained remarkably calm and carried on with her speech, laying it on the line in her genteel way. She likened Charleston to the entire South, saying it had "its roots in the traditions and beauty of the past, but it also has the will to move forward and take part in the future."

She too pointed to the city's position as a nuclear submarine port and the military's substantial contribution to the local economy. This partnership "works both ways. It means economic vitality for this area, and it means strength for our nation," said Lady Bird. It was a partnership that "takes federal resources. And it takes men in Washington who care about the people of the South, their problems, and their hopes."

Gracious and sincere, Lady Bird conveyed to the cheering thousands—and to the disrupters—the message at the heart of her trip: to her and to the president, the South was a beloved part of the country.

The rally at the Pinehaven Shopping Center was the only whistle-stop locale where Lynda and Luci appeared together, a fact that "honored" Charlestonians, said Kara Burney. Luci took over as her mother's campaign companion while Lynda returned to university classes in Washington. Lynda and Luci each spoke briefly at the rally in Charleston and then, along with Lady Bird, they thrilled the crowd by fanning out in three directions and shaking hands.

The next day, reports kept reaching Burney "that people had changed their minds about their vote because of their shame and disgust with the rally hecklers" and from seeing and hearing the First Lady.

Throughout the trip, Lady Bird, Lynda and Luci, the other speakers, and the support team would discuss after every stop what was effective and what they could do differently or better.

On the train, after the rally in Charleston, Lady Bird hastily called a meeting in her Pullman car. She asked the men in the party to tone down the combative rhetoric and rebuking of the hecklers.

Lady Bird assured her would-be "knights in shining Democratic armor" that although she appreciated their chivalry, she could handle any unpleasant instances that arose, and it was best if they ignored the hecklers. She later recalled Senator Johnston's courage and dedication to the Democratic Party in the face of constituents who were angry and vocal. "I will never forget how he strolled across that stage in Charleston, South Carolina, and roared at them, practically calling them fools to their faces, defiant, commanding—a wonderful stage appearance."

Reflecting on the day's drama, Lady Bird told a reporter, "This is a political year and we are in a political climate. You've got to look at all this in its proper perspective. Think of the thousands and thousands who have come out to see us and have given us so much warmth, such fine welcome. Think of the dozens—just dozens, that's all—who have done the heckling."

At 9:40 that evening, the telephone rang in Lady Bird's onboard quarters. It was the president calling from Chicago while campaigning in the Midwest.

Lady Bird gave him a thorough update on the train happenings and then said, "Tell me about your day."

Johnson reported on a massive crowd in Des Moines, Iowa, and said that his throat "held up pretty good." He asked if Lady Bird had seen his half-hour televised campaign address, recorded the day before at the White House and aired nationwide that evening. When she told him she hadn't seen it, he asked, "Didn't you know about it?"

His disappointment was understandable since he had come to rely on Lady Bird's advice regarding his speaking and media performances.

Earlier that year, shortly after he finished a press conference, she called him on the phone while he was in the Oval Office. "You want to listen for about one minute to my critique, or would you rather wait until tonight?" she asked.

"Yes, ma'am. I'm willing now," he replied.

Lady Bird's assessment: He "looked strong, firm, and like a reliable guy. Your looks were splendid." He was also breathless and glanced down too much. "Every now and then, you need a good crisp answer for a change of pace." She was glad when he responded to one reporter, "The answer is *no* to both of your questions." She commented on the substance of his answers and noted, "When you're going to have a prepared text, you need to have the opportunity to study it a little bit more and to read it with a little more conviction and interest and change of pace." The drama picked up considerably during the questioning session when his voice and facial expressions were "noticeably better." She concluded, "In general, I'd say it was a good B-plus. How do you feel about it?"

"I thought it was much better than last week," said Johnson.

While Lady Bird was whistle-stopping, the president followed the train's progress "through every yard of the South." He received regular updates and, he said, "called three or four times a day myself just to see how everything was getting along." When he telephoned that night, he asked Lynda what Congressman Rivers said to the hecklers. Lynda informed him that Rivers "just gave them hell" and that she believed they would "get a lot of sympathy reports because these people were bad."

Chicago Tribune reporter Mary Pakenham, who was riding on the train, came up in conversation. "[She] writes some mean stories," said Johnson. "You know her?"

Lady Bird chuckled. "Yes, I know her. She wouldn't have a job with the *Chicago Tribune* if she didn't write these stories, would she?" The paper endorsed Goldwater in 1964.

The president took particular exception to a passage in Pakenham's article deriding Lynda for singing "Hello, Lyndon!" in an "off-key girlish soprano."

"So what, Daddy?" said Lynda. "That'll just get me the sympathy vote of all of those people who can't sing on-key."

During the conversation, Lady Bird lightheartedly warned her husband not to accept an invitation to appear at a peanut festival that coming weekend during what was supposed to be one day of downtime together at their Texas ranch before resuming campaigning.

Johnson confirmed the rest of the whistle-stop tour schedule with Lady Bird and, before hanging up, he said, "I love you and I'll see you on Friday."

18

We'll Yell a Little Louder

Thursday, October 8, 1964
Charleston, South Carolina, 8:00 a.m.

The next morning, horses Spot and Jimmy conveyed a canopy-covered carriage along the Battery, a defensive seawall and promenade overlooking the harbor in Old Charleston.

Wearing a blue-gray dress with a matching hat and a ruby-red coat, Lady Bird appeared relaxed and enthusiastic as she set out on what Liz Carpenter called a "chilling" ride—and she wasn't referring to the temperature on the sun-drenched day.

Seated in the carriage with the First Lady were Congressman Rivers and Mayor Gaillard, who "somewhat reluctantly" rode along. Driving the buggy was top-hatted Harry Waagner, who shared his seat with his sidekick, a dog named Bingo, and a Secret Service agent. Asked by reporters if he was a Democrat, Waagner "grinned sheepishly" and said, "Well, not right now."

Some seventy-five photographers, reporters, and Secret Service agents scampered on foot behind the carriage as it traveled on nearly deserted streets lined with Spanish moss–draped trees. Old Charleston was giving Lady Bird the cold shoulder.

Spot and Jimmy clip-clopped past the Battery's elegant historic mansions. Fastened to the wrought-iron grillwork encircling the houses were what, from a distance, appeared to be SOLD signs. Up close, the smaller text on the signs could be seen: THIS HOUSE SOLD ON GOLDWATER. "They didn't say, GO HOME LADY BIRD. But they might as well have," remarked Liz Carpenter. The signs, a reporter noted, looked new and "apparently had been put up especially for the occasion."

And yet the overt Republican allegiance did not dissuade some residents from happening to be outside when the horse-drawn carriage bearing the First Lady passed down their streets. Some gardened and others carried envelopes to the mailbox. An elderly woman wearing a flowing silk robe sipped coffee from a gold-rimmed cup on a veranda.

Harry Waagner had Spot and Jimmy bring the carriage to a halt in front of the Nathaniel Russell House, the entourage still trailing behind. Spectators had already gathered outside, a small group comprised of both Johnson and Goldwater supporters. The exact time and route of the hour-long tour of Old Charleston was not publicly announced, but word spread. Some of the GOPers brandished Goldwater bumper stickers, as if they hadn't had enough time to craft a proper sign. Others were more prepared, holding up a sign suggesting the First Lady "Join the Teenage Republican Club." Before heading into the house museum, Lady Bird approached the group, greeting the student supporters of both political parties and handing them cards with her autograph.

The Nathaniel Russell House, built in 1808 by a wealthy merchant and slave trader, was the first stop on a whirlwind tour of five historic buildings. One of the guides who conducted Lady Bird's tour of the house told a reporter that "practically everyone in Charleston is for Goldwater." When asked why she thought Lady Bird devoted so much time to seeing the city, the woman replied, "She's probably trying to ride on Jackie Kennedy's cultural coattails. Besides, being photographed in front of our cultural buildings might help her in other parts of the South."

From the Russell House, Lady Bird traveled in a powder blue automobile to the Dock Street Theatre, where several hundred more people were waiting outside. A tour of the theater, the country's first structure built exclusively for theatrical performances, operating since 1736, was followed by a trifecta of church visits. While walking through St. Michael's Church, Congressman Rivers told Lady Bird that a month after he was married there "the roof fell in."

With the tour of the church completed, Lady Bird exited St. Michael's and crossed the street to city hall, followed by a large crowd of onlookers that had waited for her to emerge.

Someone from the Deep South later told Bess Abell that at the time, it was thought by some that the Lady Bird Special was a "Machiavellian technique" to exploit the divisions in the region, the intent being to capitalize on public displays of animosity toward a woman to garner votes. Abell refuted this idea, replying, "I don't think you ever take a trip to get spit at."

Which is exactly what happened to Ruth Williams, one of the dignitaries touring Old Charleston with Lady Bird. As the official party exited onto the street outside St. Michael's Church, a man spit on Williams.

When the *News and Courier* dared LBJ-supporting politicians to stand on the platform with the First Lady and take the consequences in "Goldwater country," Williams was one of them. She paid a steep price, losing her 1964 bid for reelection to the state House of Representatives.

Lady Bird later wrote to Williams expressing her regrets. "How terribly sorry we all were to hear that you had not won reelection to the South Carolina House of Representatives. We are well aware of the difficult circumstances in your area," Lady Bird stated. "I know how disappointed you must be and I can only share that feeling with you. I deeply appreciated all you did for me during my visit to Charleston, and I do hope that the future will hold only the good things you so richly deserve."

Williams responded to the First Lady's letter, saying, "You are mighty nice to write to me concerning this past election. Please do not feel any personal responsibility for my defeat. You are a lovely southern lady who is far above reproach. Your conduct in Charleston is acknowledged to be superior. I truly regret that Charleston's manners, during your visit, did not rise to the occasion. I especially appreciate your understanding of the 'difficult circumstances' in our area. I shall always keep your letter."

In Old Charleston, as Lady Bird approached city hall, a group of about twenty girls from a Catholic high school chanted, "We're for Lyndon Johnson, we couldn't be prouder; and if you don't believe us, we'll yell a little louder." Lady Bird stopped to shake hands with the enthusiastic well-wishers, including a sixteen-year-old girl who said, "So glad you came and please come back."

Lady Bird was presented with gifts during a reception in city hall (among them a hammock for the Texas ranch, a book about Charleston's interior architecture, a painting, and baskets woven from sweet grass and palmetto fronds). Then the mayor bowed and bid a courteous farewell. Police stopped traffic. And the motorcade returned to the Lady Bird Special waiting at the depot.

"What did you think of it?" Liz Carpenter asked Lady Bird in a private moment on the train.

Lady Bird laughed and said, "It was a rather frosty morning. I kept feeling that I was looking at a beautiful corpse."

Carpenter later reflected, "Where was the hospitality of aristocratic old Charleston that morning? In retreat, nursing its bitterness, quarrelsome with one of its own. Like the moth to the flame, I have always yearned to go back there in search of some—even a few—who might remember that day and are a little bit sorry."

Yemassee, South Carolina, 10:56 a.m. and Ridgeland, South Carolina, 11:12 a.m.

The Lady Bird Special passed through Yemassee, where some three hundred people were gathered along the rails. Despite the town being scheduled for a stop, due to a communications breakdown aboard the train, all the spectators received was campaign paraphernalia handed out by the Ladies for Lyndon as it slowed down. Lady Bird telegrammed with her apologies. "I was disappointed and heartsick that I missed the opportunity to greet all the residents of your area at Yemassee," she assured the county Democratic chairman. "Please tell all of those who came to meet me how very grateful the President and I are for our wonderful friends in South Carolina."

Less than twenty miles down the tracks, the Lady Bird Special made an unscheduled stop in Ridgeland due to the size of the crowd. Before the train came to a standstill, some irate mothers showed up after discovering that students at the local elementary school had been taken by their teachers to see the train and greet the First Lady. They left with their children in a huff.

Nevertheless, a several-hundred-person crowd applauded as Luci, standing next to her mother, made her debut on the observation car platform.

"We've got something in common," Luci shouted to the high school and remaining elementary students in attendance. "I got off school today to come see y'all, [and] you got out of school to see us."

Luci's appearance in Ridgeland was a warm-up for the next stop, where she faced a scene that might have intimidated even an experienced campaigner—and handled it with style and spirit.

19

It Takes Women to Have Guts

Thursday, October 8, 1964
Savannah, Georgia, 11:50 a.m.

U.S. Senators were as scarce in Georgia when the 'special' arrived as during General Sherman's famed March to the Sea," observed a reporter on the train.

Senator Dick Russell, who President Johnson vowed to run over if he didn't get out of his way when working to pass the Civil Rights Act, never intended to ride the train. Neither did Senator Herman Talmadge, although he was more subtle in distancing himself from the Lady Bird Special by being busy elsewhere. Senator Talmadge's wife, Betty, however, loudly and proudly aligned with the campaign train and stood by Lady Bird, with whom she was close friends.

"It takes women to have guts," said Liz Carpenter to a reporter.

Betty boarded the train in Charleston and rode through Georgia, appearing with Lady Bird on the platform at every stop. Her friends and admirers in Georgia exceeded even those of her popular husband, so much so that Governor Carl Sanders acceded to her the prestige of introducing the First Lady.

A reader later wrote to *Atlanta Constitution* reporter Celestine Sibley suggesting that Betty was merely being a mannerly Southern host by associating with the Lady Bird Special and that there were no political implications.

"How could I make my position clearer?" Betty asked. "I rode on the train with Mrs. Johnson and introduced her."

Sibley replied, "This gentleman didn't seem to think that was synonymous with supporting President Johnson politically."

Betty laughed.

"I'm a Democrat," she said on the record. "I support the Democratic ticket."

Even Betty's immense popularity couldn't counter the lack of hospitality from some in Savannah, Georgia's oldest city. At a rally in Johnson Square, named for a long-ago governor, Betty was booed right along with Lady Bird and Luci.

"It was the first time I have ever seen anybody booed in Georgia, least of all the wearer of the magic name of Talmadge," said Sibley. "I was shaken."

As Lady Bird walked toward the speakers' platform, a group of youngsters waved THIS IS GOLDWATER TERRITORY placards and yelled the presidential candidate's name. Ever gracious, she stopped, smiled, and shook hands with several people in the group.

The hecklers were a conspicuous minority, and like the groups in Charleston and other places, they made up for their lack of number by massing close to the platform to maximize the spectacle they could create. Members of the group pushed and shoved and tried to prevent other dignitaries from reaching the speakers' platform as they walked through the "sardine-can-like" crowd. Kicking off the program, two high school bands played the national anthem, during which the hecklers shouted, "We want Barry."

"We were never certain what the hecklers were going to do when they began waving their placards within a foot of our faces," said Lindy Boggs. "It was tense at times but we held our ground and kept our heads high. We weren't afraid, but the adrenaline flowed." (Earlier, when the Lady Bird Special arrived in Savannah, there was a brief scuffle as Goldwater supporters surged toward the train and were held back by law enforcement officers, although bystanders perceived it as more playful than menacing.)

At every stop, Scooter Miller, chief engineer of the Ladies for Lyndon, kept a record of what was written on signs and placards, which gave an indication of people's thoughts and feelings. Some of the signs at the Savannah rally "were rough," noted a reporter, like one featuring a red heart lettered with KHRUSCHEV LOVES LBJ (Whenever one of the hostesses saw a kid with a Goldwater banner, she swapped him some Johnson-branded candy for it.)

A European newsman traveling with the train offered his perspective: They "ought to welcome" the opposition. "It livens things up." He said hecklers were common in West German political campaigns, and fights among audience members were frequent. The Lady Bird Special team was concerned that violence would break out among the factions at rallies and become the news instead of the campaign train's messaging. In fact, one fight was reported during the whistle-stop tour. It occurred in Charleston between two groups of teenage boys, white Goldwater supporters and Black Johnson supporters each chanting for their candidate. Before it got out of hand, a group of men separated the combatants, who continued to glower at each other.

At the rally in Johnson Square, students from a local college waved pro-Goldwater placards but were not among the hecklers. Reporters asked them why they were there. Since the crowd was organized by "Johnson advance men," they wanted to offer a counter perspective. "If we hadn't come, the newspapers might have said, 'Savannah is solidly behind Johnson.' It's not," responded one of the students. When asked about their parents, another said, "They're going to vote for Goldwater too, but—you know how it is—most of them work for the government. And those that don't—well, this is a one-party state. But that's going to change."

The handful of hecklers and opposition sign bearers were the exception in a warm, friendly gathering of 10,000 people on what was declared "First Lady Day" by a mayoral proclamation. The White House coordinator advancing in Savannah and drumming up the crowd was Gladys Avery Tillett, a longtime Democratic Party leader who helped organize North Carolina's first county chapter of the League of Women Voters in 1922. Tillett was the United States' representative to the UN Commission on the Status of Women, her latest role in the nearly fifty years she had been a devoted women's rights activist. "There is more custom and tradition to break down when it comes to eliminating discrimination because of sex than there is in ending racial or religious prejudice," said Tillett.

In an interview with a local Savannah paper, Tillett expressed her excitement at a First Lady whistle-stopping solo for the first time and aided by a women-led team. In between other advance duties, Tillett witnessed the mayor sign the First Lady Day decree. The campaign train occasion turned out a crowd like police chief Leo B. Ryan hadn't seen for a long time, "not even during our civil rights demonstrations."

Ten days earlier, Dr. King praised Savannah "as having made reasonable progress in racial integration" since the passage of the recent Civil Rights Act. He was speaking in the city at the Southern Christian Leadership Conference (SCLC) annual convention. While there, he gave his first official endorsement of the Johnson-Humphrey ticket, vowing to "put the machinery of his organization" behind President Johnson and pledging "an all-out effort to get all of our affiliates to move in their communities to turn out a larger Negro vote than ever before."

At a press conference in Savannah, Dr. King shared that Black voting registration in the South had nearly doubled since the 1960 presidential election, rising from 1.1 million to about two million. "This can mean the balance of power in the upcoming election," he said.

Previously, Dr. King had a philosophy of not endorsing political candidates. The SCLC, of which he was president, was a nonpartisan organization. "The role that is mine in the emerging social order of the South and America demands that I remain non-partisan," he stated. This allowed him the freedom to criticize both political parties when necessary.

Shortly after the Savannah gathering, Dr. King spoke at an SCLC convention in St. Paul, Minnesota, and further clarified his stance in the 1964 presidential election. "I have had a philosophy of not endorsing any candidates because there must be some few individuals not bound to either party," he said. "But I confess. Mr. Goldwater has… made it necessary for me to revise my policy… If he wins, I foresee a time darker than the desperate evil days of Hitler's Germany."

Other civil rights leaders at the St. Paul convention concurred.

"Your problem is to *bury* Goldwater," said A. Philip Randolph, a labor organizer and political strategist. "If you vote just enough to barely get Johnson in, it will amount to defeat. Johnson must win by an overwhelming majority. He deserves to win." Added James Farmer, "We must organize so that when President Johnson is elected—as he must be—we can exert pressure on even him."

In Savannah, Lady Bird did not let the contentious atmosphere at the rally in Johnson Square distract her from her speech, delivered against an almost constant undertone of "We want Barry." She started by establishing kinfolk connections and praising the lip-smacking products produced in Georgia (among them Coca-Cola and country-cured hams from a company Betty Talmadge founded and ran). She remarked on Savannah's history as a melting pot and highlighted some of its famous inhabitants like cotton gin creator Eli Whitney, who invented his machine on a nearby plantation, and Girl Scouts founder Juliette Gordon Low. "The future is here too," said Lady Bird, referencing eleven dams approved by Congress, which meant powerful resources for the area.

Lady Bird then veered to the political.

"My husband is widely known as a busy and active man—yes, even a rather urgently active man. But he is also something else," she said. "In this campaign, he is a tomorrow man, a builder man, a going-ahead man, a man unafraid to run that race with the racing time that must be run by all men and all nations who do not wish to be left in the slack waters of history like solitary, grounded ships in the restless, unstayable flow and flood of change."

Next up, Luci approached the podium, telling the crowd that she welcomed an opportunity to be in the South. The heckling grew louder.

The adults on the platform gestured for the disruptive group to quiet down, to no avail.

Over and over, "raucous and loud," they hurled at Luci: "We Want Barry! We Want Barry! We Want Barry!"

Luci took on the taunters, most of whom were around her age or slightly older.

"It seems to me easy to holler a lot, it's easy to make a lot of noise, when you are not the one who's having to handle the problems," she responded in a soft, measured voice.

The hecklers quieted down, and cheers erupted.

"But we are the generation who is going to have to handle the problems. And we're going to have to handle them probably much sooner, and much more unprepared, than we would like to be," said Luci. She soberly advised on the importance of voting based on understanding and reason rather than emotion.

When she paused for a breath, the chants erupted again, louder than before.

Luci waited for them to diminish. The hecklers were quiet while she delivered a concluding point: "All the emotionalism in the world is not going to help us when it comes time for us to lift our banners, for us to take the hands of government."

Said a Georgia politician, "That young 'un shoots from the hip."

Some of the Goldwater hecklers followed Lady Bird and her party as they exited Johnson Square on foot. They continued waving their signs, one of which read, LADY BIRD, LADY BIRD FLY AWAY, AND WHEN YOU'RE GONE TAKE LBJ Another said, JOHNSON IS FOR KING AND GOLDWATER IS FOR PRESIDENT, referring to Dr. Martin Luther King Jr.

Lady Bird and her party's destination, four blocks away, was Juliette Gordon Low's birthplace. Lady Bird was serving as honorary president of the Girl Scouts, continuing a long tradition of First Ladies' involvement with the organization. At the historic home, Girl Scouts were lined up to greet Lady Bird and had a hard time keeping still as they excitedly waited for her arrival from Johnson Square. A little boy tried to climb a lamppost for a better view and looked disappointed when he couldn't make it.

Rounding out a rapid visit in Savannah, Lady Bird snipped the ceremonial ribbon at the opening of new facilities for the Savannah Press Club before heading back to the train. As the Lady Bird Special left Savannah behind, Governor Sanders dismissed the appearance of the disruptive Goldwater supporters as "fifteen or twenty kids jumping up and down." He then added, "If that's the kind of support Goldwater has I'm not worried."

Jesup, Georgia, 2:27 p.m.

The Lady Bird Special picked up speed, hitting eighty miles an hour as the train crew tried to make up time that had already been lost throughout the day.

The mood morphed from dubious to delighted in Jesup.

The anti-Johnson feeling was so intense in this neck of the woods ("some of it pure hate for the President," noted a reporter) that

Democratic supporters were generally silent due to fear of harassment. The militant right-wing John Birch Society was zealously rounding up votes for the Goldwater-Miller ticket. The Chamber of Commerce warned that it would only host the Lady Bird Special if the ceremony was not political.

And yet a large, friendly crowd turned out to greet the campaign train in Jesup, a town that initially sprang up around a railroad stop and became the county seat. Even the Goldwater rooters at the rally were courteous. THE GOLDWATER CLUB WELCOMES THE FIRST LADY stated one sign and another, more ambiguously, YOUNG MEN FOR LUCI.

Betty Talmadge warmed up the crowd in Jesup, saying, "It's just wonderful to be back in Georgia." She and her husband had been in Washington for much of the year. "When you can't get home, the next best thing to being at home is to be made to feel at home." Lady Bird and the president had been those sorts of friends to her and her senator husband since they arrived in Washington in 1957. "It's wonderful to see that you are going to join me down here today in making *her* feel at home," Betty told the audience. "It is with great pride that I present the most capable and gracious First Lady this country has ever known—Mrs. Lyndon Johnson."

Lady Bird began by sharing with the audience that town officials in Jesup had made a donation to a children's hospital in Atlanta in her honor. "You couldn't have done anything that would have made me happier. I thank you," she said. She kept her speech short but did deliver a brief political message and pitch for the president and his time on the job that received loud cheers. "You know what sort of a president he will make because you have lived through those last ten months with us," Lady Bird said before thanking the crowd for turning out. "It gives us a mighty happy feeling to see y'all out here."

Outside Jesup, an elderly woman sat in a wheelchair pushed up to the edge of a field bordering the railroad tracks. She and her family waved as the train passed by and continued south.

Blackshear, Georgia, 3:10 p.m.
The town of Blackshear was slated for a slowdown by the Lady Bird Special and instead received an unscheduled stop due to the sizable crowd that had gathered. For several minutes, while the train idled, an automobile adorned with a Goldwater '64 bumper sticker was held up at a grade crossing.

The air fleet accompanying the Lady Bird Special included the two small, crop duster–style planes advancing the train. In a plan dubbed "Operation Skyhook," the pilots would scout for crowds along the tracks that were large enough to warrant a slowdown or a stop, such as in Blackshear and earlier in Ridgeland, South Carolina, and radio the information to the train crew.

The pilots' other task was to tout the Lady Bird Special's impending arrival. The planes left Washington, DC, an hour before the campaign train and launched a "jumping" operation that continued all the way to New Orleans. The first plane to leave Washington circled Alexandria, Virginia, and the outlying areas trailing a banner that read See Lady Bird, Alexandria Depot, 7 A.M. Pilots flew low and also used a bullhorn to announce that the Lady Bird Special was coming. The second plane, similarly equipped, proceeded directly to Fredericksburg to do the same.

The main driver behind Operation Skyhook, a promotional plan used successfully in other political campaigns, was to alert and encourage people in rural communities to head to the depot. With the advance notice, they would have sufficient time "to lay up their horses, mules and tractors, clean up the kids, and drive the car to town" for the rally.

Mingling with the crowds was the best part of the whistle-stop tour for reporter Celestine Sibley, who had "never made a jollier, more colorful, more fascinating journey." She felt a sense of excitement burgeoning when "Happy Days Are Here Again" began playing over the train's loudspeaker, which signaled that another stop was coming up.

Even though the platform speeches were piped into the press car, she found it more exciting to head down the tracks and meet the locals. "The crowds were very appealing to me—the cheering school children, black and white; the old people with work-roughened hands raised in awkward salutes, the little babies held up in arms or hoisted on shoulders," said Sibley. "In spite of the wonders of television, there's still a great hunger among us to see our national figures in person, to search their faces and return their smiles and maybe yell a question to them."

Waycross, Georgia, 3:23 p.m.

The Lady Bird Special rolled into Waycross in midafternoon. The "strong Goldwater flavor" was more mild than usual, with a huge blue and gold WELCOME FIRST LADY banner from the local Goldwater Club.

Lawyer John Kopp, head of the Goldwater campaign in Waycross, said he arranged for the sign at the train station and issued orders to his group to be polite. He wanted the First Lady to know that not all Goldwater supporters acted like the unbecoming hecklers the previous day in Columbia and Charleston.

That kind of hostility had backfired before, as it did in the 1960 presidential campaign, during what a reporter called "one of the most trying" ordeals in Lady Bird's political life to date. It was four days before the election, and polls showed Texas—which had gone Republican by significant margins in 1952 and 1956—in a dead heat between Kennedy and his rival, Richard Nixon.

As Lady Bird and Lyndon crossed a street to reach the Adolphus Hotel in Dallas to attend a campaign rally, several hundred people surrounded them, blocking their path, waving placards, and yelling, "We want Nixon." The horde was largely women, Republicans and Johnson-hating Democrats who accused him of being, as signs proclaimed, a "counterfeit Confederate" and a sellout to Yankee socialists. Some of the vitriol from the crowd, primarily well dressed or wearing Nixon-branded outfits and dubbed the "Mink Coat Mob" by a newspaper, was directed at Lady Bird. She was jostled by people she recognized and had previously known to be courteous Republicans. Placards saying LET'S GROUND LADY BIRD were waved in her face, her hat was knocked off, and someone snatched her white gloves and threw them on the ground.

"It came upon me as a tremendous surprise and sort of an assault on my spirit," Lady Bird later said, "because we had felt that we were working for them all these years."

Lady Bird and Lyndon held on to each other as they made their way to the Adolphus Hotel entrance. Once they were inside, the abuse continued. They began to cross the lobby, heading for the elevator, as the crowd, bristling with hostility, became bolder. People pressed in on the Johnsons, swearing, shouting insults, and spitting on the floor, continuing to jostle and all but physically attacking them.

Showing what was described as "admirable coolness in a dangerous situation," Lyndon, dignified and poised, slowly walked through the lobby as newspaper and television correspondents reported on the scene. Lady Bird, who came up to her six-foot-three husband's shoulder and couldn't see over the crowd, recalled how she had to tamp down her emotions "and be just like Marie Antoinette in the tumbrel."

Senator Johnson refused police assistance. "If the time has come when I can't walk through the lobby of a hotel in Dallas with my lady without a police escort, I want to know it," he said. When Lady Bird and Lyndon made it to the door of the ballroom where the rally was taking place, they paused, and he offered her a comb to smooth her tousled hair. One of the newspapers that reported on the incident ran the headline, "Lady Bird Combs Mob Right Out of Hair."

The nationally covered "spite and spittle" incident resulted in a number of net gains for the Kennedy-Johnson ticket. Seeing Johnson under attack in his own state portrayed him in a new light to the Northern critics who believed he was a racist and beholden to oil and gas interests. Furthermore, thousands of Texans were outraged at the ugly breach of courtesy, especially toward a woman. And so were other Southerners, including Georgia senator and the Johnsons' friend Dick Russell, whose stubbornness in not supporting his party's national ticket—a stance he had taken since 1944—was undone by his fondness for Lady Bird. He called up Lyndon that night and offered his services, and the two campaigned together through Texas. What occurred at the Adolphus Hotel, especially with the election just four days later, is widely thought to have helped tip Texas into the Democratic column.

In Waycross, politeness prevailed while the Lady Bird Special was there. The mayor proclaimed it "Lady Bird Johnson Day," and due to the exuberance of the 3,000-person crowd, the train lingered past the allotted fifteen minutes.

A young woman standing in a Goldwater group was asked why she had come to the rally. "I heard so much about" the First Lady, "I just wanted to see what she looked like," she said.

Lady Bird mentioned her summers spent in neighboring Alabama and highlighted ancestral ties with Georgia. "We think we have some friends down here," she said. The audience cheered as she delivered her line about valuing, respecting, and needing Southerners.

Even here, deep in anti-Johnson territory, Lady Bird pressed her points. She reminded the audience that the state's per capita income had gone up during Democratic years. Her husband had brought the many lessons of the past, including the harsh Depression years, with him to the White House. "It is that more than anything else that lies behind the programs he has fought for, what he calls the requirements of the Great Society," she said. "Always on his mind is trying to figure out practical, compassionate ways to help those in America that are still in need."

After leaving Waycross, it was necessary to cool down the hospitality car by re-icing, a laborious task that waylaid the train for an hour. During the downtime, Governor Sanders held an onboard press conference. Reporters asked if he thought it was odd that neither of the state's senators were participating with the Lady Bird Special.

"Not at all," Sanders replied. Senator Russell was a bachelor and had "no wife to send along." Senator Talmadge's wife, Betty, was representing him superbly. Glossing over party divisions, he added, "I think our senators have made themselves clear. They are Democrats and they will support the Democratic ticket."

Homerville, Georgia, 4:17 p.m.

The Lady Bird Special made an unscheduled stop in Homerville—just one minute long—before continuing on to another gracious reception in Valdosta. Out-of-state reporters asked their colleagues why, after leaving Savannah, the hostile heckling ceased as the train made its way through southeast Georgia, despite it being heavy Goldwater territory. One Georgian responded that "people have better manners in small towns than in cities." The other reason he gave is that "there is no protection by the cloak of anonymity in the little town. Someone who embarrassed the rest of the town down at the railroad station ran the risk of getting [the] hell kicked out of themselves on the way home."

Valdosta, Georgia, 4:56 p.m.

"My friends of Valdosta, we've had a wonderful time on this train," Lady Bird told a crowd estimated by the police chief at 8,000, some of whom had waited more than two hours. She lauded Georgia politicians present on the platform as well as the ones who had ducked for cover. The president "has learned so much from your senator Dick Russell," she said. "I believe it was Dick Russell more than anybody who was responsible for Lyndon being majority leader of the Senate." The crowd was slow to cheer.

Goldwater banners were in evidence, including a sign held up twenty feet from the train's rear platform showing Goldwater 315 and Johnson 19, which were the results of a poll of local labor union members. A half dozen halfhearted hecklers in the crowd, who presumably risked getting the hell kicked out of them, were so sedate they could hardly be heard above the throng.

Luci scored points with the audience by lauding a beloved local sports team. Since being in Georgia, she had heard about "what a fine football team Valdosta has," she said while flashing a smile. She expressed the hope that the same spirit and enthusiasm they had for their team would be transferred into the coming election.

"And they loved it: That huge, squirming, tired but excited mob which converged against the sides and rear of the Lady Bird Special and extended for over a block in all directions," reported the *Valdosta Daily Times*.

Five women from Valdosta had already been converted to the Johnson cause before the Lady Bird Special reached their hometown. They boarded the train in Waycross for what one described as "the ride of a lifetime." The ride to Valdosta "was as smooth as the silk ribbons that bedecked the hostesses' baskets of favors and as gay as the flowers in the windows of the lounge cars."

First the Valdosta passengers were "charmed" by Lindy, Virginia, and the hostesses in Car #3's lounge. Then they met with Lady Bird in her private quarters and had their photo taken with her. They chatted with her about varieties of day lilies and some of the gifts they brought for her, among them a jar of mayhaw jelly made from a fruit native to the region. The jar was adorned with a hand-drawn caricature of the president eating a hot, jam-topped biscuit, which Lady Bird promised he would see.

Last, the Valdostans were ushered into the hospitality car, where Martha Hodges, whose husband was Luther, the secretary of commerce and campaign train emcee, posed a question. "Tell me, how do you think Georgia is going on November 3rd?" she asked.

One Valdostan answered, "When we got on the train, we weren't all strong for Johnson. But a lovely woman like Mrs. Johnson couldn't be married to anybody but a fine man. We're all solidly for him."

Thomasville, Georgia, 6:02 p.m.
Lady Bird told the audience in Thomasville that she hoped to return at a more leisurely time with the president and hunt the quail for which the area was known. "Right now, we're hunting something else," she said to audience laughter. "And I know that I can abide by your good judgment in the weeks ahead in choosing the man that you want for your leader."

Governor Sanders remarked to reporters that the Lady Bird Special "started out as a train and is winding up a bandwagon." Before leaving the train in Thomasville, the last stop in Georgia, he concluded, "Mrs. Johnson is cutting the heart out of the Goldwater campaign in the South."

20

Courageous Willingness

Thursday, October 8, 1964
Drifton, Florida, 7:34 p.m.

The village of Drifton was so small it was unmarked on state highway maps and ignored by the 1960 census. Here the Lady Bird Special entered tracks operated by the Seaboard Air Line Railroad, one of the six different rail lines over which the train was traveling. Each time the train came to a new rail line, it meant switching out the engine as well as the crew.

"You could get in a heap of trouble if you sent an engineer and his train into a strange territory," explained a Southern Railroad official. "You have to be familiar with the road."

Drifton was one of five stops in Florida coordinated by Jan Sanders of the White House advance team. Comprising part of the crowd were Tallahassee high schoolers brought in by bus and car caravan. "This proved successful" for two reasons, said Sanders. Drifton needed attendees at the rally, and it "gave a special role for these young people who would have been lost amid" the older students at Florida State University (FSU), the Lady Bird Special's next stop.

Adding to the excitement for the 3,000 people assembled at this remote railroad crossing was the arrival of the governor, Farris Bryant, and a bevy of other state politicians and notables who boarded the Lady Bird Special there.

"We were glad to reach Florida and Alabama," said Lindy Boggs. The hope was that Lady Bird's relatives and friends in these states would bolster their spirits and keep "would-be hecklers in line."

Tallahassee, Florida, 8:50 p.m.

JOHNSON GIRLS NEEDED

A front-page announcement in the *Florida Flambeau*, the campus newspaper, instructed any FSU coeds interested in being Johnson Girls during the First Lady's visit to attend a meeting in an auditorium three days later.

When Jan Sanders arrived in Tallahassee, the ball was already rolling for the Lady Bird Special's arrival. She offered guidance at the meeting arranged by a student coordinator where eighty women showed up, representing every dorm and sorority house. To generate enthusiasm for the First Lady's visit, which included a trackside greeting and an indoor, on-campus rally, the students wore yellow WELCOME LADY BIRD campaign buttons, distributed to every dorm "Hello, Lyndon!" records and matchbooks, and worked with the campus newspaper to promote the event.

Later that week, the Lady Bird Special pulled in two hours late, stopping at a spot near the FSU football stadium. The railroad track was the physical dividing line separating the city of Tallahassee's Black and white sections. FSU was on one side while Florida A&M

University (FAMU), a historically Black school, was on the other less than two miles away.

FAMU students were among those leading the fight for racial equality in Tallahassee, including Carrie Patterson and Wilhelmina Jakes, who began a bus boycott. In May 1956, they boarded a crowded city bus and sat in the front where the only seats were available. When they refused the driver's instruction to move to the back, he pulled over the bus and called the police. Patterson and Jakes were arrested, charged with "placing themselves in a position to cause a riot," and released on bond later that day. The next night, a cross was burned in the front yard of the home near campus where they rented rooms. FAMU students held a mass meeting and voted to boycott city buses, a movement that expanded among the city's Black community and was one of the early major economic protests of the civil rights movement. Black riders contributed more than 60 percent to the bus company's income, paying the same fare as white passengers but not receiving the same treatment. Despite intimidation tactics by the police, the boycott continued for seven months and—aided by the U.S. Supreme Court ruling that neighboring Alabama's segregated busing laws were unconstitutional—led to the desegregation of the Tallahassee bus system the next year.

The first activists in the student sit-in movement to choose jail over bail also attended FAMU. In May 1960, after a sham trial, sisters Patricia and Priscilla Stephens were among a group of students found guilty of disturbing the peace and other charges for participating in a peaceful sit-in at a Woolworth lunch counter. Their punishment: $300 or sixty days in jail. "We would not pay a fine to support a system that did not treat us as equal human beings. We would not pay for segregation," said Patricia. The Stephens sisters, along with five other FAMU students and a high schooler, chose jail over bail, and they spent forty-nine days in a county prison.

The day after the group was jailed, a bolstering telegram arrived from Dr. King, who eleven months later did the same for Rock Hill's lunch-counter activists. The missive praised their "courageous willingness" to "suffer and sacrifice for the cause of freedom." For Patricia, it was a "very meaningful" reminder "that we were not alone, that we were part of a far-reaching social movement." While incarcerated, she explained her position to her concerned parents, saying, "We cannot be contented with the condition here in the South any longer. Our very souls are being taken from us by discrimination."

Both FAMU and FSU students participated in welcoming Lady Bird and Luci to Tallahassee, making up the majority of the 2,000 spectators that greeted the train. During the long wait at the railroad siding, the FSU coeds, who grew into a contingent of more than three hundred Johnson Girls, sang and led a cheering section to pass the time, backed up by a university band. (Others did the same for those waiting at the student union ballroom.)

Also entertaining the trackside crowd was FAMU's Marching 100, a renowned marching band and a "perennial show stealer" that often performed at high-profile sporting events. Commenting on the Orange Bowl halftime show, where the Marching 100 performed, the *Miami Herald* wrote, "The band members seem to move faster than the football players on the field." They were widely considered the most precision-tooled marching band in the country, known for sophisticated choreography and fast, high-stepping moves (320 steps per minute versus the usual 120). The band's intricate marching patterns and routines included a "seemingly inexhaustible repertoire of kaleidoscopic formations" depicting words, symbols, and designs.

Amid the fanfare orchestrated for the Lady Bird Special, another gun-toting young man was spotted on the outskirts of the crowd an hour before the train was due. He was detained by the authorities and asked why he was carrying a scope-mounted .22-caliber rifle. They accepted the explanation that the gun was being used as a prop for a skit in the upcoming homecoming festivities, and he had just stopped by the football field to "get a look at Lady Bird and Luci." The unloaded weapon was locked in the trunk of an officer's car for the night.

When the Lady Bird Special arrived, a band began playing "The Eyes of Texas." One of the Johnson Girls yelled across the crowd, "Cover that Goldwater sign," as Confederate flags waved here and there. Lady Bird paused at the microphone long enough to apologize for the train's tardiness and to thank the crowd for the warm welcome. She exited the train via a specially constructed platform, part of the elaborate advance preparations noted in one of three front-page articles about the campaign train in that morning's *Tallahassee Democrat*. Lady Bird was whisked into the governor's limousine and driven to the student union.

Another 3,500 people stood shoulder to shoulder in the student union ballroom, sweltering and restless as cameramen frantically wiped lenses fogging in the heat. Like the spectators greeting the train, the audience was racially mixed and comprised mostly of students. They "really let go" when Lady Bird and Luci arrived, giving the official party a stomping, screaming, sign-waving welcome. A newspaper declared the rally worth the wait, proclaiming in a headline, "Johnson Women Score Hit at FSU."

The crowd wasn't simply being polite. Their rousing cheers turned into vehement booing for those on the speakers' platform with whom they had grievances—like Haydon Burns, the Democratic gubernatorial candidate, whose promise to fire "campus commies and pinks" if elected was widely disliked by students. Goldwater disrupters at the student union rally were fairly restrained. They uttered some "We want Barry" chants and held up signs, although ones lauding LBJ and proclaiming WE LOVE LADY BIRD outnumbered them ten to one.

The chanters' disruption at the rally prompted Patricia Pendergast to send a letter to Lady Bird apologizing on behalf of the FSU community, which was "mortified" at the "poor taste and lack of manners displayed by eleven members of the student body." They were not part of the organized campus Goldwater Youth Group or the Young Republicans. "The 'hecklers' were what we students have nicknamed 'contraries' since they are absolutely contrary to anything the majority wants or does," relayed Patricia. "These 'contrary' students seem to demonstrate their views like a spoiled child vying for attention. I am happy to report that more disgust was thrown their way and more respect was given to your cause through their actions."

Nineteen-year-old Patricia was not old enough to vote. (At the time, the only states that allowed voting under age twenty-one were Georgia and Kentucky at eighteen, Alaska at nineteen, and Hawaii at twenty.) "I can certainly help though and make others aware of this great privilege. Better yet I will keep well-informed and try to persuade the stubborn, sway the negatives, and boost the supporters in favor of your husband for President. He has done a fine job and we need him," wrote Patricia. "I enjoyed your speech very much… Thank you for coming to our school and I am truly sorry our reception couldn't be flawless but in our hearts it was flawless."

Acknowledging the dissenting campaign views and the freely booed politicians on the platform at the student union, Governor Bryant quipped, "Anybody who says we don't have academic freedom here at FSU hasn't attended one of these meetings." While introducing the First Lady, he extolled "this great nation." A voice in the throngs shouted, "Let's keep it that way—Goldwater!" which elicited a round of disapproving boos. The governor responded, "One of the things that has made the nation great is the willingness of its people to accord everyone the right to speak." The audience erupted into thunderous cheers.

When Lady Bird approached the podium, the exuberant crowd grew silent. Her speech was billed in the *Tallahassee Democrat* as the "key talk" of the tour. She highlighted Florida's role in the exciting new era of space exploration along with themes of communication and education, which she deemed "the key to freedom, success, goodwill among men, and peace in the world."

Lady Bird went on to say that she didn't need to tell those who witnessed the rocket launches at Cape Kennedy how thrilling it was to be part of an age with such tremendous scientific developments.

"Man first circled the earth in a satellite launched from a Florida shore. Man will be sent to the moon from Florida," she said to great applause.

"Cape Kennedy is not the only launching pad in Florida," she went on. "This campus, as well as the other campuses throughout the state, are our educational launching pads. From them we hope to send bright young men and women home to the towns and cities of this state with a new thrust of ideas. We hope that you will put into the business and political and, yes, spiritual community of Florida your zest and intelligence.

"Surely a nation which masters all the intricacies of Saturn V can master the engineering of human relationships," she said to audience applause. "We've learned so much in the technological fields it seems to me sometimes we have yet to catch up in the fields of learning how to get along with each other. You too," she told the students in the audience, "can be like the communications satellites—protection against human storms."

When Lady Bird finished speaking, the crowd responded with an ovation. They saved even greater enthusiasm for the student on the speakers' platform, shouting, "We want Luci."

Luci was one of the most famous teenagers in the nation. Five months earlier, in May 1964, she was featured on the cover of *Life* magazine with the headline "Luci Baines Johnson: Teen-ager in the White House." (Lynda turned twenty earlier that year.) A teenage daughter hadn't been part of the First Family since seventeen-year-old Helen Taft lived in the White House more than half a century prior.

"Suddenly it's teensville on Pennsylvania Avenue," declared the magazine in a six-page feature story about Luci.

A full-page announcement heralding the Lady Bird Special in the *Florida Flambeau* touted, "LUCI WILL BE HERE TOO."

In what the paper described as a rally "for Luci and her mother, Lady Bird," she was made an honorary member of the 1964 FSU homecoming court in a surprise ceremony. The reigning queen crowned Luci with a Seminole feathered headdress according to homecoming court tradition. The students loved Luci's extemporaneous speech, during which she "threw some real campaign punches" as she spoke about their generation's responsibilities. "I'm thrilled to death to be here, and again, I hope our decisions...justify the faith that our parents and our teachers have had in us," said Luci.

While Luci spoke, Lady Bird smiled and at times was seemingly "leaning forward in suspense." Asked by a reporter about her daughters' speeches during the whistle-stop tour, she insisted they were on their own. Speaking of Luci, she said, "She opens her mouth and out it comes. I keep holding my breath." The Tallahassee audience liked what they heard and gave Luci a thunderous ovation.

Following the rally, Luci, a senior at the National Cathedral School for Girls in Washington, brought her chemistry books with her to the governor's mansion, where a reception was held in Lady Bird's honor. Liz Carpenter joked that she hoped Luci wasn't studying the Goldwater formula. The chemical symbols AUH_2O (gold and water) were being used by the senator's supporters in the campaign.

The press had other plans while the First Lady was feted at the governor's mansion. Two events were arranged at the Hotel Duval for reporters: a cocktail party and much-needed showers. When Helen Thomas called the whistle-stop tour a "grueling, grimy journey," she meant it literally. The only bathing facilities on the train were in Lady Bird's quarters. Mary Pakenham was the sole reporter "farsighted enough to bring along her own makeshift bathtub," said Liz

Carpenter. She filled a large plastic sack with water and then "slipped into it and swished about, emerging better than before."

Carpenter had wired ahead to the advance man in Tallahassee:

> Press stinks. Please reserve three rooms and 150 towels for bathing period at nearby hotel.

Reporters let out whoops of joy when they read the message she posted in the press car. "The press that bathes together stays together," she announced and directed them to the Hotel Duval that night. Said Carpenter, "The gratitude of the train's grimy passengers was touching. The entire atmosphere was literally sweeter."

21

I'm Afraid I Bopped Him

Friday, October 9, 1964
Chattahoochee, Florida, 6:45 a.m.

The next morning, after waiting on the tardy governor and a senator, the Lady Bird Special set out from Tallahassee at 5:49 a.m. for its last day on the tracks. An hour later, when the train pulled into the tiny hamlet of Chattahoochee for another engine change, Lady Bird appeared on the back platform to address a gathering and humorously announced, "I never talk politics before breakfast."

Chipley, Florida, 7:45 a.m. and Crestview, Florida, 9:35 a.m.
Heading on, the Lady Bird Special continued to draw enthusiastic and "surprisingly large" crowds. Unsurprisingly, they encountered a fair amount of Goldwater sentiment, including a group of junior college students wearing sweatshirts branded with AUH$_2$O.

Jan Sanders had diligently advanced the Lady Bird Special in

Chipley and Crestview, the train's next two stops. She rallied the support of Chipley's mayor and other town officials and their wives, met the publishers of the local paper, the *Washington County News*, and attended a coffee get-together with women from Chipley and outlying towns who were arranging carpools to bring people to the rally. In these meetings, "I did not ignore the tremendous problems these people were having to face politically, but tried to give them a larger perspective, encouragement, and recognition that I felt was so desperately needed," Sanders said.

In Crestview, Sanders spoke with a group of women who were new to politics. They were "interested in Lady Bird's visit but lukewarm about doing anything themselves," she said. But by the time the meeting concluded, all committee chores were assigned and "they left with a lot of enthusiasm."

Despite the difficulties, Sanders achieved the primary objective given to the advance women: "The success of the Whistle-Stop is going to depend upon the number of [people] at the station stops. This is your first responsibility."

Thousands of people assembled from across the Panhandle, an estimated 3,000 in Chipley and another 5,000 in Crestview. Crowds in both locales gave wildly cheering receptions to Lady Bird and Luci.

Speaking on the train platform in Chipley, Lady Bird began by telling the audience she had woken up that morning to good news. The *Washington County News* was the first Florida weekly to endorse President Johnson for a full four-year term.

Lady Bird delivered a message to the "folks of the South," expressing her appreciation for those working for and helping the Democratic cause. Speaking in a much firmer, more determined tone than she had previously, she continued, "Now there are *some* who would have us ignore the South, that think that we can win without it. Maybe we can. But we have too much respect for it to take it for granted and too much love for it to ignore it."

While the First Lady spoke, robust cheers mainly obscured the "We want Barry" chants delivered by a group of men that no one recognized. And proving the theory that it's hard to hide in a small-town area, half a dozen Chipley high school boys were identified as aiding the out-of-town hecklers.

Standing near the unidentified hecklers was a local resident, Mrs. Trawick, who heard them use racial slurs while Lady Bird spoke. They were making so much noise that she and others in the vicinity had difficulty hearing what Lady Bird was saying. "This man began waving a Goldwater sign and yelling at Mrs. Johnson every time she tried to talk. I asked him to be quiet, but he wouldn't," said Mrs. Trawick. "I'm ashamed of forgetting to act ladylike, but I'm afraid I bopped him." She hit the man twice in the body and then gave him a backhanded slap across the face, all while holding her fourteen-month-old daughter.

"I don't know what possessed me to do it. But when the First Lady is speaking, I believe those in her audience should have the courtesy to keep quiet," said Mrs. Trawick. The man "looked awfully surprised" when she bopped him. "But he stopped heckling."

There was speculation that the stop in Chipley, originally scheduled for ten minutes, was reduced to five due to the hecklers. In actuality, the shortened time frame—a decision made before the train reached the town—was done to help keep to the tight schedule and ensure the train reached New Orleans on time that evening.

Another fracas unfolded at the next stop in Crestview. Two young men held up a six-foot-long WE WANT BARRY sign, obstructing the view of the people standing behind them. A woman politely asked them to lower the sign, a request they ignored. She then swatted at the banner while another woman hit it with an umbrella. Still, the boys doggedly kept the paper sign in the air until the first woman grabbed it and tore it to pieces.

"Heck, I'm for Barry, too," said one of the women. "But I came here to see Lady Bird and I was going to see her."

Milton, Florida, approx. 10:30 a.m.
The Lady Bird Special's stop in Milton helped assuage hurt feelings. Four years earlier, the LBJ Special's vote-getting swing through the Panhandle omitted Milton. The exclusion "raised a shower of sparks" and was perceived as "an open insult." Now, the First Lady received loud cheers, especially when she praised the town's football team. Luci bought a box of doughnuts from a football player fundraising for the team, "and the whole atmosphere was that of circus day."

22

Hard-Hitting and Down-to-Earth

Friday, October 9, 1964
Pensacola, Florida, 11:22 a.m.

The Lady Bird Special's entrance into Pensacola was even more dramatic than usual.

A Coast Guard vessel loaded with armed men was waiting to escort the campaign train across a bridge spanning Escambia Bay. As the train traversed the trestle, the boat kept pace until they reached the city on the other side, where a second boat stood guard. The two helicopters traveling with the Lady Bird Special flew overhead, while the Marine Corps chopper went on to survey the rally site.

Overpasses and bridges all along the Lady Bird Special's route were inspected by law enforcement, sometimes yard by yard. In Pensacola, precautions were considerably amped up. An anonymous telephone call to the Escambia County sheriff's department reported that an attempt would be made to blow up a trestle on the Lady

Bird Special's route. When the train slowly pulled into the station in Pensacola, guards in plain clothes were seen standing in the doorway of each coach.

A sign hanging at the top of a building proclaimed PENSACOLA LOVES LADY BIRD. Standing immediately above the sign was a policeman holding a rifle. The heavy police presence, which was for protection as well as to deter anyone thinking of doing harm, did not diminish the festive feel of the occasion. The advance team's efforts, along with Liz Carpenter's well-oiled publicity machine, yielded a turnout of some 10,000 for the Lady Bird Special's twenty-minute visit.

While working in Pensacola with two advance men, Jan Sanders primarily used a grassroots approach. She set up a calling tree, using the phone book, her own contacts, and ones provided by the White House. She talked with employees at a chemical company as part of a bipartisan political action course, a heavily Goldwater group where she offered a different perspective from a mean-spirited Republican who presented. She attended the Democratic Women's Club dance, where she made an announcement about the whistle-stop (and danced with a tipsy voter to "Hello, Lyndon!"). And she met with small groups at people's houses.

"This is slow campaigning but very effective," said Sanders, "particularly in view of the political climate of Pensacola which was 'grim' at that time." To each group, she spoke about Lady Bird's impending visit and told them about the Johnsons, the importance of the campaign, and how she personally became involved in the endeavor.

Two weeks earlier, Sanders boarded a midnight flight in Dallas and arrived the next morning in Washington, DC. A friend met her at the airport with a jug of coffee to fuel up before a briefing with the Lady Bird Special advance team.

Lady Bird specifically asked that Sanders join the team. Her dozen years of campaign experience ranged from contributing to her newlywed husband's ultimately successful race for the Texas House of Representatives (they were married only a week when he hit the campaign trail) to organizing some of the highly attended Texas teas for Lady Bird and the Kennedys with only a few days' notice. Like her fellow female White House coordinators and others on the Lady Bird Special team, Jan worked the whistle-stop tour into an already hectic schedule of family responsibilities and other commitments. She had four children ranging in age from two and a half to eleven, and her husband was currently the U.S. attorney for the northern district of Texas. Among her volunteer activities was making Braille school books, setting up the type on metal drums and running off copies for the Dallas Services for Blind Children.

And yet Sanders didn't hesitate, boarding the plane to Washington just over forty-eight hours after receiving Virginia Russell's invitational telephone call and remaining on the road for two weeks. "I really love politics," said Sanders. "I feel it is one of the highest callings and the responsibility of all citizens in a free society."

The day Sanders departed for Washington, she readied her wardrobe and packed, went to a Democratic Women's Board gathering, and attended meetings related to her school-age children. She didn't know until the briefing in the capital where she would be working.

Before leaving Washington several days later with Virginia, Lindy, and the advance team to head south, Sanders spent time preparing. She attended numerous briefing sessions, including one where Liz Carpenter inspired and instructed in "her hard-hitting, down-to-earth way." She also met with a Florida senator and congressmen in their Capitol Hill offices to glean insights into the political atmosphere in the state and the people there with whom she would be working.

Once in Pensacola, Sanders also became part of the story, as directed in the advance team instructions. (Every detail was potentially newsworthy, including the curiosity about her husband's name, Barefoot, which was his grandmother's maiden name and traced back to Anglo-Saxon derivation.) Impressively multitasking, Sanders was interviewed by reporters while driving and flying around the state. Her efforts largely contributed to the Lady Bird Special's successful run, and the stop in "grim" Pensacola was a triumph and a fitting finale in Florida.

"Lady Bird Johnson came to town today with all the hoopla of an old time circus train," wrote a reporter. Bands played and banners waved. Bunting was hung, and the lawn around the railroad tracks freshly mown after a photo appeared in the *Pensacola Journal* that morning showing the "unsightly grass 'n weeds" marring the area. A woman fainted at the rally and was treated by an ambulance on the scene. An overly boisterous man was taken to the city jail. Teenage Democrats greeted the train chanting, "We want Johnson…Johnson we want." A small boy carried a bird-themed sign saying NAS Ornithologists Welcome You. Vendors hawked soft drinks and souvenirs around the perimeter of the crowd. Another group of teenagers, girls wearing white dresses and straw hats with red, white, and blue ribbons, sang and led cheers.

As the time for the train's arrival drew closer, police repeatedly requested that the crowd clear the tracks. An estimated 12,000 people came to the depot, massing so close to the rails it took several minutes to wedge the train into the station. As the train came to a stop, reporters sprinted for the yellow trackside phones to call in their latest news flashes. Reporter Frances Lewine, the first woman to be a full-time White House correspondent for the Associated Press, was running down a sidewalk when she hit a "blip" and went crashing down. "Helen Thomas was right behind me, she hit it, she fell down," recalled Lewine. "The photographers came running up and they looked down with their cameras and they said, 'Oh, it's you,' and went on. The hazards of travel."

A group of teenage boys at the rally worked hard to deliver their contrary message. They stood and waited for an hour atop scaffolding that had a large sign attached: Welcome Lady Bird. Just as the train halted, they unfolded the bottom portion of the sign to reveal the rest of the message—TO GOLDWATER COUNTRY.

Blunting the effects of their attention-seeking sign was the sight of Lady Bird and Luci on the rear platform as the train approached the station. When Luci came into view, the crowd "really cut loose." Amid the cheering throng, a mother held her child up high and pointed out the First Lady. "Look, there she is. The lady in the red dress."

Addressing the crowd, Lady Bird acknowledged the fiftieth anniversary of the Naval Air Station Pensacola before making the point, as she had in Charleston, that this and other military bases pumped millions into the Florida Panhandle economy. She wrapped up by promoting her husband's record and his reelection.

When Hale Boggs, the last speaker in Pensacola, finished his remarks, the crowd began chanting, "We want Lady Bird." Lady Bird laughed and stepped up to the microphone.

"Once more, I want to tell you how it warms my heart, how much I thank you, all you young folks and all you mamas and papas and all these good homemade signs," she said. "You're sending us on our way with a happy feeling. My husband will try to repay you with the best hard work and the most devoted service to his country that he can produce."

Most people in the Pensacola crowd were there to cheer. Some came specifically to hoot and holler. "All in all," noted a reporter, "it was a warm, heartening reception" for the First Lady in "politically doubtful Florida." Governor Bryant agreed, saying the visit "will help return the area to the Democrats."

By this time, even members of the press corps who weren't from the South were "sprinkling their conversation with 'you' alls," said a Pensacola newspaper correspondent.

For the "Nawthern" reporters on the train, Liz Carpenter

concocted a "Dixie Dictionary," a quick primer in "conversational English down heah."

"Everyone got a laugh out of it except the sober-minded Associated Press," recalled Carpenter. After Frances Lewine submitted a story that went out on the wire, the AP messaged its clients:

Please Eliminate the Dixie Dictionary—Objectionable Material.

Said Carpenter, "Translated, I suspected that meant some Goldwater publisher had filed a complaint."

Dixie Dictionary:
Yawl—Not a boat, but more than one Democrat.
Tall cotton—What Southerners walk in due to Johnson prosperity.
Grits—Only staple available in Hoover administration.
Beri-beri—(pronounced Barry-Barry)—A disease wiped out in the South.
Yankee—Object of good neighbor policy.
High on the hawg—The gross national product under the Democrats.
Whole hawg—All the way LBJ.
Honey chile—Young citizen for Johnson.
Fat back—Rich Democrat who turned Republican and is now returning to the Democratic fold.
Hush-puppies—Him and Her when they are quiet.
Southern belle—A ding dong Democrat.
Kissin' kin—Anyone who'll come to the depot.

Lady Bird's kissin' kin were so abundant that reporters began asking her, "Is this next stop going to be a one-cousin town or a four-cousin town?"

23

The New South

Friday, October 9, 1964
Flomaton, Alabama, 12:51 p.m.

Flomaton was at least a ten-cousin town.

Six of Lady Bird's relatives joined the train in Pensacola and rode into Alabama, including Minnie Wade Derby, whose daughter, Patsy, was one of the official Ladies for Lyndon hostesses. Here in what Lady Bird called "the land of cousins," she introduced some of them on the train platform, and others she called out to in the crowd.

Three of the cousins joining Lady Bird in Flomaton had seen her at the White House that summer when they stopped by while on their way to New York City for the World's Fair. On the Truman balcony overlooking the South Lawn, she and her kinfolks had a "wonderful visit about our youth and Alabama today," said Lady Bird. The cousins shared with her that there were mixed reactions in Alabama to the public accommodation requirement in the Civil Rights Act, including some filling stations that circumvented the mandate to desegregate restrooms by handing keys to customers according to their race. And while driving home one evening around twilight, her cousin Nettie Mason Woodyard and a friend saw fire and thought someone's farmhouse was burning down. Cars were parked along the road, and one passerby explained what was happening. Members of the White Citizens Council, a white supremacist organization, were building a bonfire they wanted "high enough so it can be seen in Washington." Lady Bird understood from Woodyard, a longtime teacher, that she was "trying to bring a spirit of understanding and acceptance of the changing world to her students."

Lady Bird's talk with her kinfolks at the White House turned to reminiscing about the past. She said, "It was a pleasant voyage into the days of my childhood."

Lady Bird was born on December 22, 1912, in an antebellum plantation house in rural East Texas near the Louisiana border. (She acquired her distinctive moniker as a baby. She tried to cast it off in later years in favor of her given name, Claudia, to no avail. Said Lady Bird, "Long ago I made my peace with the nickname.")

In the town of Karnack, described by Lady Bird's brother as where the "Old South begins to fade into the West," their father made his fortune growing cotton and running a general store. A sign above the door advertised DEALER IN EVERYTHING. Work was her father's "passion and his god," said Lady Bird. Her mother was more cerebral, a voracious reader and a progressive who became involved in local politics at a time when women did not yet have the right to vote.

Lady Bird was five years old when her mother died unexpectedly. From then on, she spent three months every year in Alabama, the state from which both of her parents hailed, until she was twenty-one and married Lyndon. "My life there was visiting kinfolks in little towns," Lady Bird recalled.

During the whistle-stop tour, she frequently spoke about the summers with her Alabama relatives to convey her affection for and affinity with the South. She shared with audiences her cherished memories of watermelon cuttings, hayrides, swimming in the creek, and gathering with so many cousins at a time they ran out of beds and slept on pallets on the floor.

"We're so proud of your Alabama heritage," Maryon Allen, the wife of the state's lieutenant governor, said to Lady Bird on the train's back platform in Flomaton. "Welcome home."

As the Lady Bird Special traveled south, "a thawing of the chill" took place among Democratic politicians who had previously been icy toward the Johnson-Humphrey ticket.

Not so with Alabama Governor George Wallace, one of President Johnson's "political enemies." The notoriously hostile governor was absent from the lineup of dignitaries who greeted the campaign train in Flomaton. He hightailed it out of Alabama that morning, leaving three days early for the Southern Governors Conference in San Antonio. And yet with momentum for the train running so high, even Wallace didn't snub the Lady Bird Special entirely. Said Liz Carpenter, "He didn't want to ignore a popular daughter of the South."

Wallace telegrammed a greeting to Lady Bird and sent four dozen red roses—bearing the message "Welcome Home"—which were delivered by Maryon Allen.

Allen had boarded Car #3 in Pensacola. She relinquished the bountiful bouquet to waiting hands as she worked her way through the train's politicking corridor. She met with Lady Bird in her private quarters and then moved on to the hospitality car. As the train neared Flomaton, Allen realized the governor's roses—which she was to present to the First Lady during the platform ceremony—were nowhere to be seen.

The abundance of flowers presented to Lady Bird during the whistle-stop tour could easily have filled a florist shop, and a method was devised for regifting the blooms. Either Ashton Gonella or Mary

Rather, the First Lady's secretaries, would attach a note from her to the bouquets received at a particular stop and walk the flowers to the front of the train. Through a window near the engine, they would hand them over to a waiting advance man or a policeman for delivery to a local nursing home or hospital.

Allen asked Liz Carpenter, "Where are Governor Wallace's roses?"

Carpenter realized immediately what must have happened.

"In any campaign, there is always the danger of overorganizing—becoming a victim of your own efficiency. That's what put Governor Wallace's roses in peril that day," said Carpenter. She rushed off to find Mary Rather. As she explained the situation, Rather turned ashen and then "started out in a dead heat" to overtake the person she had sent to the front of the train with the roses. "In what seemed like hours," recalled Carpenter, "she was back breathless—with roses. She had rescued them just as they were being handed out the window. This was one time when it was *not* better to give than to receive."

Allen was invited by the Democratic Campaign Steering Committee to extend the First Lady's official welcome in Alabama. "I don't think the committee held much hope I would do it," said Allen. The reason: Her husband, the lieutenant governor, was head of the state's electors, who declined to pledge support for President Johnson. "But right from the very start," Allen said, they both "agreed it would be unthinkable if I refused the invitation."

Allen, a former newspaper writer new to politics, was surprised at the "to-do" that arose over her decision to participate in the whistle-stop, which was her first major political role since marrying the lieutenant governor two months earlier. Her phone began ringing day and night with friends and acquaintances speculating and asking questions.

"I really thought the entire thing ridiculous anyone would consider it strange I had agreed to greet the First Lady of the land on behalf of the State of Alabama," Allen remarked. Finally, Lieutenant Governor Allen issued a statement to the press, saying "the state must show respect to the nation's first lady and Alabama is noted for its southern hospitality." He gave his "full approval and support" of his wife taking part in the Lady Bird Special.

While standing near the rear door in the hospitality car, waiting to exit onto the platform, Allen was gripped by nervousness. "Then I saw something I shall never forget," she said. Next to her, Lady Bird held her speech in her hands, fingers trembling and her eyes tightly closed. "I was overcome with compassion for this great lady, this superb, polished campaigner," Allen recalled. "She was afraid of just what sort of reception she would receive" in a state to which she had such close ties. "In these crazy times we're living in right now, the wife of the President of the United States, the First Lady, a woman of Southern heritage, couldn't be sure she would be accorded the respect and honor due her position."

Allen was "as thrilled as the rest" when she saw the enormous turnout at the Flomaton train station. The scene brought to mind campaign movies of the 1930s and '40s with a high school band blaring "Dixie," handcrafted signs, and "people from every walk of life" who were "yelling their heads off," said Allen. Even the presence of a few Goldwaterites didn't dispel the "holiday mood."

Ultimately, Lady Bird was pleased with her Alabama reception. She later told her longtime friend Virginia Durr, an Alabama resident and a civil rights activist, that Flomaton "was a happy event and all that I could have asked for."

Mobile, Alabama, 2:36 p.m.

If there was any concern that "white backlash" in Alabama would spoil the whistle-stop tour, "Mobile gave the answer," reported Gloria Negri. "Delighted and cheering" crowds estimated as high as 20,000 amassed to see the First Lady in the Gulf Coast city, which she declared her favorite stop of the trip. Spectators greeted the train and lined the motorcade route into downtown Mobile, where Lady Bird had been invited by the mayor to dedicate a restored, century-old firehouse turned museum and receive a key to the city.

The Lady Bird Special came into town under continued, extremely tight security. Coast Guard patrol boats lined each side of a bridge when the train crossed a river into Mobile County. Additional patrol boats were stationed along the city's docks, and the area was teeming with uniformed officers and policemen on top of buildings and near the railroad tracks.

More family and friends were in Mobile to support Lady Bird. "I'm home," she told the rally crowd gathered in front of the restored firehouse. "Everywhere I look I see a cousin." Aside from the cousins already on the train, three more greeted Lady Bird at the station in Mobile. On the way to the rally site, they spotted two more on the street and stopped and brought them along too.

In addition to Lady Bird's kin, "seeing you and Cliff in the crowd was one of the happiest moments of the Whistle-Stop," she told Virginia Durr. (Virginia and Clifford, an attorney, accompanied civil rights activist E. D. Nixon to bail out Rosa Parks from a Montgomery jail on the night of her arrest for refusing to sit at the back of the bus. Virginia was friends with Parks, and she later recalled the "terrible sight" of seeing this "gentle, lovely, sweet" woman "being brought down by a matron" at the jail.)

The abundant audience in Mobile was the largest of the whistle-stop tour so far. It also included hostile hecklers, who during the rally went well beyond the usual "We want Barry" chants. Once again, they were small in number—mostly teenagers in what appeared to be an organized group—but determined to cause a commotion. They bobbed signs up and down, hooted and howled, and shouted "Black Bird, go home" and "Down with Johnson."

University of Alabama students carried a huge sign and held it in front of the heckling group, somewhat muffling the noise. The sign was a welcome for Luci, who "proved herself a natural campaigner" by plunging into the crowds at the Mobile depot and at the rally, speaking with people and "shaking hands with all the gusto of her father."

Senator John Sparkman directly admonished the primary group of heckling teenage boys. "I read in the paper that my good friend, Barry Goldwater, had sent a telegram to his different state directors asking them to be courteous. I hate to think that Alabama failed to take notice of that request from their leader," he said. The audience responded with loud cheers and dueling "We want Barry" and "Lady Bird" chants. Sparkman declared it his great pleasure to introduce the First Lady, "the wife of the president of all of us regardless of what party we may belong to."

Other than Senator Sparkman, Alabama public officials were conspicuous by their absence during the Lady Bird Special's stops in Mobile and Flomaton. (The state's senior senator, Lister Hill, wasn't hiding like other politicians; he was recovering from surgery.)

Virginia Durr spoke with Senator Sparkman after the rally, telling him, "John, you really deserve a gold cross for having courage enough to stand on that platform by Lady Bird when all the other politicians had disappeared." The senator responded, "Well, I hope it's going to be a gold cross. I'm afraid it's going to be an iron cross."

When Lady Bird stepped up to the podium in Mobile, even the most vociferous Goldwater hecklers were outmatched. The crowd cheered and whistled. The band played. The cheers kept going, and the crowd chanted "Lady Bird, Lady Bird" over and over again.

As in previous speeches, she stressed the importance of "fusing the best of the old and the new South," and here in Mobile, she also highlighted her ties to the state.

"As many of you know, Alabama is close to my heart. I am proud to be in the state where my mother and father were born and raised, and being in Mobile is part of a sentimental journey for me," she said. "I'm mighty glad to be in that part of the country where, although you might not like all I say, at least you understand the way I say it."

Several times as Lady Bird spoke, she smiled and held up her left hand, on each occasion quieting the hecklers for a time.

"I'm sure that these little boys had been paid to heckle her and to interrupt her because every other breath they would interrupt her and say something nasty or just yell, 'Down with Johnson,'" said Virginia Durr. "Well, just because she was so ladylike about it and so sweet and gentle, they did hush up a little while so she could finish her speech."

Some spectators appeared mortified at the breaches of courtesy. One woman confronted a Goldwater heckler who stood beside her, straining at the ropes, when the train arrived at the railroad station. "Doesn't it mean anything to you that she is the wife of the president of the United States?" she asked. It wasn't reported whether she received an answer.

When Barry Goldwater campaigned through the South, "not a single boo" was heard. The contrast with the treatment Lady Bird received "was striking," noted Mary McGrory. A longtime political columnist for the Washington *Evening Star*, McGrory (who was assigned to the beat only after an editor determined that she wasn't going to get married, have a baby, and leave the paper any time soon) covered both presidential candidates on the campaign trail. "The most intelligent single decision of the Southern campaign may have been the decision on the part of Democrats and Negro civil rights leaders to give the Republican candidate a safe conduct through the South." The telegram Senator Sparkman mentioned, issued by Goldwater's campaign manager forbidding demonstrations, "was published too late to nullify the effect of the First Lady's harassment."

In Mobile, Lady Bird spoke calmly and confidently to the boisterous crowd, projecting above the near-constant din of Goldwater disturbers and the Johnson counter chanters.

"Standing here today, I feel that having spent so much of my life of the past here and having traveled quite some since, I can speak of what the new South means to the nation," said Lady Bird.

THE NEW SOUTH

The Southern warmth and courtesy she associated with her youth would never change, while allowing for the new South she saw in Alabama: on an earlier trip to Huntsville, "where man turns his face to the moon," and in Mobile. "But we still have a big task ahead of us. Thirty-nine per cent of the people of the state are below the poverty line—this must be changed for the good of us all," she cautioned. "The landmarks of the past serve us only as a challenge to build the landmarks of the future."

Lady Bird summed up her speech, stating, "I can't close without saying how much this means to me that all of you would want to come out and greet me. It's a colorful, beautiful picture I will carry away in my heart always."

During a lull before the firehouse dedication began, the boisterousness increased. "We want Lady Bird" chants resounded to counter the refrains of "We want Barry."

"Just a moment, please. Just a moment," Lady Bird said to the audience. "This is a free country, and I respect your right to your opinion. Now will you give me just one minute to finish this." Someone in the crowd shouted, "Go home." Lady Bird continued on, citing the history of the Phoenix Fire Station, which was built in 1859. "I thank you one and all," she said as boos and cheers and "We want Lyndon" chants erupted again.

In Mobile, "Mrs. Johnson was the most relaxed, the most fiery and the most appealing of all the days of her history-making whistle-stopping tour of the South," wrote Gloria Negri.

Other reporters who had been on board the train the entire way agreed. It was here that Lady Bird "won her campaign diploma," declared *Austin American-Statesman* reporter Sam Wood. "She took the political fireworks in stride."

In the late afternoon, eight-year-old Gary Southern and his brother, five-year-old Michael, watched the Lady Bird Special as it passed through Pascagoula, Mississippi. Some three hundred people stood along the tracks in the town, many of whom held pro-Goldwater signs. That night, Gary penned a letter to the First Lady.

"We saw you go by our house today," he wrote. "We hope you had a good time in Mississippi. We love you and President Johnson." His father, he added, worked at the post office in Pascagoula. "I know you are very busy but, I hope you will come back to Pascagoula to see us."

Gary then expressed his political preference. "I like Mr. Johnson very much. And I pray he will not have to go to heaven, like President Kennedy until he has lived a long, long time.

"I have to go to bed now. Please answer my letter soon. I love you."

24

Voice Their Convictions

Friday, October 9, 1964
Edgewater Park, Biloxi, Mississippi, 5:17 p.m.

The powder keg of Southern politics was at its most volatile in Mississippi, another state hostile to President Johnson. A statewide survey concluded that in the 1964 election, Mississippi voters were "dominated by the race question to the exclusion of almost any other political consideration."

"Anti-Johnson sentiment was strong in Mississippi at that time, even stronger than anti-Negro sentiment," observed Drew Pearson, a Washington, DC, columnist, while in the state during the 1964 election. "It took a lot of courage in Mississippi last fall to go 'All the way with LBJ.'"

And yet even in "the nation's most segregated state," some 9,000 people turned out for the Lady Bird Special in Biloxi. The First Lady's "greatest political triumph" of the trip "was to produce on the train's back platform." Mississippi governor Paul Johnson. The governor, who had publicly denounced the Johnson-Humphrey ticket as "the most dangerous political combination in the history of this nation," succumbed to the influence of the Lady Bird Special. He told his fellow Mississippians that with "a real sense of pleasure," he welcomed the First Lady to the state, which had "risen to the occasion" with a generous welcome.

"We're delighted to have her, regardless here in America, of any political opinions or differences. The people of this country and the love and devotion of the people of Mississippi transcends all political questions," said Governor Johnson. "We are honored to have this fine lady in our state."

The governor's wife, Dot, presented Lady Bird with yellow roses on behalf of Mississippi, the hospitality state. "No campaign is an easy one. We know, we've been there," said Dot. "I hope that she will take pleasant memories with her of this one."

In addition to the Goldwater-supporting Governor Johnson, two other reluctant dignitaries greeted Lady Bird in Mississippi. Senators James Eastland and John Stennis each mustered a single sentence in welcome, although Stennis managed to add "Good luck."

Introducing the First Lady in Biloxi was Douglas Wynn, a lawyer and the head of the Johnson-Humphrey campaign committee in Mississippi. (His wife, Leila, was a Ladies for Lyndon hostess and made the entire journey aboard the Lady Bird Special.) Wynn was one of the Mississippi delegates at the Democratic National Convention, where civil rights activists challenged the stranglehold on the state's political regime.

White supremacists' influence was so entrenched in state and local government that the KKK, originally founded to resist advances in racial equality during the Reconstruction era, had been largely inactive for decades. But Klan membership began to resurge as the civil rights movement gained momentum and nationwide notice in the 1950s and

'60s. Various splinter groups arose, including the White Knights of the KKK, a notoriously secretive and violent group responsible for the murders of James Chaney, Andrew Goodman, and Michael Schwerner in Mississippi. Beginning in the fall of 1963, it took only six months for a zealous new Klan recruit to organize chapters in seventy-six counties in the state.

Mississippi also had a larger percentage of Black residents than any other U.S. state.

Trouble brewed when an attempt was made to rectify the racial imbalance in the state's politics. At the 1964 Democratic National Convention, two different panels of delegates each vied for the right to represent the state of Mississippi. On one side was the Mississippi Freedom Democratic Party, comprised of elected Black and white delegates. On the other was the regular state delegation, which barred Black participants, in violation of federal law.

Which delegation was seated would be decided by the convention's credentials committee. Each side argued its case in an "emotional session" aired on national television. Witnesses for the Freedom Party told of the relentless "brutality and terror" they experienced for simply trying to register and vote.

Fannie Lou Hamer, a Mississippi Freedom Democratic Party delegate and cofounder, spoke of being evicted from her home and fired from her job after she became active in voter registration and a field worker for the Student Nonviolent Coordinating Committee. On her way home from a civil rights meeting, she was arrested and jailed, where she was beaten so severely it left her with lifelong injuries.

"We are going to make you wish you was dead," a state highway patrolman said to Hamer. She was told to lie face down on a bunk bed in a cell. A Black man was ordered to strike her repeatedly with a blackjack, a weighted bludgeoning device, and after he exhausted himself, a second one took over. When Hamer screamed, an officer began beating on her head and told her to hush.

"All of this is on account we want to register, to become first-class citizens," said Hamer in the credentials committee hearing. "If the Freedom Democratic Party is not seated now, I question America. Is this America, the land of the free and the home of the brave where we have to sleep with our telephones off of the hooks because our lives be threatened daily because we want to live as decent human beings, in America?"

A state senator representing the regular delegation tried to prevent the next witness, Rita Schwerner, from speaking to the credentials committee. He argued that she was not a Mississippian and that her being asked to testify was a calculated attempt to evoke "passion and prejudice against the delegates here from Mississippi." The committee chairman overruled the attempt to silence Schwerner, whose husband, Michael, was one of the murdered civil rights workers.

After Michael's disappearance, Rita tried to get someone to help her find him and his two companions. She tried several times to meet with Governor Johnson and was rudely and repeatedly rebuffed, including by the governor himself on the steps of the executive mansion in Jackson where he was huddling with Governor Wallace. A reverend accompanying Rita attempted to introduce her to Governor Johnson, who turned on his heel and walked away as soon as he heard her name. The pair of governors strode into the mansion and slammed the door in Rita's face, and she was surrounded by policemen. It was federal authorities who relayed the devastating news when her husband's body was found, two and a half weeks before the convention.

The last witness called before the credentials committee was Dr. Martin Luther King Jr. No other state in the union had gone to "such extremes" to prevent Black participation in political life, he said. "You who must sit here judging their validity as delegates to this Convention cannot imagine the anguish and suffering they have undergone to get to this point." The Democratic Party allowed "an atmosphere of violence and lawlessness to rule the land" and stood by, "calm and unmoved, by the countless murders of citizens seeking to secure civil rights," Dr. King charged. "If you value your party, if you value your nation, if you value the future of democratic government, you have no alternative but to recognize with full voice and vote the Mississippi Freedom Democratic Party."

A spokesman for the all-white delegation denied that Black people had difficulty voting in Mississippi, claiming they were "absolutely" free to participate in the state Democratic Party, including the selection of national convention delegates.

Joseph L. Rauh Jr., a lawyer representing the Mississippi Freedom Democratic Party, posed a question to the committee. "Are you going to throw out [of] here the people who want to work for Lyndon Johnson, who are willing to be beaten in jails, to die for the privilege of working for Lyndon Johnson?" The current delegation wouldn't even commit to supporting the president for reelection. Rauh accused them of presenting a false face at the convention and accurately implied that they would support Barry Goldwater.

President Johnson feared a backlash from Southern state delegations at the convention if the Mississippi Freedom Democratic Party was seated and, after some dealing and arm-twisting, advocated for a compromise solution. The credentials committee's decision—approved by a convention-wide vote—offered the Freedom Party two at-large seats, and the rest of its members would be welcomed as honored guests at the convention. They also ruled that members of the regular delegation would be required to sign a loyalty pledge promising to support Democratic candidates in all upcoming elections, including the current presidential contest, and established an antidiscrimination requirement for delegations at future conventions.

The Freedom Party, which had sixty-eight delegates, voted to reject the committee's decision. "We didn't come all this way for no two seats since all of us is tired," said Fannie Lou Hamer.

Only four of the regular delegation's sixty-six members and

alternates signed the pledge to support the Democratic presidential ticket while the others refused and walked out of the convention.

When Thelma McMullan stood up to sign the loyalty pledge, her husband, who refused to sign, told her to sit down. "Don't you tell me what to do, Milton," she replied. After Thelma was back home in Mississippi, Milton's brother sent her a telegram warning her to look out for the KKK. Thelma's granddaughter, Margaret McMullan, said, "She told me she was never afraid."

But there was good reason to fear. A week after the convention ended, the White House received a call from Douglas Wynn reporting that a fellow delegate and signer, Fred Berger, was being targeted by the KKK. Berger was a lawyer in Natchez, a vital center in the civil rights movement and where the KKK had a stronghold and was particularly brazen. He received menacing letters and telephone calls, and friends reported that people were planning to kill him. Berger hired guards to protect his home and keep it from being bombed like had happened to the town's mayor.

After Wynn's call, President Johnson immediately got Nicholas Katzenbach, the acting attorney general, involved. "They threatened his life, and they're really moving in on him. And it's real dangerous," said Johnson. "I don't want somebody to get killed because they exercised their right to stay in the convention." Johnson asked Katzenbach to alert the FBI and relayed what Wynn had reported: "He said the Klan had been very active, and please don't go through the chief of police. He's the leader."

Katzenbach responded, "All right. I think we can do something to cool them off a little bit."

By this time, the FBI had stepped up counterterrorism methods in Mississippi. But even so, the harassment finally drove Fred Berger, who had continued to campaign for the Democratic ticket, to leave the state out of fear for his family's safety. He moved to Washington, DC, and took a job with the Justice Department.

These scare tactics were used against a member of the Lady Bird Special team. Several days before the train's arrival in Biloxi, Mary Love Bailey traveled there from Austin at the request of the First Lady, with whom she was friends, to assist in advancing the train. Her first night there, she received anonymous phone calls suggesting she leave town. Instead, Bailey, another experienced campaigner, worked the phone, talking about Southern hospitality and party unity, and helped garner a huge, cheering turnout for the train.

Among those at the rally was Thelma McMullan, who boarded the Lady Bird Special in Mobile, rode into Biloxi, and was introduced on the platform with the other dignitaries. McMullan later corresponded with Lady Bird, who wrote to her, "How proud the President and I are of friends such as you who were anxious and willing to voice their convictions and stand by their guns!... You may be sure of our deep gratitude."

In Biloxi, Lady Bird told the crowd that along the way on the train journey, there were "happy encounters with old friends and joyful reunions with kinfolks." In Biloxi, there was one more. From the platform, she called out to Mrs. Forest A. Miller, who once taught her now-famous pupil history at St. Mary's Episcopal College in Dallas. (She described the future First Lady to a reporter as lovely, shy, and a good student.)

Here at the penultimate rally of the whistle-stop tour, Lady Bird did not let up. She drove home economic points, reminding the audience of the "dollars-and-cents evidence of good economic management" by the Johnson administration and the objectives and programs assuring that "all Americans share more equitably in these gains in the future."

Lady Bird remained optimistic. Over the past four days, "I have found doubts in the South, but I have also found faith," she said.

While she spoke, Goldwater chants broke out and were countered by Johnson refrains. She spoke louder to deliver her concluding message over the din, urging the audience to continue her husband's tenure as president.

Surprisingly, opposition at the rally was fairly sedate in a state seething over President Johnson's signing of the Civil Rights Act. About two dozen sign-carrying Goldwater supporters uttered some heckling that was mild but still vocal enough to attract notice.

Air Force Captain Leo P. Hays wrote to Lady Bird that the "insulting detractions did not, for one moment, diminish your charm and grace or political astuteness in delivering your address." He added, "I am only sorry that the people of Mississippi appear to be caught up in this emotionalism of the moment. But your appearance here, I am sure, will stir the loyal Democrats and other thinking Americans to act."

Captain Hays attended the rally with his wife and his five- and three-year-old daughters, who were thrilled to see Lady Bird and Luci. He reported that the oldest, Sara Ann, could hardly wait to tell her friends at school that she "saw *my* First Lady."

25

What a Team They Were

Friday, October 9, 1964
New Orleans, Louisiana, 7:27 p.m.

President Johnson walked half a mile down the spectator-lined railroad tracks at the Union Passenger Terminal in New Orleans, shaking hands along the way. He bounded up the steps of the Lady Bird Special's platform as the train, which was backing into position, rolled to a stop. He received a kiss from Luci and asked her, "How are you baby?" He then enveloped Lady Bird in an embrace as the milling mass of people greeting the train cheered and the sounds of jazz filled the air. "I was terribly proud of her as I welcomed her that evening in New Orleans," he said.

Reporters and news crews captured the historic scene. While the train was still moving, the NBC camera crew made it onto the tracks, ran ahead, and got into position. Ready and waiting at the station, Nancy Dickerson took the microphone they tossed to her. She began recording just as the train halted and the president reached the platform.

Lady Bird embraced her husband "as if they had been separated for three years instead of three days," reported Mary Pakenham. Noted Gloria Negri, a "radiant" Lady Bird and a "jovial" President Johnson "greeted the throngs." The Ladies for Lyndon waved pennants in the air as local politicians crowded on the platform with the First Family. Russell Long, a Louisiana senator, told Lyndon about Lady Bird, "[She] had real guts when she went over to Mississippi to carry on this fight."

Katharine Graham, publisher of the *Washington Post*, was on the station platform when the Lady Bird Special arrived. "It was a hot and steamy night, and we all watched the President greet Lady Bird with a big hug and kiss," said Graham. "It was very clear to me what a team they were."

Master of ceremonies Hale Boggs introduced Lady Bird to the crowd as "a valiant woman" and declared that "the South and the rest of the nation are proud of her and her daughters." As he spoke, the president, who had his arm around Lady Bird, winked at her and showed her a bandage on one of his fingers. The skin had rubbed off from so much handshaking.

Lady Bird briefly addressed the audience, speaking one last time from her namesake train.

"This has been four unforgettable days," she said. "It has been a journey of the heart, one that I will always love, one that I will always remember, one that proves to me that my South is going forward to a greater day, a day of peace among us all."

Four days earlier in Alexandria, the president had joked that Lady Bird on her train would beat him to New Orleans. Contrary to his jest, Air Force One arrived several hours ahead of the Lady Bird Special. The combined star power of the president and the First Lady exceeded even the rousing reception in Raleigh.

The president flew into New Orleans from the campaign trail, fresh off a string of hugely successful appearances from Chicago to Nashville.

The hoopla began at the airport, where he was greeted by a 2,500-person crowd that "roared its approval" when he appeared in the doorway of Air Force One.

In this contentious election, even the Louisiana State University band that played "Hail to the Chief" struck up some controversy. In a presidential poll taken earlier that week, the LSU campus swung heavily for Goldwater with 70 percent of students favoring the senator. The band director explained why they had come to the airport welcome, saying, "We feel we're honoring the President of the United States. There is absolutely no political aspect." When asked if any band members had objected to participating, he smiled and answered, "We had a little moaning and groaning."

Reluctant politicians continued to be lassoed by the influence and the momentum of the president and Lady Bird. In a West Wing memo outlining strategy for the New Orleans trip, a Johnson aide identified Louisiana's governor, John J. McKeithen, as "the strongest factor in Louisiana politics" with a whopping 85 percent popularity rating and "tremendous voting pull." The governor had been cagey when invited to ride the Lady Bird Special, and in the ensuing weeks, he hedged when asked by reporters if he would be on hand for the president's visit. McKeithen professed himself neutral in the presidential race and had recently ducked Goldwater by taking a trip to Mexico while the senator was in town. (His mother later told reporters, speaking for herself and her husband, "We are for Johnson. And how.")

On the tarmac in New Orleans, Governor McKeithen was the first of the state and local officials to greet President Johnson. Around the time they were shaking hands, the governor's wife and two eldest children boarded the Lady Bird Special in Biloxi.

After making quick work of greeting the bigwigs, President Johnson spent a twenty-minute session with the populace. True to form, he moved along the entire length of a barricade as people applauded, cheered, and eagerly reached out to grasp his hand. At one point, a Secret Service agent glanced up and then lunged toward the president before realizing the potential threat was a paper airplane.

The president didn't miss a beat, smiling and talking to the crowd as he used both hands to press the flesh. He paused to give a gold-plated LBJ pin to a young boy and shake a high school girl's hand. "I just touched the President's hand," she exclaimed, "and I'll never wash it again."

President Johnson was once taught "a lesson about people" that he never forgot. During World War II, he participated in bond-selling tours with former heavyweight champion Jack Dempsey, who routinely made their group late by insisting upon shaking the hand of every person who sought him out. "It was part of the old champ's image, and Dempsey was determined not to disappoint a single soul."

After the president finished working the fences at the New Orleans airport, he worked on Governor McKeithen some more. The governor, who was swept along on Johnson's handshaking jaunt, had his own vehicle at the airport. Speculation had it that he wanted to avoid riding into town with the president. Instead, an observer watched as Johnson "fandangled him into the presidential car," which had inched alongside by the time he shook the last hand.

Shortly after, an officer reported, "The motorcade was just about to leave the airport here, but now has stopped." Using a radio channel reserved for communicating about the president's visit, he advised the deputy police superintendent of a security headache. "The President is out of the car, greeting people."

The motorcade finally exited the airport with a U.S. Navy helicopter flying overhead and a white police truck with flanged wheels rolling down a railroad track paralleling the road, keeping pace with the president's limousine.

Some of the estimated 200,000 spectators lining the route from the airport to the Jung Hotel in downtown New Orleans also received the Johnson treatment. Spotting a throng of people at a shopping center, the president ordered the car stopped while he greeted a class of second graders and other well-wishers.

The limo stopped seven more times on the president's instructions. At each stop, crowds surged forward. Johnson stood in the car's doorway, reaching out with his left hand and speaking through a bullhorn he held in his right. "Thank you for coming out here," he said. When people stood in awe and surprise, he waved them in, saying, "Come on up."

"There is always a sense of excitement about these moments, and it gets through to the most blasé of observers," declared a newsman traveling with the president's campaign. "For although the situation is familiar to Mr. Johnson and his staff and the press, it is a time of high drama in the lives of countless Americans who are seeing the President for the first time and may never get another look at him."

Along the way, the president shouted into the bullhorn, "Are you Democrats?" Ear-splitting cheers sounded back. He grinned and said, "I thought this was Goldwater country?" The crowds responded with boos and yells of "No, no, no, no."

When Johnson was asked if he thought he could carry the state, he smiled. "Well," he said, "I'll go away from here with a mighty good feeling about Louisiana."

Spying a Goldwater sign, he said in a jovial tone, "I see we have an anti-Democrat in the crowd." He added, "I want y'all to do what's right in your hearts for peace and the country."

Once, he stopped the car to speak with two nuns. At another stop, he talked to a woman holding a baby. Over the din, he relayed to reporters that he had taught her public speaking in Houston in 1931. "She still thinks I am a wonderful teacher," said the president.

Audiences were nearly all interracial. Some were mostly white and others mostly Black, depending on the neighborhood. Everywhere men, women, and children rushed toward the limousine and "strained forward in an effort to touch the President. He tried to touch every hand within reach."

Despite spirits running high, some of those along the route weren't pleased to have traffic at a standstill. An exasperated football official bound for a game paced back and forth. A woman who shouted "Go, Goldwater" was asked if she was mad at being held up for forty-five minutes. "I'm cussing," she replied.

The coach and the cussing woman were the exception. Even a veteran reporter was awed by the streetside scenes. "This is unbelievable," he said. "I wouldn't have missed it for a million dollars."

The novelty of a presidential visit was spurring the massive turnout, plus Johnson was popular in New Orleans. Both of the city's main newspapers endorsed him in the election, and polls showed that—despite trailing in the state overall—he was ahead in New Orleans.

After taking an hour to travel the fifteen miles from the airport, the motorcade reached downtown New Orleans. A blue pickup truck plastered with Goldwater signs kept circling the area, but the sound of its repeatedly beeping horn was largely drowned out by the hubbub of the "Mardi Gras-sized crowd" and the two brass bands that played near the Jung Hotel.

After bantering with the crowd while standing on the limousine's roof, President Johnson left to attend to a pressing task. "I've got to go get a clean shirt—Lady Bird's coming to town in a little while," he said.

With that, he waved goodbye and headed for his room to freshen up before leaving to meet the Lady Bird Special.

Newspaper photographer Erby Aucoin followed behind, elbowing his way to within eight feet of the president and then "shooting pictures like mad." At one point, he lost his subject in the viewfinder and then had his vision obscured entirely when someone stepped in front of the camera. Aucoin, still peering into the viewfinder, reached out and nudged the person aside. "All right, podnah," he said, "you're obstructing the view." He then glanced up and realized it was the president, who had strolled over to request that his photo be taken with a well-wisher. Startled and sheepish, Aucoin did so before the president moved on.

Inside the hotel, it was just as crowded and celebratory. As the president walked through the lobby greeting people, a woman complained he wasn't paying enough attention to the ones on her side of an aisle that had been cleared by policemen from the front doors to the elevator.

"We're on the wrong side," she called out.

Johnson replied, "No, you're not on the wrong side unless you're for Goldwater."

When the president later reemerged from the hotel, a crowd was still gathered outside. They thunderously applauded, and he enthusiastically shook some more hands.

Before entering his limousine, he turned on the bullhorn. "Hello, folks. We'll be back in a little bit. We're going to meet the train."

At the station, the First Family moved from the campaign train to a specially constructed platform a short distance away. The outdoor platform was placed in a spot where it was protected by buildings on three sides, one from the south and another from the north and the west. To further the president's safety, all occupants were instructed to vacate the buildings.

Lady Bird approached the podium first. Making her forty-seventh speech in four days, she said, "You have brought to the depot just the person I wanted most to see, because he can take over the speaking." Before relinquishing the spotlight, she had her say. Mile after mile on the "sentimental" and "political" journey through a region that she and the president valued, she witnessed the "forward motion of this country, a keeping in step with the times." She found the "spirit of progress" everywhere from the bustling cities to the "small rural towns where the superhighways and the airlines do not always go."

At various times during the whistle-stop tour, Lady Bird traded "lace mitts" for "iron gloves," and she did so now. Lyndon respected her for not cutting a corner, and she laid it on the line.

"I am aware that there are those who would exploit [the South's] past troubles to their own advantage, but I do not believe that the majority of the South wants any part of old bitterness," she said to the largest crowd of the tour. "What is afoot in this coming election is not really a contest between two political parties... We are testing as a nation whether we shall move forward with understanding of each other and of each other's needs, ever increasing our total power—economic, social, military—in common trust and faith, or whether we shall move backward toward a denial of each other's needs, toward a national climate of fear and dislike.

"This is, I believe, a contest between the positive and the negative, between the 'Yes' and the 'No.' This land of the South, which is my land, will not, I believe, turn back from its steady, proud road ahead."

Lady Bird concluded, "I know, and I found on this trip, that while the memories of the South are as old as Thomas Jefferson, their spirit is as young as Lyndon Johnson."

Luci addressed the crowd after Lady Bird. "I had the privilege of riding on the whistle-stop train from Charleston, South Carolina to New Orleans, Louisiana, and there is one thing that impressed me all the way," she told the audience. "Every stop we made, no matter how tiny the town, or how large the city, lots and lots of young people came out and took an active interest." They showed "that they did not want to shrink away from responsibility, as some people might like to think that we would, but that we want to face up to it; that we realize that we are going to have to learn today if we are going to lead tomorrow."

The next day, the president and George Reedy, one of his aides, discussed the whistle-stop tour and the finale in New Orleans.

"Damn, that Luci's got it, hasn't she?" asked Johnson.

"She sure has," Reedy replied.

"Did you hear her in New Orleans last night?"

"That was terrific," said Reedy. "And there's a tremendous asset here because you've got your whole family, all of them able to do something."

Luci later recalled the celebratory atmosphere in New Orleans, sharing the stage with her parents after a dramatic and dangerous journey. "It was a heady time. You were a part of something that was bigger than yourself," she said.

When the president took over the speaking at the passenger terminal, he began by paying tribute to his wife and his daughters. "You have heard from the stars and the sensations of this special train," he said. "I want all of you to know that I think so much of the South that gave me birth that I have given the South the best I had for the last four days."

The West Wing strategy memo emphasized the importance of the president speaking at the Union Passenger Terminal to address the public "before going off to talk to the 'fat cats'" at a fancy fundraising dinner.

In some areas, the station crowd was mostly Black, and in other areas, it was mostly white. Except in front of the speakers' platform, where "the races were packed together with no rhyme or reason" as they listened to the president. "And to that mixed audience the President spoke with emotion and without note[s]."

He recalled the tragic day he took office, vowing that he would do his best "to be President of all the people." He added, "A good and wise and courageous leader had started moving this country again, and he had been President of all the people; and he had given all that he had to give—his life—in the service of it. I promised my Maker and I promised my family if I were spared that as long as I occupied the position that he had left vacant, that I would carry on for him and for you, in his program and in your program, of peace and prosperity for all the people of all the world." He reminded the audience that for the past twenty years, the country had a bipartisan approach to foreign policy and meeting threats to democracy around the world. "I do not think we can unite other peoples if we are divided ourselves," said the president. Then, just as Lady Bird had done, he cut to the heart of the matter.

"I am going to repeat here in Louisiana what I have said in every State that I have appeared in, and what I said the night that I walked to the White House to take over the awesome responsibilities that were mine," he declared. "As long as I am your President, I am going to be President of all the people. We are not going to have any business government, we are not going to have any labor government, we are not going to have any farm government. We are going to have a government of all the people, and your President is going to protect the constitutional rights of every American."

The audience "went wild, black and white alike," recalled Liz Carpenter. Even Louisiana Senator Allen Ellender, who supported the president's reelection without "beating the bushes for the national ticket," was swept up in the festive mood. He had the crowd roaring with laughter after he excitedly yelled out, "All the way with LJB!"

It turns out President Johnson's speech at the terminal was a warm-up act. Yet to come that evening was what Jack Valenti, special aide to the president, deemed "the most dramatic moment" of the entire campaign.

At the Jung Hotel, the president delivered a formal address to two thousand "fat cats," politicians, and other Democratic supporters that was televised in Louisiana and Mississippi. The strong, scripted speech called for a new era of courage, common sense, and confidence. "If our position in the world is not to be weakened, if we are to spare ourselves wasteful years of antagonism and division and animosity here at home, the American people on November 3rd must give a decisive reply that will be understood and heard throughout the world," he said.

"So long as I serve in the White House, your Government will be dedicated not to encroaching upon the rights of the states, but to helping the states meet their responsibilities to their own people, and let me be specific: If we are to heal our history and make this nation whole, prosperity must know no Mason-Dixon Line, and opportunity must know no color line."

Hearkening back to Lady Bird's whistle-stop kickoff speech in Alexandria, he added, "Robert E. Lee counseled us well when he told us to 'Cast off our animosities, and raise our sons to be Americans.'"

This was the speech carefully crafted by West Wing aides, the one Johnson was expected to give and that echoed similar speeches given along the campaign trail.

Aides were divided on whether the president should talk about civil rights at all in the campaign. Some advised caution, saying, "You have the election going so well now, don't take chances, say nothing about civil rights." Although Valenti and others were "also cautious and more than fearful," they believed it was necessary for the president to address the issue. And yet even they wanted it done "blandly, so as not to ruffle too many feathers." A public opinion expert observed that "the racial issue is the only one that can elect Goldwater."

A section titled "The Issues" in the New Orleans strategy memo noted that civil rights "underlies everything" and bluntly stated: "The less said about Civil Rights the better."

The president disagreed. Added to the white backlash in the South was his concern that the riots in the North foreshadowed even further divisiveness for the country. He considered civil rights an integral campaign issue. "I had confidence that given the proper leadership, the American people would repair the injustice so long borne by the Negro," he said. "I did not think the majority of Americans would retreat from justice because of the destructive work of a lawless few, black or white. I wanted to make this point absolutely clear."

The prepared speech President Johnson gave at the Jung Hotel contained what he described as "only one rather mild reference" to civil rights. ("If we are to heal our history and make this nation whole, prosperity must know no Mason-Dixon line and opportunity must know no color line.") That night, he looked out over the crowd assembled in the ballroom, "people who had been in my camp so long," he said. "Knowing how sorely our unity was going to be strained and how often the racial issue had been used to divide us before, I knew I could only say what I deeply believed." It was time.

Johnson chose to make his stand "not in New York or Chicago or Los Angeles, but in New Orleans—near home, in my own backyard."

Finished with the formal address, he set aside the script. He took off his glasses and figuratively rolled up his sleeves. With little political capital to be gained and much to be lost, he launched into a follow-up speech. "I spoke off the cuff and from the heart," he said.

Valenti and other presidential staffers, caught unaware, froze as Johnson "began, in evangelical fashion, to pour it on." He spoke with no text, guided only by "that remarkable instinct that served him so well," said Valenti.

The president pounded the podium. He stretched out his arms and sliced the air.

"The people that would use us and destroy us first divide us," he told the audience. "If they divide us, they can make some hay, and all these years they have kept their foot on our necks by appealing to our animosities, and dividing us.

"Whatever your views are, we have a Constitution and we have a Bill of Rights, and we have the Law of the Land, and two-thirds of the Democrats in the Senate voted for it and three-fourths of the Republicans. I signed it, and I am going to enforce it, and I am going to observe it, and I think any man that is worthy of the high office of President is going to do the same thing."

The audience applause "was less than overwhelming," Johnson later recalled. "But I was in it, and I had to continue." He wanted the nation to realize "how profoundly animosity and hatred waste the common effort and dissipate the national energy." As politicians used the issue of race to divide people, as passions were wasted on prejudice, more important considerations were ignored "to the detriment of the people."

To hammer home his point that politicians' use of race to divide people was done at the expense of economic prosperity, he shared a story about an unnamed Democratic senator from a Southern state. (Later revealed to be Joe Bailey, who was raised in Mississippi and elected to Congress from Texas.) Johnson told how, late in life, the senator lamented this long-overused tactic during a conversation with Congressman Sam Rayburn. "Sammy, I wish I felt a little better," said the senator. "I would like to go back down there and make them one more Democratic speech. I just feel like I have one in me."

The president then delivered the regretful senator's concluding words to Rayburn and the lightning-bolt line of the night: "The poor old state, they haven't heard a Democratic speech in thirty years. All they ever hear at election time is Negro, Negro, Negro."

The audience gasped. There was silence before the racially mixed audience, led by Black attendees, broke out into thunderous applause.

Johnson wasn't done yet.

"We have the law of the land, and we are going to appeal to all Americans that fight in uniform and work in factory and on farm to try to conduct themselves as Americans. Equal opportunity for all, special privileges for none, because there is only one real big problem that faces you," he said, pointing toward the audience. "It is not even an economic problem and it is not the Negro problem. The only problem that faces you is whether you are going to live or die, and whether your family is going to live or die."

He recalled sitting through thirty-seven National Security Council meetings during the Cuban missile crisis, leaving home each morning not knowing if he would see Lady Bird again. Generals and admirals laid out their war maps and talked through tactics. Fleets were moving, and planes loaded with bombs were in the sky. "The coolest man in that room," said Johnson, was John F. Kennedy, the one who could put his thumb on the button.

The audience in the ballroom stood up and applauded.

That button could "wipe out 300 million lives in a matter of moments. And this is no time and no hour and no day to be rattling your rockets around or clicking your heels like a storm trooper," orated Johnson. "This is a moment when all nations must look all ways to try to find some ways and means to learn to live together without destroying each other. I have no reference to any nation, any country, or any individual. I just say that when you look at history, and you see what has happened to us in our lifetime, and we have gone through two wars, and then you see what the next war could bring us, it is no time to preach division, or hate."

Ultimately, the president left the audience laughing.

"I know the people of Louisiana want to do what is right" on November 3, he said. "And I hope if you do what you think is right, that somehow or other it is the same thing that I think is right. But if it is not, I won't question your patriotism, I won't question your Americanism, I won't question your ancestry. I may quietly, in the sanctity of our bedroom, whisper to Lady Bird my own personal opinion about your judgment."

The audience laughed, clapped, whooped, and cheered.

When the president stepped down from the dais, "the applause was there," observed Valenti. There wasn't total enthusiasm, especially from some of the politicians present. But the applause "was there in sufficient quantity to allow the president to believe that enough southerners were with him."

A woman in attendance said of the president's speech that she had "never heard anything like it in her life."

Additional comments ranged from "dynamic" and "sincere" to "level-headed and represented stability." A state representative said, "His sincerity was enlightening to all of us. It was also good to see that he had a sense of humor." The registrar of the state land office believed it to be an effective speech. "I think that he convinced a lot of people that he did recognize the problems of the people of the entire country and particularly of the South," she said.

A man approached Valenti as crowds in the ballroom jostled around the president. "You know, I never really liked Johnson. I always thought he didn't really have it here," he said, pressing his heart. "But tonight, gawd-damn, he shoved it right up us and made us like it. That takes a fair amount of guts and I got to say Johnson showed us that tonight, that he did."

Nancy Dickerson was off the clock once the Lady Bird Special reached the end of the line, but she decided to stay for President Johnson's speech at the Jung Hotel. "I'm glad I did, because it was the best I ever heard him give. It was not only the highlight of his campaign, it was one of his finest hours," said Dickerson. Covering a campaign means hearing candidates give variations of the same speech over and over. Reporters heard certain passages so often they would involuntarily memorize them.

"That night Johnson was different, both in manner and delivery," said Dickerson. "[He] was almost messianic as he warmed to his subject, a preacher who could not turn back." Since polling had the president substantially ahead, "it could be argued that it was safe for him to lecture the South on racism that night," said Dickerson. "Even so, in the first half of the sixties, prejudice was high throughout the country, and it took courage as well as a special instinct for the President to know that the time was right for him to go to the South and lecture the people there on racism."

After the speech, Dickerson spoke with the president, who was "justifiably proud of himself." He said, "I really gave it to them, didn't I?" and added, "They'd better not claim any more that I say one thing in the North and something else in the South."

The fundraising dinner at the Jung Hotel was already in the works when plans for the Lady Bird Special developed. An advance team planning memo stated that the fortuitous coincidence would "make a grand finale" to the whistle-stop tour.

The success of the hoped-for dramatic finish in New Orleans underscored the Lady Bird Special's dual purpose: to bring to the South a message of unity and the need to move forward and to augment the president's campaign platform and aid his reelection bid.

As the Lady Bird Special sat on the tracks in New Orleans, emptied and swept of the traces of its history-making journey, the president and Lady Bird headed to their Texas ranch for a brief rest before more campaigning.

Liz Carpenter traveled with them, feeling, as Lady Bird said, "like cooked spaghetti." President Johnson "was bursting with pride," recalled Carpenter. "He had watched his wife take on an assignment that no other woman had done in history, and perform it with skill and with heart—and with courage in the ugly hours." He laughed, shook his head, and said, "Now, Liz, that's the way to run a railroad!"

If Barry Goldwater lost the South, the key to his campaign strategy, "he will hardly know which of them to blame," asserted Mary McGrory. Was it Lady Bird blowing kisses from the train's back platform and talking of "better human understanding"? Or was it the president "storming into New Orleans to join her and making the most moving speech of his campaign and the toughest speech of his career on civil rights"?

"Together," she concluded, "the President and the First Lady made an assault on the heart and the mind of the South that must be the most remarkable joint campaign effort in American political history."

Epilogue

The Lady Bird Special rolled into history, widely deemed a success by political strategists and the press.

The campaign train was called "a virtuoso political performance" and "a remarkable display of courage, stamina and old-fashioned political savvy" by a North Carolina newspaper. The undertaking "was not a stunt or a gesture or a personal advertisement. It was a serious political enterprise, carefully planned and gallantly undertaken, and rewarded with great success," stated journalist Max Freedman.

As the primary Democratic campaign effort in the South, the Lady Bird Special "brought evidence of new Democratic unity and rising support for the President," observed Claude Sitton, a *New York Times* reporter regarded as the best daily newsman on the Southern scene even by rival publications. "The swing through eight states aroused enthusiasm for the campaign that had been sorely missing."

On November 3, 1964, Lyndon Johnson received the landslide election victory he hoped for, carrying forty-four states and the District of Columbia and garnering 61.1 percent of the popular vote (a record that still stands). Three of the eight states through which the Lady Bird Special traveled went Democratic, including Virginia and North Carolina. On October 5, one day before the Lady Bird Special set out, a West Wing memo stated that "only a miracle" could deliver Florida for Johnson. He won the state by 42,599 votes, a margin of 2.2 percent.

Women voted for president in greater numbers than men for the first time, with 62 percent casting their ballots for Johnson. He also garnered 94 percent of the Black vote.

Two days after the election, President Johnson telephoned Dr. King to thank him for his support. "We're certainly all very happy about the outcome," said Dr. King. "It was a great victory for the forces of progress, and a defeat for the forces of retrogress." With the election concluded, civil rights demonstrations were set to resume. "There will be a renewal of demonstrations in situations that demand them…as long as the evils are there," Dr. King had recently told the press. (A significant stride came with the passing of the Voting Rights Act the next year.)

During the call with Dr. King, Johnson brought up Lady Bird's whistle-stop tour through the South. "She took on a pretty hard assignment, didn't she?" he asked.

"I'm telling you!" Dr. King replied. "But she did it beautifully and eloquently. We are all mighty proud of her."

In Pascagoula, Mississippi, eight-year-old Gary Southern heard back from the First Lady within two weeks of seeing the campaign train. He received a reply thanking him for his "sweet, friendly letter" and wishing him "a successful school year."

Lindy Boggs threw her husband, Hale (who was reelected), a surprise birthday party featuring crayfish bisque and other Southern dishes he touted from the Lady Bird Special's back platform and had promised to reporters.

Those members of the press who made the journey received a

EPILOGUE

certificate from Lady Bird lauding their endurance as, "day on day, daze on daze, eyeball to eyeball, elbow to elbow," they "weaved and wiggled the crowded aisle of the Lady Bird Special in pursuit of the better story."

After riding the campaign train the entire 1,682 miles down the tracks, Helen Thomas "never had any doubt" that with or without Lyndon Johnson, "Lady Bird was one of those women who would make a mark on society."

The Lady Bird Special impacted more than the political landscape as it steamed southward and captured national headlines. Misogyny was ground under its wheels as an extraordinary group of women, led by Lady Bird, came together to make history.

An Arizona newspaper editorial allowed that "perhaps it took considerable courage" for Lady Bird to campaign in the South. Even if it were the "rousing success" that "promoters" of the Lady Bird Special claimed, they considered it too forward. "We have an old-fashioned idea that First Ladies should not engage in out and out campaign speeches. This holds for wives of all presidential nominees."

Perhaps even these chauvinistic editors could sense the winds of change. They concluded, "We're probably in the minority on this reaction."

They were.

In December, Lady Bird was chosen "Woman Newsmaker of the Year" by the editors of AP member newspapers and TV stations. The designation was in large part for her campaign efforts and for the precedent-breaking whistle-stop tour in particular.

"She may have set a pattern for future would-be first ladies. It may be that she has, and if so it's a very happy innovation," determined Celestine Sibley. Max Freedman agreed that it upended the status quo, saying, "Perhaps this marks the emergence of women as central figures in a national contest instead of being on the edges of a campaign."

Years later, as Lady Bird prepared her diaries for publication, she reminisced about the 1964 election season. "There were moments of high elation during the campaign. I wouldn't take anything for the Whistle-stop through the South—forty-seven stops in four days!" she recalled.

"Scores of times since that October as I have stood in a receiving line someone would come up and say, 'I rode with you on the Whistle-stop'—and we would clasp hands with a warmth and a rush of memories of that very special time, those four most dramatic days in my political life."

Author's Note and Acknowledgments

Journeying with the Lady Bird Special on the page was a truly memorable ride. After writing about Eleanor Roosevelt's trip to the Pacific Theater, I began researching other journeys undertaken by First Ladies. And there was Lady Bird Johnson whistle-stopping through the South in 1964 and breaking tradition along the way. Fittingly, Lady Bird's role model was the intrepid Eleanor, whom she first met when she was a young congressman's wife.

I was intrigued by the Lady Bird Special, and nothing lights my fire like stories about brilliantly badass women—and there were many trailblazers on board the train. But, I thought, how could a four-day trip possibly cover an entire book? As Lady Bird said though, the whistle-stop tour was "like doing a month's work in four days." In addition, the undertaking didn't take place in a vacuum, and the story encompasses some of the shifts taking place in the cultural, social, and political landscapes of the time.

As soon as I discovered there was a vast amount of resource

materials pertaining to the Lady Bird Special—a writer's dream—it was full steam ahead. I eagerly stepped aboard the campaign train and traveled down the tracks with an extraordinary group of women who came together to make history.

I thank two of those women, Lynda Johnson Robb and Luci Baines Johnson, for speaking with me and sharing memories of their time on the Lady Bird Special.

Lady Bird took great pride in introducing her daughters at each stop, twenty-year-old Lynda Bird for the first half of the journey and seventeen-year-old Luci Baines for the second. They both made a terrific impression, including facing down hecklers with poise, and were enormously popular with the vast number of young people who turned out all along the route. The title of this book comes from a phrase said by Lynda as a pair of boys, waving pro-Goldwater signs, chased after the train as it left a station. She flipped on the loudspeaker and schooled them, saying, "You're running after the twentieth century. You can't catch us."

A historical narrative like *You Can't Catch Us* could never be written without the wealth of materials available at various institutions and the archivists and librarians who oversee their preservation. I owe an enormous thank-you to Alexis Percle, archivist extraordinaire at the LBJ Presidential Library, who specializes in materials related to Lady Bird Johnson. From the moment I first reached out, Alexis was exceedingly generous in helping me source the information I needed. And information I didn't know I needed, including Lady Bird's advance notebooks for the whistle-stop tour, which were a treasure trove. In addition, I thank Jenna de Graffenried, Dwina Bridgemohan, and Calvin Clites for their assistance during the days I researched at the LBJ Presidential Library.

At the Lyndon B. Johnson National Historical Park visitor center in Johnson City, Texas, Kristian Enbysk and Mary Orms graciously showed me items from the Lady Bird Special not currently on display. I sincerely thank them for this behind-the-scenes visit, during which I saw dresses worn by the Ladies for Lyndon, the train's official hostesses; the Southern-themed menu; LADY BIRD pennants; and other items that were featured on the whistle-stop tour.

Among the exhibits at the LBJ Museum of San Marcos is a replica of the Lady Bird Special's back platform. My thanks to Debby Butler for kindly welcoming me to the museum the day I stopped by during a drive through the Hill Country.

Others who provided materials that enhanced this story are Linda Bridges at the Bull Street Library in Savannah, Terre Heydari and Cynthia Franco at the DeGolyer Library at Southern Methodist University, Drew Russell at the Louise Pettus Archives and Special Collections at Winthrop University, Chris DuBose at the Wilson Library at Duke University, and Raya A. Schilke at the Valdosta State University Archives and Special Collections. My terrific local libraries, the New York Public Library and the Hoboken Public Library, always come through with books, e-books, and other resources integral to the research process.

I thank my editors, Meg Gibbons and Sophia Ellinas, for journeying with me on the Lady Bird Special and for helping to craft an even more dynamic story. I also thank the entire team at Sourcebooks for their continued enthusiasm and collaboration as we embark on our second First Lady adventure book together. My publicist (and longtime friend) Ron Longe deserves a huge thank-you, as does my agent, Dan Lazar, who has championed my writing since the beginning, four books ago. I greatly appreciate his efforts and those of Victoria Doherty-Monroe and their colleagues at Writers House.

The many family members and friends who have backed me most certainly deserve a major shout-out for coming to events (some multiple times and taking flights to get there), buying books, and understanding when I disappear down a writing rabbit hole for weeks and months at a time.

As always, the biggest thanks of all go to my husband, Brian, for reading and editing drafts, having cocktail hour discussions about writing, keeping me supplied with coffee, doing a read along of *The Feminine Mystique*, and pretty much everything else. Brian, I'm endlessly grateful for your love and support in writing and in life.

Source Notes

On October 10, 1964, the day after Lady Bird and Lyndon Johnson's joint appearance in New Orleans that concluded the whistle-stop tour, his press secretary, George Reedy, informed him that on his recent campaign trips, some eighty to ninety members of the press went along.

"Mrs. Johnson had 200 [press]," replied the president. "How the hell did she draw more than we do?"

The answer: Liz Carpenter.

Lady Bird's dynamo press secretary, a former journalist, was known for her smarts, her sense of humor, and her P. T. Barnum–like flair. Reporters could be certain that this history-making ride, of which Carpenter was a key orchestrator, would generate colorful copy and probably be a rollicking good time. They signed up in such numbers that she finally had to "put a lid on it." And sure enough, their editors were soon clamoring: "More stories on Lady Bird train."

The resulting deluge of newspaper accounts was invaluable in telling this story. They number in the thousands, from articles by legendary White House correspondent Helen Thomas that went out over the wire and reached readers nationwide to local papers in towns and cities along the way from Washington, DC, to New Orleans.

In addition, there are memoirs written by members of the Lady Bird Special team and journalists who were on board, oral histories, correspondence, and much more. It all amounted to a wonderful abundance of source materials that allowed me to follow the train in detail as it traveled 1,682 miles down the tracks, making forty-seven stops along the way and riding into history.

Primary Sources

From the archives of the Lyndon B. Johnson Presidential Library and Museum:

Oral histories, including Lady Bird Johnson, Liz Carpenter, Bess Abell, Lindy Boggs, Virginia "Scooter" Miller, and Virginia Foster Durr

White House Social Files, including the "Whistle-Stop" folders 1–6 from the Liz Carpenter Subject Files and "Schedule and Lists for 1964 Whistle-Stop" and "Gimmicks—1964 Whistle-Stop" folders from the Bess Abell Subject Files

Lady Bird's Advance Notebooks

Papers of Lindy Boggs

Cecil Burney Papers, among which is a detailed report written by Kara Burney, who advanced the Lady Bird Special in Charleston, SC

Lady Bird Johnson's Diary

Lyndon B. Johnson's Telephone Tapes

Lady Bird's Speeches: In her talks along the whistle-stop tour, she always went off script to some degree. Available speech transcripts were cross-referenced with audio where possible (see the YouTube videos available at www.youtube.com/@TheLBJLibrary). In the instances where no audio was available, speeches were referenced against newspaper accounts.

Newspapers

Articles came from a variety of sources, including Newspapers.com, ProQuest, Readex, Google Media, the North Carolina Digital Heritage

Center (www.digitalnc.org), and the Virginia Chronicle: Digital Newspaper Archive (www.virginiachronicle.com). Additional articles came from archival scrapbooks and individual newspaper collections, such as the *New York Times* and the *Times-Picayune*. Others, like the *Savannah Morning News*, were provided by librarians and archivists in whistle-stop locales.

Books

Ruffles and Flourishes by Liz Carpenter (Texas A&M University Press, 1993). Liz Carpenter was a driving force behind the Lady Bird Special. Her memoir about her years working with Lady Bird and Lyndon Johnson is colorful, clever, and a chance to spend time with the force of nature that was Liz Carpenter.

Washington Through a Purple Veil by Lindy Boggs (Harcourt Brace, 1994). Lindy Boggs cochaired the Lady Bird Special and worked around the clock for weeks to help ensure its success. During the journey, she told a reporter that she had a total of fifteen minutes sleep the night before the train left Washington—and that was only because she "fell asleep sitting up."

Washington's Iron Butterfly: Bess Clements Abell, An Oral History by Donald A. Ritchie and Terry L. Birdwhistell (University Press of Kentucky, 2022).

Lady Bird Johnson: Hiding in Plain Sight by Julia Sweig (Random House, 2022).

Lady Bird Johnson: Our Environmental First Lady by Lewis L. Gould (University Press of Kansas, 1999).

Lady Bird: A Biography of Mrs. Johnson by Jan Jarboe Russell (Scribner, 2016).

A White House Diary by Lady Bird Johnson (University of Texas Press, 2007).

Lady Bird Johnson: An Oral History by Michael L. Gillette (Oxford University Press, 2012).

Additional Resources

ABC News VideoSource, www.abcnewsvsource.com, has raw footage of the whistle-stop tour.

Miller Center, University of Virginia, including famous presidential speeches, millercenter.org/the-presidency/presidential-speeches.

"Women in Journalism," the Washington Press Club Foundation Oral History Project: www.wpcf.org/woman-in-journalism.

Bess Abell Oral History Project, Louie B. Nunn Center for Oral History, University of Kentucky Libraries, www.kentuckyoralhistory.org.

Congressional Records: www.congress.gov/congressional-record/archive, as well as print copies.

Life magazine archives: books.google.com/books/about/LIFE.html?id=N0EEAAAAMBAJ.

Saturday Evening Post archives: www.saturdayeveningpost.com.

The Internet Archive, www.archive.org, has a wealth of historical books and other materials like the *Florida Flambeau*, FSU's student newspaper.

National First Ladies' Library: www.firstladies.org.

Civil Rights Movement Archive: www.crmvet.org.

Student Nonviolent Coordinating Committee (SNCC) Digital Gateway: www.snccdigital.org.

The Martin Luther King, Jr. Research and Education Institute, Stanford University: kinginstitute.stanford.edu.

Jan Sanders Papers, Collection A2018.0058, DeGolyer Library, Southern Methodist University, Dallas, TX.

Gladys Avery Tillett Papers, Southern Historical Collection, Wilson Library, University of North Carolina at Chapel Hill.

Ruth Williams Cupp Papers, Louise Pettus Archives and Special Collections, Winthrop University, Rock Hill, SC.

Articles

Barnes, Michael. "Texas History: Tales of a Famous Texas Feminist, Liz Carpenter." *Austin American-Statesman*, August 17, 2020. https://www.statesman.com/story/news/history/2020/08/17/texas-history-tales-of-famous-texas-feminist-liz-carpenter/42603585.

Bates, Karen Grigsby. "Why Did Black Voters Flee the Republican Party in the 1960s?" *Morning Edition*, NPR, July 14, 2014. https://www.npr.org/sections/codeswitch/2014/07/14/331298996/why-did-black-voters-flee-the-republican-party-in-the-1960s.

Gittinger, Ted, and Allen Fisher. "LBJ Champions the Civil Rights Act of 1964." *Prologue* 36, no. 2 (Summer 2004). https://www.archives.gov/publications/prologue/2004/summer/civil-rights-act.

Heleniak, Roman. "Lyndon Johnson in New Orleans." *Louisiana History: The Journal of the Louisiana Historical Association* 21, no. 3 (Summer 1980): 263–75. https://www.jstor.org/stable/4232006.

SOURCE NOTES

Hindley, Meredith. "The Lady Bird Special." *Humanities* 34, no. 3 (May/June 2013). https://www.neh.gov/humanities/2013/mayjune/feature/lady-bird-special.

Jones, Ryan M. "Mississippi Burning: From Murder Mayhem to a Mighty Mission." National Civil Rights Museum, accessed March 11, 2025. https://www.civilrightsmuseum.org/mississippi-burning-from-murder-mayhem-to-a-mighty-mission.

Kellerman, Barbara. "Campaigning Since Kennedy: The Family as 'Surrogate.'" *Presidential Studies Quarterly* 10, no. 2 (Spring 1980): 244–53. https://www.jstor.org/stable/27547568.

Kellerman, Barbara. "The Political Functions of the Presidential Family." *Presidential Studies Quarterly* 8, no. 3 (Summer 1978): 303–18. https://www.jstor.org/stable/27547410.

Little, Becky. "How the 'Party of Lincoln' Won Over the Once Democratic South." History.com. April 10, 2019. https://www.history.com/news/how-the-party-of-lincoln-won-over-the-once-democratic-south.

Markman, Sherwin. "Tragedy and Triumph: The Summer of 1964." Sermon, Unitarian Universalist Church, Chestertown, Maryland, May 18, 2014. https://www.lbjlibrary.org/life-and-legacy/tragedy-and-triumph-the-summer-of-1964.

Martin, Harold H. "The Johnson Touch." *Saturday Evening Post*, October 31, 1964, 21–29.

NCC Staff. "On This Day, Filibuster Fails to Block the Civil Rights Act." National Constitution Center, June 19, 2024. https://www.constitutioncenter.org/blog/on-this-day-congress-passes-the-civil-rights-act.

O'Connor, Karen, Bernadette Nye, and Laura Van Assendelft. "Wives in the White House: The Political Influence of First Ladies." *Presidential Studies Quarterly* 26, no. 3 (Summer 1996): 835–53. https://www.jstor.org/stable/27551636.

Peter, Katie. "Mapping Lady Bird Johnson's Whistle-Stop Tour." White House Historical Association, accessed March 11, 2025. https://www.whitehousehistory.org/mapping-lady-bird-johnsons-whistle-stop-tour.

Ragan, Sam. "Dixie Looked Away." *American Scholar* 34, no. 2 (Spring 1965): 202–12. https://www.jstor.org/stable/41209268.

Robertson, Nan. "Our New First Lady." *Saturday Evening Post*, February 8, 1964, 20–25.

Smith, Nancy Kegan. "Private Reflections on a Public Life: The Papers of Lady Bird Johnson at the LBJ Library." *Presidential Studies Quarterly* 20, no. 4 (Fall 1990): 737–44. https://www.jstor.org/stable/20700157.

Sweeney, James R. "A New Day in the Old Dominion: The 1964 Presidential Election." *Virginia Magazine of History and Biography* 102, no. 3 (July 1994): 307. https://www.jstor.org/stable/4249450.

Bibliography

Atkinson, Frank B. *The Dynamic Dominion: Realignment and the Rise of Two-Party Competition in Virginia, 1945-1980*, rev. 2nd ed. Rowman & Littlefield, 2006.

Beschloss, Michael R. *Taking Charge: The Johnson White House Tapes, 1963–1964*. Touchstone, 1998.

Beschloss, Michael R. *Reaching for Glory: Lyndon Johnson's Secret White House Tapes, 1964–1965*. Touchstone, 2002.

Burns, Lisa M., ed. *Media Relations and the Modern First Lady: From Jacqueline Kennedy to Melania Trump*. Lexington Books, 2020.

Cagin, Seth, and Philip Dray. *We Are Not Afraid: The Mississippi Murder of Goodman, Schwerner, and Chaney*. Bantam, 1989.

Caro, Robert A. *Master of the Senate: The Years of Lyndon Johnson*. Alfred A. Knopf, 2024.

Caro, Robert A. *Means of Ascent: The Years of Lyndon Johnson*. Vintage Books, 1991.

Caro, Robert A. *The Passage of Power: The Years of Lyndon Johnson*. Vintage Books, 2013.

Caroli, Betty Boyd. *First Ladies: From Martha Washington to Michelle Obama*. Oxford University Press, 2010.

Caroli, Betty Boyd. *Lady Bird and Lyndon: The Hidden Story of a Marriage That Made a President*. Simon & Schuster, 2016.

Carpenter, Liz. *Getting Better All the Time*. Pocket Books, 1988.

Carson, Clayborne, Tenisha Armstrong, Susan Carson, Erin Cook, and Susan Englander, eds. *The Martin Luther King, Jr., Encyclopedia*. Greenwood Press, 2008.

Dallek, Robert. *Lone Star Rising: Lyndon Johnson and His Times, 1908–1960*. Oxford University Press, 1991.

Dallek, Robert. *Lyndon B. Johnson: Portrait of a President*. Oxford University Press, 2004.

Dickerson, John. *On Her Trail: My Mother, Nancy Dickerson, TV News' First Woman Star*. Simon & Schuster, 2006.

Dickerson, Nancy. *Among Those Present: A Reporter's View of 25 Years in Washington*. Random House, 1976.

Due, Tananarive, and Patricia Stephens Due. *Freedom in the Family: A Mother-Daughter Memoir of the Fight for Civil Rights*. One World, 2003.

Edwards, India. *Pulling No Punches: Memoirs of a Woman in Politics*. G. P. Putnam's Sons, 1977.

Farmer, James. *Lay Bare the Heart: An Autobiography of the Civil Rights Movement.* Plume, 1986.

Faust, Drew Gilpin. *Necessary Trouble: Growing Up at Midcentury.* Farrar, Straus and Giroux, 2023.

Friedan, Betty. *The Feminine Mystique.* Dell, 1963.

Goldman, Eric F. *The Tragedy of Lyndon Johnson.* Alfred A. Knopf, 1969.

Howar, Barbara. *Laughing All the Way.* Fawcett, 1974.

Hummer, Jill Abraham. *First Ladies and American Women: In Politics and at Home.* University Press of Kansas, 2017.

Johnson, Lyndon Baines. *The Vantage Point: Perspectives of the Presidency 1963–1969.* Holt, Rinehart and Winston, 1971.

Kotz, Nick. *Judgment Days: Lyndon Baines Johnson, Martin Luther King Jr., and the Laws That Changed America.* Mariner, 2006.

Lewis, John, with Michael D'Orso. *Walking with the Wind: A Memoir of the Movement.* Harcourt Brace, 1998.

McAdam, Doug. *Freedom Summer.* Oxford University Press, 1990.

McLendon, Winzola, and Scottie Smith. *Don't Quote Me!: Washington Newswomen and the Power Society.* E. P. Dutton, 1970.

Miller, Merle. *Lyndon: An Oral Biography.* G. P. Putnam's Sons, 1980.

Newby, I. A. *Black Carolinians: A History of Blacks in South Carolina from 1895 to 1968.* University of South Carolina Press, 1973.

O'Dell, Cary. *Women Pioneers in Television: Biographies of Fifteen Industry Leaders.* McFarland, 1997.

Pietrusza, David. *1960: LBJ vs. JFK vs. Nixon: The Epic Campaign That Forged Three Presidencies.* Union Square Press, 2008.

Pope, Michael Lee. *The Byrd Machine in Virginia: The Rise and Fall of a Conservative Political Organization.* History Press, 2022.

Rabby, Glenda Alice. *The Pain and the Promise: The Struggle for Civil Rights in Tallahassee, Florida.* University of Georgia Press, 1999.

Richardson, Christopher M., and Ralph E. Luker, eds. *Historical Dictionary of the Civil Rights Movement*, 2nd ed. Rowman & Littlefield, 2014.

Robertson, Nan. *The Girls in the Balcony: Women, Men, and the New York Times.* Random House, 1992.

Sanders, Marlene, and Marcia Rock. *Waiting for Prime Time: The Women of Television News.* Perennial, 1990.

Shaw, John T. *JFK in the Senate: Pathway to the Presidency.* Palgrave Macmillan, 2013.

Sibley, Katherine A. S., ed. *A Companion to First Ladies.* John Wiley & Sons, 2016.

Thomas, Helen. *Front Row at the White House: My Life and Times*. Scribner, 1999.

Travell, Janet. *Office Hours: Day and Night*. New American Library, 1968.

Updegrove, Mark K. *Indomitable Will: LBJ in the Presidency*. Crown, 2012.

Valenti, Jack. *A Very Human President*. W.W. Norton, 1975.

Wilkinson, J. Harvie III. *Harry Byrd and the Changing Face of Virginia Politics 1945–1966*. University Press of Virginia, 1968.

Woods, Randall B. *LBJ: Architect of American Ambition*. Harvard University Press, 2006.

Notes

Abbreviations

LBJL: Lyndon B. Johnson Presidential Library and Museum, Austin, TX

Note: Audio recordings of the whistle-stops sourced below, which are archived at www.youtube.com/@TheLBJLibrary, were all accessed and verified on March 24, 2025.

Prologue

xiii **September 1964:** "Backers Here Learn Lady Bird Trip Plans," *Columbia (SC) Record*, September 23, 1964.

xiii **"What are six men":** Liz Carpenter, *Ruffles and Flourishes* (Texas A&M University Press, 1993), 146.

xiii **cross burning:** "Five Men Are Charged with Burning of Cross," *Index-Journal* (Greenwood, SC), September 25, 1964.

xiv **"rim states" and "a lesser degree":** Claude Sitton, "Civil Rights Act: How South Responds," *New York Times*, July 12, 1964, https://www.nytimes.com/1964/07/12/archives/civil-rights-act-how-south-responds.html.

xiv **"Much of the Lady Bird Special's route":** Claude Sitton, "Mrs. Johnson's Southern Trip Spurs New Support," *New York Times*, October 11, 1964, https://www.nytimes.com/1964/10/11/archives/mrs-johnsons-southern-trip-spurs-new-support.html.

xiv **"They had their fingers"**: Carpenter, *Ruffles and Flourishes*, 147.
xv **Mississippi Freedom Summer Project:** "Summer 1964: Freedom Summer," SNCC Digital Gateway, accessed February 24, 2025, https://snccdigital.org/events/freedom-summer; Kent Germany and David Carter, "Mississippi Burning," Miller Center, University of Virginia, https://millercenter.org/the-presidency/educational-resources/mississippi-burning.
xv **publicity stunt:** Lyndon B. Johnson, "Conversation with James Eastland," June 23, 1964, Miller Center, University of Virginia, audio, 8:19, https://millercenter.org/the-presidency/secret-white-house-tapes/conversation-james-eastland-june-23-1964.
xv **in the Oval Office:** Nick Kotz, *Judgment Days: Lyndon Baines Johnson, Martin Luther King Jr., and the Laws That Changed America* (Mariner, 2006), 165.
xvi **targeted Schwerner:** Seth Cagin and Philip Dray, *We Are Not Afraid: The Mississippi Murder of Goodman, Schwerner, and Chaney* (Bantam, 1989), 15.
xvi **That summer:** Doug McAdam, *Freedom Summer* (Oxford University Press, 1990), 96.
xvi **"While not himself a racist":** Clayborne Carson et al., eds., *The Martin Luther King, Jr., Encyclopedia* (Greenwood Press, 2008), 114.
xvi **on the day Goldwater accepted:** Barry Goldwater accepted the Republican presidential nomination on July 16, 1964.
xvi **"as political as all" and "hold the South":** Ruth Montgomery, "Capital Letter," *Terre Haute Tribune*, October 11, 1964.
xvii **"in the slack waters":** "Lady Bird's Whistle-Stop, Savannah, GA: 10/8/64, 11:50 AM," TheLBJLibrary, October 7, 2014, YouTube video, 7:16, https://www.youtube.com/watch?v=H7DmM7CU7RQ.

Chapter 1

1 **a brightly bedecked:** The preview of the train on Sunday, October 4, 1964, was reported in numerous accounts, including Roy Parker Jr., "Trio Bids to Hold South," *News and Observer* (Raleigh, NC), October 6, 1964.
1 **"victory blue," "landslide red," and other train details:** "History Making Whistle-Stop Tour Mrs. Johnson's Campaign Contribution," *Daily Record* (Long Branch, NJ), October 6, 1964.
2 **"probably the most colorful":** "History Making Whistle-Stop Tour."
2 **"train sortie":** "William S. White Says: 'Lady Bird Special' Will Be Significant Train," *Evening Express* (Portland, ME), September 25, 1964.
2 **"No memorial oration" through "evil and violence":** Lyndon B. Johnson, "Address to Joint Session of Congress," November 27, 1963, Miller Center, University of Virginia, transcript and audio, 24:30, https://millercenter.org/the-presidency/presidential-speeches/november-27-1963-address-joint-session-congress.

NOTES

3   **"I don't intend"**: Robert Dallek, *Lyndon B. Johnson: Portrait of a President* (Oxford University Press, 2004), 163.

3   **sixty working days**: "Civil Rights Filibuster Ended," United States Senate, accessed February 7, 2025, https://www.senate.gov/about/powers-procedures/filibusters-cloture/civil-rights-filibuster-ended.htm.

3   **"earnest, dogged work"**: Lady Bird Johnson, *A White House Diary* (University of Texas Press, 2007), 174.

3   **"No army can withstand"**: E. W. Kenworthy, "Dirksen Shaped Victory for Civil Rights Forces in Fight to Bring Measure to Vote," *New York Times*, June 20, 1964, https://www.nytimes.com/1964/06/20/archives/dirksen-shaped-victory-for-civil-rights-forces-in-fight-to-bring.html.

4   **On June 19:** Kenworthy, "Dirksen Shaped Victory."

4   **"had seen the beginning"**: Johnson, *White House Diary*, 174.

4   **Sixty-six percent:** Shannon Mullen O'Keefe, "Gallup Vault: Americans Narrowly OK'd 1964 Civil Rights Law," Gallup, July 29, 2020, https://news.gallup.com/vault/316130/gallup-vault-americans-narrowly-1964-civil-rights-law.aspx.

4   **"the most monstrous"**: George C. Wallace, "The Civil Rights Movement: Fraud, Sham, and Hoax," speech, July 4, 1964, PBS, transcript, https://www.pbs.org/wgbh/americanexperience/features/lbj-wallspeech/.

4   **"avoid the racial issue" and "I was concerned"**: Lyndon Baines Johnson, *The Vantage Point: Perspectives of the Presidency 1963–1969* (Holt, Rinehart and Winston, 1971), 109.

4   **"states' rights"**: "Goldwater Says He'd Curb Court," *New York Times*, September 16, 1964, https://www.nytimes.com/1964/09/16/archives/goldwater-says-hed-curb-court-also-stresses-states-rights-in-swing.html.

5   **recently released:** President Johnson received a copy of the Warren Commission Report on September 24, 1964, and it was released to the public three days later. It received national coverage, including "Johnson Gets Assassination Report," *New York Times*, September 25, 1964, https://www.nytimes.com/1964/09/25/archives/johnson-gets-assassination-report.html.

5   **Warren Commission:** "Warren Commission Report," JFK Assassination Records, National Archives, accessed February 8, 2025, https://www.archives.gov/research/jfk/warren-commission-report.

5   **rode for the first time:** "Johnson Uses Rebuilt Kennedy Car, Now Bulletproof," *New York Times*, October 6, 1964, https://www.nytimes.com/1964/10/06/archives/johnson-uses-rebuilt-kennedy-car-now-bulletproof.html.

5   **"so why make the effort"**: Bess Abell quoted in Donald A. Ritchie and Terry L. Birdwhistell, *Washington's Iron Butterfly: Bess Clements Abell, An Oral History* (University Press of Kentucky, 2022), 94.

5 **"We must go"**: Carpenter, *Ruffles and Flourishes*, 143.
6 **"I don't think anybody"**: James Roe Ketchum, interviews by Donald A. Ritchie, November 13, 2004, to September 30, 2007, transcript, Oral History Interviews, Senate Historical Office, Washington, DC, https://www.senate.gov/about/resources/pdf/ketchum-james-oral-history.pdf.
6 **"a Floridian and a"**: India Edwards to Liz Carpenter, September 9, 1964, box 11, folder "Whistle-Stop [2 of 6]," Liz Carpenter Subject Files, White House Social Files, LBJL, https://www.discoverlbj.org/item/whsf-lc-subject-b11-f09.
6 **a threat was reported**: "Klan Probers Charge Plot to Dynamite Mrs. Johnson's 'Lady Bird Special' in 1964," *St. Petersburg (FL) Times*, January 14, 1966; "Activities of Ku Klux Klan Organizations in the United States, Part 3," Hearings Before the Committee on Un-American Activities, House of Representatives, 89th Congress, 2nd Session.
6 **weighed heavily**: Mark Updegrove quoted in Kate Bennett, "Revisiting Lady Bird Johnson's Whistle-stop Tour," CNN, June 13, 2020, https://www.cnn.com/2020/06/13/politics/melania-trump-racism-coronavirus-protest-lady-bird-johnson/index.html.
6 **"You may not believe this"**: Carpenter, *Ruffles and Flourishes*, 142.
7 **"small Southern towns"**: Carpenter, *Ruffles and Flourishes*, 145.
7 **"next to the President"**: Liz Carpenter to Lady Bird Johnson, September 2, 1964, box 34, folder "Schedules and lists for 1964 Whistle-Stop," Bess Abell Subject Files, White House Social Files, LBJL, https://www.discoverlbj.org/item/whsf-ba-b34-f03.
7 **"picturesque"**: "'Lady Bird' Johnson Is Capable, Busy, Charming and Devoted Wife and Mother," *Knoxville News-Sentinel*, November 24, 1963.
7 **often compared**: Esther Von Wagoner Tufty, "Michigan in Washington," *Holland (MI) Evening Sentinel*, August 14, 1965.
7 **"learning from people"**: "Lady Bird Speaks Her Mind on Life as the First Lady," *Buffalo (NY) Evening News*, June 8, 1964.
7 **"be a link" through "the people I talk to"**: "Remarks by Mrs. Lyndon B. Johnson at Press Breakfast in Honor of Mrs. Johnson by Mrs. Richard Hughes and Mrs. John Bailey, Shelburne Hotel, Atlantic City. N.J.," press release, August 27, 1964, "Mrs. Johnson—Speeches," Reference File, LBJL, https://www.discoverlbj.org/item/ref-ctjspeeches-19640827-1000.
8 **"No First Lady within memory"**: Lewis L. Gould, *Lady Bird Johnson: Our Environmental First Lady* (University Press of Kansas, 1999), 38.
8 **front-page stories**: Helen Thomas, "On Snake River Trip: Lady Bird Loves the Rapids," *Birmingham (AL) Post-Herald*, August 17, 1964.
8 **"Mrs. Johnson was extremely"**: Stewart Udall to Lyndon B. Johnson, August 19, 1964, box 62, folder "7/15/64–10/1/64," EX PP 5/Johnson, Lady Bird, Papers of Lyndon Baines Johnson, President, 1963–1969, LBJL.

NOTES

8 **"Mrs. Johnson represents"**: Douglass Cater to Lyndon B. Johnson, August 18, 1964, box 62, folder "7/15/64–10/1/64," EX PP 5/Johnson, Lady Bird, Papers of Lyndon Baines Johnson, President, 1963–1969, LBJL.

9 **"She is and she will"**: "LBJ Says 1st Lady Is, Will Campaign," *Courier-Journal* (Louisville, KY), August 16, 1964.

9 **"so enthusiastic" through "Mrs. Johnson, Bess, and me"**: Elizabeth (Liz) Carpenter, interview by Joe B. Frantz, December 3, 1968, transcript, LBJ Library Oral Histories, LBJL, https://www.discoverlbj.org/item/oh-carpenterl-19681203-1-74-193-a.

9 **"turned up his nose"**: Carpenter, *Ruffles and Flourishes*, 143.

9 **"[He] had no respect"**: Carpenter, interview by Frantz.

9 **"But I would be less"**: Carpenter, *Ruffles and Flourishes*, 143–44.

10 **"the best 'train man'"**: Liz Carpenter to Lady Bird Johnson, n.d., box 11, folder "Whistle-Stop [2 of 6]," Liz Carpenter Subject Files, White House Social Files, LBJL, https://www.discoverlbj.org/item/whsf-lc-subject-b11-f09.

10 **"I had LBJ"**: Carpenter, *Ruffles and Flourishes*, 144.

10 **"The President knew"**: Carpenter, interview by Frantz.

10 **"sharp, efficient show"**: "LBJ's Special Caravan Sharp, Efficient Show," *Pensacola News*, October 14, 1960.

10 **"a master of details"**: Arthur Edson, "First Lady Real Pro on Stump," *Austin Statesman*, October 14, 1964.

10 **population 4,800**: James Ross, "'Special' Setting Records," *News and Record* (Greensboro, NC), October 7, 1964.

10 **telegram and "Stop there"**: Carpenter, *Ruffles and Flourishes*, 144.

10 **"Don't give me"**: Carpenter, *Ruffles and Flourishes*, 143.

11 **just after the ratification**: Kathleen McElroy, "Celebrating Liz Carpenter at 100," School of Journalism and Media, University of Texas at Austin, September 1, 2020, https://journalism.utexas.edu/news/celebrating-liz-carpenter-100.

11 **"packed us all up" and "involved in everything"**: Carpenter, *Ruffles and Flourishes*, 19.

11 **"took me everywhere"**: Carpenter, *Ruffles and Flourishes*, 20.

12 **"Lyndon and I" and "We wonder if"**: Carpenter, interview by Frantz.

12 **"It was too great"**: Carpenter, *Ruffles and Flourishes*, 29.

12 **"enjoyed the change"**: Carpenter, *Ruffles and Flourishes*, 6.

12 **"a willing captive"**: Carpenter, *Ruffles and Flourishes*, 29.

12 **"As for me"**: Carpenter, *Ruffles and Flourishes*, 111.

13 **"understood a reporter's" and "She knew the language"**: Carpenter, *Ruffles and Flourishes*, 114.

13 **"the best of all worlds"**: Carpenter, *Ruffles and Flourishes*, 111–12.

13 **"The West Wing serves"**: Carpenter, *Ruffles and Flourishes*, 12.

13 **"I help her":** Carpenter, *Ruffles and Flourishes*, 6.
14 **"cut her eyeteeth":** "She's Played in Big Leagues," *Fort Lauderdale News*, December 16, 1963.
14 **"inside and out":** Winzola McLendon and Scottie Smith, *Don't Quote Me!: Washington Newswomen and the Power Society* (E. P. Dutton, 1970), 94.
14 **"Second the Second Lady":** "She Seconds the Second Lady," *Washington Post*, December 19, 1960.
14 **"She is well-equipped":** Dorothy McCardle, "LBJ Hospitality Is Her Style Too," *Washington Post*, December 9, 1963.
14 **"What was not assumed":** Bess Abell, interview by T. H. Baker, May 28, 1969, transcript, LBJ Library Oral Histories, LBJL, https://www.discoverlbj.org/item/oh-abellb-19690528-1-84-28.
14 **"She had the right blend":** Ritchie and Birdwhistell, *Washington's Iron Butterfly*, 39.
15 **"Social secretaries are expected":** Carpenter, *Ruffles and Flourishes*, 7.
16 **"I will match":** Carpenter, *Ruffles and Flourishes*, 144.
16 **"a figure in political life":** Michael L. Gillette, *Lady Bird Johnson: An Oral History* (Oxford University Press, 2012), 243.
16 **"Early on, Hale established":** "For Lindy, Long Way to Power," *Durham Morning Herald*, July 13, 1976.
16 **"When someone has a job":** "Mrs. Hale Boggs Tours the South," *Lake Charles (LA) American-Press*, October 3, 1964.
17 **"People are afraid":** Isabelle Shelton, "Whistle-Stoppers' Rally," *Evening Star* (Washington, DC), September 22, 1964.
17 **schoolteacher:** "Virginia U. Russell," *Herald-Journal* (Spartanburg, SC), June 30, 2003.
17 **brilliant, well-read:** Janet S. Spencer, "Donald Russell's Widow Dies," *Herald-Journal* (Spartanburg, SC), June 28, 2003.
17 **"If you were to sit":** Shelton, "Whistle-Stoppers' Rally."
17 **worked as a team:** Charles Hauser, "Russells Call Victory 'Family Affair,'" *Charlotte Observer*, June 14, 1962.
17 **"the best politician":** Shelton, "Whistle-Stoppers' Rally."
17 **"was a whole new":** Carpenter, *Ruffles and Flourishes*, 143.
17 **"a fantastic job":** Carpenter, interview by Frantz.
18 **"You've got to have":** Carpenter, *Ruffles and Flourishes*, 144.
18 **"Have them hold"** and **"This was pure":** Carpenter, *Ruffles and Flourishes*, 147.
18 **"Some fifty advance":** Arthur Edson, "Never Before Has Wife of President Hit Trail So Hard," *Pensacola Journal*, October 12, 1964.
18 **"All of these good-looking":** Carpenter, interview by Frantz.
18 **newspaper headline touted:** Celestine Sibley, "Advance Women for Lady Bird Are Something New in Politics," *Atlanta Constitution*, October 11, 1964.

NOTES

18 **"whipped up" and "went flying":** Instructions to Advance Women, box 1, folder "Lady Bird Special–Whistlestop Tour [1 of 2]," Personal Papers of Lindy Boggs, LBJL.

18 **"Lyndon knew":** Lindy Boggs, *Washington Through a Purple Veil: Memoirs of a Southern Woman* (Harcourt Brace, 1994), 190.

19 **"I know the Civil Rights Act":** Carpenter, *Ruffles and Flourishes*, 147.

19 **"Advance men are":** Carpenter, *Ruffles and Flourishes*, 148.

19 **"We were told":** Bess Abell, interview by T. H. Baker, June 13, 1969, transcript, LBJ Library Oral Histories, LBJL, https://www.discoverlbj.org/item/oh-abellb-19690613-2-84-29.

20 **"the equivalent":** Memorandum to Train Hostesses, box 1, folder "Lady Bird Johnson's Advance Notebook, 'Lady Bird Special,' Oct. 6–9, 1964 [2 of 3]," Lady Bird Johnson's Advance Notebooks, 1964, White House Social Files, LBJL.

20 **Adjacent to the hospitality car:** A detailed outline of the Lady Bird Special's route and the content/purpose of each car can be found in box 11, folder "Whistle-Stop [2 of 6]," Liz Carpenter Subject Files, White House Social Files, LBJL, https://www.discoverlbj.org/item/whsf-lc-subject-b11-f0.

21 **"Speech-making was only":** Estelle Jackson, "'Friends and Sunshine' Greet Nation's First Lady," *Richmond Times-Dispatch*, October 7, 1964.

21 **"President Johnson is willing":** Ethleen Underwood, "Tar Heel Rides with Mrs. LBJ to Ahoskie," *Chowanian* (Chowan University Student Newspaper, Murfreesboro, NC), December 1, 1964.

21 **"not for their looks":** Memorandum to Train Hostesses.

21 **"This campaign needed":** Dale Miller and Virginia "Scooter" Miller, interview by Joe B. Frantz, August 26, 1969, transcript, LBJ Library Oral Histories, LBJL, https://www.discoverlbj.org/item/oh-millerd-19690826-1-78-29.

22 **"the best available":** Barbara Howar, *Laughing All the Way* (Fawcett, 1974), 14.

22 **serving up dishes:** The Lady Bird Special Menu, box 34, folder "Gimmicks—1964 Whistle-Stop," Bess Abell Subject Files, White House Social Files, LBJL, https://www.discoverlbj.org/item/whsf-ba-b34-f05.

22 **"most unusual whistle-stop":** Montgomery, "Capital Letter."

Chapter 2

23 **"an exercise in citizenship":** Jerry Kline, "Lady Bird Special: First Stop: Alexandria," *Sunday Star* (Washington, DC), October 4, 1964.

24 **"the hoopla" and "was as serious":** Edson, "First Lady Real Pro."

24 **hosting a state dinner:** Suzanne Holden, "Lady Bird Sets Dizzy Pace for Successors," *Ledger-Star* (Norfolk, VA), October 7, 1964.

25 **"Sunshine and lots" and "vote for both":** Lyndon B. Johnson, "Remarks at the Station in Alexandria, Va., at the Start of Mrs. Johnson's Trip Through the

South," October 6, 1964, transcript, American Presidency Project, https://www.presidency.ucsb.edu/node/242517.

25 **Bind up the nation's wounds:** Nan Robertson, "First Lady's Whistle-Stop Tour Is Cheered by Crowds in South," *New York Times*, October 7, 1964, https://www.nytimes.com/1964/10/07/archives/first-ladys-whistlestop-tour-is-cheered-by-crowds-in-south.html.

25 **made courtesy calls:** Johnson, *White House Diary*, 195–97.

25 **"I don't think I'll have":** Carpenter, *Ruffles and Flourishes*, 149.

26 **"The conversations" and "They loved to give":** Carpenter, interview by Frantz.

26 **"how tough things were" through "through your state":** Carpenter, *Ruffles and Flourishes*, 149–50.

26 **single-handedly filibustered:** "Civil Rights Filibuster Ended."

26 **"A lovely place":** Johnson, *White House Diary*, 195.

27 **"somewhat hostile":** Johnson, *White House Diary*, 195.

27 **"best qualified":** Kent Krell, "Gov. Russell Maintains Johnson Best Qualified," *Times and Democrat* (Orangeburg, SC), September 11, 1964.

27 **"mighty good":** Johnson, *White House Diary*, 196.

27 **"I'm all out":** "Johnston Blasts GOP Candidates," *State* (Columbia, SC), October 7, 1964.

27 **"The decision could be":** Johnson, *White House Diary*, 196.

27 **Five days later:** Claude Sitton, "Thurmond Break Is Made Official," *New York Times*, September 17, 1964, https://www.nytimes.com/1964/09/17/archives/thurmond-break-is-made-official-he-will-work-as-republican-for.html.

27 **attempt to portray:** Robert S. Allen and Paul Scott, "Thurmond's Bolt Is One Setback to Lady Bird's Whistle-Stop Journey," *Progress-Index* (Petersburg-Colonial Heights, VA), October 2, 1964.

28 **"So here we go":** Johnson, *White House Diary*, 196.

28 **"His differences with Lyndon":** Johnson, *White House Diary*, 196.

28 **senator who started:** "On This Day, Filibuster Fails to Block the Civil Rights Act," National Constitution Center, June 19, 2024, https://constitutioncenter.org/blog/on-this-day-congress-passes-the-civil-rights-act.

28 **"It's going to cost" and "If that's the price":** Dallek, *Lyndon B. Johnson*, 163.

28 **"That is an elastic":** Johnson, *White House Diary*, 196.

28 **"booed from one end":** Herman Talmadge, interview by T. H. Baker, July 17, 1969, transcript, LBJ Library Oral Histories, LBJL, https://www.discoverlbj.org/item/oh-talmadgeh-19690717-1-78-13.

28 **"among our strongest":** Johnson, *White House Diary*, 196.

28 **behind-the-scenes operator:** "George A. Smathers," University of Florida Levin College of Law, June 27, 2014, https://www.law.ufl.edu/alumni/george-a-smathers.

NOTES

29 **"But I'm already"**: Edson, "First Lady Real Pro."
29 **"were among the most"**: Johnson, *White House Diary*, 197.
29 **Bryant, who ran:** Stuart Lavietes, "C. Farris Bryant, 87, Governor of Florida at Turning Point," *New York Times*, March 6, 2002, https://www.nytimes.com/2002/03/06/nyregion/c-farris-bryant-87-governor-of-florida-at-turning-point.html; "Farris Bryant: Led Fla. During Desegregation," *Washington Post*, March 1, 2002, https://www.washingtonpost.com/archive/local/2002/03/02/farris-bryant/925680eb-7ca1-415a-b9ba-ca76599742b1/.
29 **"it would even be courteous"**: Johnson, *White House Diary*, 197.
29 **"I say segregation"**: "New Note in Dixie," *Time*, January 25, 1963, https://time.com/archive/6873298/nation-new-note-in-dixie/.
29 **"the most personal" and "most adamantly"**: Johnson, *White House Diary*, 197.
29 **not listed:** Mary Pakenham, "Mrs. Johnson Gets Mixed Reception in Tour of Georgia," *Chicago Tribune*, October 9, 1964.
29 **"mighty glad"**: Johnson, *White House Diary*, 197.
29 **"he thought he could"**: Johnson, *White House Diary*, 197.
30 **"the most dangerous"**: "Elect Goldwater, Mississippi Demos Told by Governor," *Miami Herald*, September 10, 1964.
30 **"working for the Democrats"**: Johnson, *White House Diary*, 197.
30 **"I think we just"**: Randall B. Woods, *LBJ: Architect of American Ambition* (Harvard University Press, 2006), 480.
30 **"The voice was soft"**: Carpenter, *Ruffles and Flourishes*, 154.
30 **"I wanted to make this trip" and subsequent quotes from this speech:** Lady Bird Johnson, "Remarks at the Station in Alexandria, Va., at the Start of Mrs. Johnson's Trip Through the South," October 6, 1964, transcript, American Presidency Project, https://www.presidency.ucsb.edu/node/242517.
32 **"Ladies and gentlemen"**: "Remarks at the Station in Alexandria, VA, 10/6/64," TheLBJLibrary, October 5, 2014, YouTube video, 4:20, https://www.youtube.com/watch?v=2HwQSZIe3FA (only the president's remarks are heard on this audio).
33 **"year of decision" and "keep the line of contact"**: Marie Smith, "'Don't Fence Me In' Is Private Slogan of the First Lady," *Greensboro Daily News*, December 8, 1963.
33 **"but there to meet you"**: Carpenter, interview by Frantz.
33 **"I have a full time job!"**: Nancy Kegan Smith, "Private Reflections on a Public Life: The Papers of Lady Bird Johnson at the LBJ Library," *Presidential Studies Quarterly* 20, no. 4 (Fall 1990): 737–44, https://www.jstor.org/stable/20700157.
33 **"so stimulating"**: Gould, *Lady Bird Johnson*, 10.
34 **"keep up"**: Smith, "Private Reflections."
34 **"until Lyndon Johnson"**: Gould, *Lady Bird Johnson*, 10.
34 **"Out of the cauldron" and "do a job"**: Smith, "'Don't Fence Me In.'"
34 **"a keener understanding"**: Smith, "'Don't Fence Me In.'"

34 **"She fell in love with":** Carpenter, interview by Frantz.
34 **"like a book":** Isabelle Shelton, "Lady Bird Being Touted as a Great 'Influence,'" *Sunday Star* (Washington, DC), February 2, 1964.
34 **"She has had the best":** Carpenter, interview by Frantz.
35 **"just went along" and "swung into action":** Smith, "'Don't Fence Me In.'"
35 **"able vote-getter":** "Mrs. Lyndon Johnson Feted by Wichita Women, Who Find Her Able Vote-Getter," *Wichita Falls (TX) Record News*, August 24, 1948.
35 **called the LBJ ranch and "Certainly":** Jan Jarboe Russell, *Lady Bird: A Biography of Mrs. Johnson* (Scribner, 2016), 186.
35 **"Lady Bird Shows":** *Kansas City Times*, referenced in Julia Sweig, *Lady Bird Johnson: Hiding in Plain Sight* (Random House, 2022), 438.
35 **"Johnson's Biggest Booster":** *Birmingham News*, referenced in Sweig, *Lady Bird Johnson*, 438.
35 **"sheer magic" and "There was a sly":** Holmes Alexander, "President Lyndon B. Johnson Walked with Destiny," *Galveston Daily News*, December 1, 1963.
35 **"helping Lyndon":** "Amazing Lady Bird," *San Francisco Examiner*, April 29, 1964, excerpt from *Mrs. L.B.J.* by Ruth Montgomery.
35 **"Washington's No. 1 pinch hitter":** Blake Clark, "Lyndon Johnson's Lady Bird," *Reader's Digest*, November 1963.
36 **"Lady Bird is":** Clark, "Lyndon Johnson's Lady Bird."
36 **"Somebody else can have":** "Johnson's Lady Bird Is a Wife with Everything," *Winston-Salem Journal*, February 9, 1960.
36 **"From now until election day" and subsequent quotes from this speech:** Johnson, "Remarks at the Station in Alexandria."
36 **"four astonishing days":** Edson, "First Lady Real Pro."

Chapter 3

37 **"Here she comes":** Paul Muse, "Crowd Here Greets 'Lady Bird Special,'" *Free Lance-Star* (Fredericksburg, VA), October 6, 1964.
38 **"looked fairly":** Charles McDowell Jr., "First Lady Employs Soft-Sell Approach," *Richmond Times-Dispatch*, October 7, 1964.
38 **"I'm Luther Hodges":** Muse, "Crowd Here Greets."
38 **"The sun of the":** Muse, "Crowd Here Greets."
39 **"happy summer weekends":** "Remarks by Mrs. Lyndon B. Johnson, Fredericksburg, Virginia," press release, October 6, 1964, "Mrs. Johnson—Speeches," Reference File, LBJL, https://www.discoverlbj.org/item/ref-ctjspeeches-19641006-0815. For this speech, quotes were confirmed against newspaper accounts.
39 **"general beliefs":** Lady Bird Johnson, audio diary and annotated transcript, September 8, 1964, Lady Bird Johnson's White House Diary Collection, LBJL, https://www.discoverlbj.org/item/ctjd-19640908.

NOTES

40 **"Mrs. Johnson is":** Frances Lewine, "First Lady Sets Whirlwind Pace," *Evening Star* (Washington, DC), May 19, 1964.
40 **"She wanted to learn":** Carpenter, *Ruffles and Flourishes*, 188.
40 **"Read all you can":** Nan Robertson, "Our New First Lady," *Saturday Evening Post*, February 8, 1964.
40 **Tonight, I went:** Carpenter, *Ruffles and Flourishes*, 187.
41 **"Perhaps the most":** John C. Goolrick, "LBJ Ladies Obvious Asset," *Free Lance-Star* (Fredericksburg, VA), October 6, 1964.
41 **"Lady Bird Demonstrates":** Charles Barbour, "Lady Bird Demonstrates She Did Her Homework for Tour," *Durham Morning Herald*, October 7, 1964.
41 **"very much impressed":** "Mrs. Johnson Impresses," *Free Lance-Star* (Fredericksburg, VA), October 23, 1964.
41 **"is already beginning":** Levona Page, "Liz Blazes the Trail for Lady Bird," *State* (Columbia, SC), September 23, 1964.
42 **"Democrats are putting on":** "Train Tour May Help Gus Johnson," *Washington Post*, September 20, 1964.
42 **"I do not need to tell you":** "Remarks by Mrs. Lyndon B. Johnson, Fredericksburg, Virginia."
42 **"You'd think the Beatles":** Goolrick, "LBJ Ladies Obvious Asset."
43 **"for coming out":** Muse, "Crowd Here Greets."
43 **"a great success" and "I told her":** Muse, "Crowd Here Greets."
43 **doesn't usually require:** Marilyn Muse, "Company's Coming: Women Are Busy Planning for a Very Special Visitor," *Free Lance-Star* (Fredericksburg, VA), October 5, 1964.
43 **William Durland:** "Lady Bird Train Reception Is Set," *Free Lance-Star* (Fredericksburg, VA), September 29, 1964.
44 **"leaving home" and "because she":** "Biography of Mrs. William P. McClure (Bette)," press release, September 1964, box 11, folder "Whistle-Stop [4 of 6]," Liz Carpenter Subject Files, White House Social Files, LBJL, https://www.discoverlbj.org/item/whsf-lc-subject-b11-f11.
44 **noted that in between:** Muse, "Company's Coming."
44 **"Like Lyndon or not":** Goolrick, "LBJ Ladies Obvious Asset."
44 **"Goodbye":** Muse, "Crowd Here Greets."
44 **"Aren't they" and "Well, that":** Goolrick, "LBJ Ladies Obvious Asset."
44 **"This is a five-minute stop":** McDowell, "First Lady Employs Soft-Sell Approach."
45 **"some of my closest" and all excerpts from Ashland speech:** "Lady Bird's Whistle-Stop: Ashland, VA: 10/6/64, 9:23 AM," TheLBJLibrary, October 5, 2014, YouTube video, 5:21, https://www.youtube.com/watch?v=Ny9c9-DXfHM.
45 **impending arrival:** "'Lady Bird' Special Train to Stop in Ashland Tuesday," *Herald Progress* (Ashland, VA), October 1, 1964.

45 **"The general feeling"**: "Barry vs LBJ; In Hanover Round: Democrats Criticized," *Herald-Progress* (Ashland, VA), October 8, 1964.

46 **"There were politicians"**: Helen Thomas, *Front Row at the White House: My Life and Times* (Scribner, 1999), 254.

46 **"For local Democratic leaders"**: McDowell, "First Lady Employs Soft-Sell Approach."

46 **"and out of respect"**: John Goode, "Outdoors," *Herald-Progress* (Ashland, VA), October 8, 1964.

46 **"In the South"**: David Pietrusza, *1960: LBJ vs. JFK vs. Nixon: The Epic Campaign That Forged Three Presidencies* (Union Square Press, 2008), 265.

46 **"with the presence"**: Councill Chase, "1,000 Gather to Greet Lady Bird's Arrival," *Yellow Jacket* (Randolph-Macon College, Ashland, VA), October 16, 1964.

46 **Lynda had already:** Frances Lewine, "Johnson Gals Working Like Mad to Reelect Dad," *Record* (Hackensack, NJ), October 5, 1964.

46 **represented her father:** "Lynda Bird Sees Greek Royalty Wed," *Burlington (VT) Free Press*, September 19, 1964.

47 **"They were born" and "Any job":** May Herbert, "Mrs. Lyndon Johnson Says Whistle-Stop Is 'Most Enjoyable' Tour," *Greenville News*, October 12, 1960.

47 **three different groups:** Betty Beale, "Capital Capers: Lynda Bird Assists Mother in White House When Needed," *Daily Press* (Newport News, VA), February 9, 1964.

47 **"They do it graciously"**: Mildred Schroeder, "The First Family's Girl Friday," *San Francisco Examiner*, March 11, 1964.

47 **"leaving the air"**: Chase, "1,000 Gather."

Chapter 4

49 **"helter skelter"**: Frances Lewine, "Lady Bird Special Had Its Own Specialist," *Charlotte Observer*, October 12, 1964.

49 **"fell like dominos "**: McDowell, "First Lady Employs Soft-Sell Approach."

50 **from whose ranks:** David Stout, "Janet Travell, 95, Pain Specialist and Kennedy's Personal Doctor," *New York Times*, August 3, 1997, https://www.nytimes.com/1997/08/03/us/janet-travell-95-pain-specialist-and-kennedy-s-personal-doctor.html.

50 **"genius"**: Carroll Kilpatrick, "She's Eying the President's Chair," *Washington Post*, January 27, 1961.

50 **"A key ingredient"**: "White House Physician," *Time*, February 3, 1961, https://time.com/archive/6809707/medicine-white-house-physician/.

50 **"physician, nurse"**: Janet Travell, *Office Hours: Day and Night* (New American Library, 1968), 454.

NOTES

51 **"It was a good thing" and "accustomed herself"**: Lewine, "Lady Bird Special."
51 **"felt almost like"**: Pat Lloyd, "Around the Town," *Pensacola News*, October 13, 1964.
51 **"And newspaper people"**: Annie Lee Singletary, "It's 'Lady's Day' Across the State," *Twin City Sentinel* (Winston-Salem, NC), October 7, 1964.
51 **"She's the second"**: Singletary, "It's 'Lady's Day.'"
51 **"the heroine"**: Travell, *Office Hours*, 454.
51 **his office announced**: "Harrison Plans to Board 'Lady Bird Special' Here," *Richmond Times-Dispatch*, September 27, 1964.
51 **"It is never pleasant"**: "Voice of the People: Ambulances, 'Lady Bird Special,' Seibel," *Richmond Times-Dispatch*, October 1, 1964.
52 **"In President Johnson"**: Alex R. Preston, "Johnson Visit Is Seen as Virginia Hopes Rise," *Evening Star* (Washington, DC), October 7, 1964.
52 **"endorsed the"**: McDowell, "First Lady Employs Soft-Sell Approach."
52 **"First Lady Starts"**: "First Lady Starts Tour," *Richmond Times-Dispatch*, September 14, 1964.
52 **"firmly in the GOP"**: "When Polls Disagree," *Richmond Times-Dispatch*, September 30, 1964.
52 **reminded readers**: "'Lady Bird Special' Is on the Way," *Richmond-Times Dispatch*, October 5, 1964.
52 **"a 19-car railroad groundling"**: James Latimer, "Governor Will Lead Greeters in Richmond," *Richmond Times-Dispatch*, October 6, 1964.
53 **"train to socialism"**: Ed Grimsley, "Leaders Snub Haddock," *Richmond Times-Dispatch*, October 7, 1964.
53 **"Spreading Southern"**: McDowell, "First Lady Employs Soft-Sell Approach."
53 **"Today in Politics"**: *Richmond Times-Dispatch*, October 7, 1964.
53 **only one woman**: Ellen Robertson, "Retired Consumer Columnist Estelle Jackson Dies," *Richmond Times-Dispatch*, July 14, 2017.
54 **"garnered cheers" through "campaign story aboard"**: Estelle Jackson, "'Friends and Sunshine' Greet Nation's First Lady," *Richmond Times-Dispatch*, October 7, 1964.
54 **"I greatly underestimated"**: Carpenter, *Ruffles and Flourishes*, 152.
54 **"because they knew"**: Carpenter, *Ruffles and Flourishes*, 152.
55 **"The real value of it"**: Carpenter, interview by Frantz.
55 **"was a good idea"**: Nancy Dickerson, *Among Those Present: A Reporter's View of 25 Years in Washington* (Random House, 1976), 126.
55 **"A woman—no matter"**: Lee Graham, "Women Don't Like to Look at Women," *New York Times Magazine*, May 24, 1964.
56 **own daily newscast**: Cary O'Dell, *Women Pioneers in Television: Biographies of Fifteen Industry Leaders* (McFarland, 1997), 224.
56 **"Often the people"**: Dickerson, *Among Those Present*, 128.

56 **"a noisy, cheerful" and "with deep-drawled":** B. W. Mader, "Mrs. Johnson Recalls Ties with Virginia," *Richmond Times-Dispatch*, October 7, 1964.

56 **"tight as a nail" and "I was about":** "Student Snaps LBJ's Family," *Commentator* (Douglas Southall Freeman High School, Richmond, VA), October 16, 1964.

56 **fly away:** Mader, "Mrs. Johnson Recalls."

57 **"total sellout":** Grimsley, "Leaders Snub Haddock."

57 **"I think I've already":** "Lady Bird's Whistle-Stop: Richmond, VA: 10/6/64, 9:47 AM," TheLBJLibrary, October 5, 2014, YouTube video, 20:33, https://www.youtube.com/watch?v=2RXbC--pb7s.

57 **"She has a brief":** McDowell, "First Lady Employs Soft-Sell Approach."

Chapter 5

59 **A black limousine:** "Thurmond Opens Tour of Virginia," *Roanoke World-News*, October 5, 1964.

59 **"The Republican party":** "I'll Never Move Back, S.C. Senator Insists," *Sumter (SC) Daily Item*, October 5, 1964.

59 **"Civil right[s]":** Melville Carico, "Thurmond Begins 4th District Tour," *Roanoke Times*, October 5, 1964.

60 **"I know that Petersburg":** "Lady Bird's Whistle-Stop: Petersburg, VA: 10/6/64, 10:55 AM," TheLBJLibrary, October 5, 2014, YouTube video, 17:48, https://www.youtube.com/watch?v=_7NgjXhRKOE.

60 **Luther Hodges:** Shane Williams, "Luther H. Hodges (1895–1974)," North Carolina History Project, accessed February 11, 2025, https://northcarolinahistory.org/encyclopedia/luther-h-hodges-1895-1974/.

61 **"the great privilege" and "I think that what":** "Lady Bird's Whistle-Stop: Petersburg, VA."

61 **"I think we can agree":** "Lady Bird's Whistle-Stop: Petersburg, VA."

61 **"for coming down":** Gloria Negri, "Mrs. LBJ Draws Throngs on Southern Tour," *Boston Globe*, October 7, 1964.

61 **"I can be a Democrat" through "all women":** Negri, "Mrs. LBJ Draws Throngs."

61 **Gloria Negri:** Brian McGrory, "A Career for the Ages," *Boston Globe*, September 14, 2012; David Filipov, "Trailblazing Globe Reporter Retires," *Boston Globe*, September 14, 2012.

61 **"freedom fighters":** Gloria Negri, "Kennedy Tribute by N.C. Negroes," *Boston Globe*, December 25, 1963.

62 **"Send me":** Thomas Farragher, "A Half-Century of Delivering the Far Reaches of Globe," *Boston Globe*, December 12, 2017.

62 **"were calling the signals":** Carpenter, interview by Frantz.

62 **"Johnson, Humphrey Wives":** Isabelle Shelton, "Johnson, Humphrey Wives Both Top-Notch Campaigners," *Evening Star* (Washington, DC), August 27, 1964.

NOTES

62 **"come hell or high water"**: Jack Graham, "Isabelle Shelton: Memorial Service," June 1, 1993, transcript, Washington Press Club Foundation Oral History Project, http://beta.wpcf.org/oralhistory/shelmem.html.

63 **"attained her"**: Anne G. Ritchie, "Isabelle Shelton: Introduction," Washington Press Club Foundation Oral History Project, 1993, http://beta.wpcf.org/oralhistory/shelint.html.

63 **"political junkie"**: Ritchie, "Isabelle Shelton: Introduction."

63 **"the times had not" and "The job of a"**: Shelton, "Johnson, Humphrey Wives."

64 **"and the rest of the gossips"**: Barbara Kellerman, *All the President's Kin* (Free Press, 1981), 6.

64 **"How'd ya' like"**: Steven R. Goldzwig, *Truman's Whistle-stop Campaign* (Texas A&M University Press, 2008), 32–33.

64 **"the boss" and "the one who"**: Margaret Truman, *Harry S. Truman* (William Morrow, 1973), 23.

64 **He never acceded**: Truman, *Harry S. Truman*, 23.

64 **credited with**: "Elizabeth 'Bess' Wallace Truman," Truman Library Institute, accessed February 11, 2025, https://www.trumanlibraryinstitute.org/truman/bess-wallace-truman.

64 **"Yes, I go around"**: Ritchie and Birdwhistell, *Washington's Iron Butterfly*, 93.

64 **"in the spotlight"**: "Presidential Hopefuls See Wives Drawing Votes," *Progress-Index* (Petersburg-Colonial Heights, VA), July 10, 1960.

64 **largely relegated to**: Barbara McAden, "Lady Bird, Reporters Chug Across State," *Charlotte Observer*, October 8, 1964.

65 **hosted house parties**: John T. Shaw, *JFK in the Senate: Pathway to the Presidency* (Palgrave Macmillan, 2013), 41.

65 **70,737 votes**: Shaw, *JFK in the Senate*, 44.

65 **"is, I daresay" and "It was those"**: Rose Fitzgerald Kennedy, *Times to Remember* (Doubleday, 1974), 326.

65 **"Tea Party"**: "WOMEN: Tea Party Task Force," *Time*, September 12, 1960, https://time.com/archive/6832522/women-tea-party-task-force/.

65 **spraining her ankle**: Sweig, *Lady Bird Johnson*, 11; "Tired Lady Bird," *Clarion-Ledger* (Jackson, MS), September 1, 1960.

65 **"If vivacity"**: Anita Brewer, "Lady Bird's Campaign," *Austin American-Statesman*, October 23, 1960.

65 **"stag Government"**: Marjorie Hunter, "President Gives Jobs to 10 Women," *New York Times*, March 5, 1964, https://www.nytimes.com/1964/03/05/archives/president-gives-jobs-to-10-women-jerseyan-will-be-envoymrs-kross.html.

65 **"and be prepared" through "The hunt was on"**: Carpenter, *Ruffles and Flourishes*, 35.

66 **Charlotte Moton Hubbard**: "Negro Woman Is Promoted to State Dept. Assis-

tant," *Berkshire Eagle* (Pittsfield, MA), May 7, 1964; "C. M. Hubbard, 82, Ex-State Dept. Aide," *New York Times*, December 21, 1994, https://www.nytimes.com/1994/12/21/obituaries/c-m-hubbard-82-ex-state-dept-aide.html.

66 **"Our determination":** Hunter, "President Gives Jobs."

66 **Whittington received:** Michael R. Beschloss, *Taking Charge: The Johnson White House Tapes, 1963–1964* (Touchstone, 1998), 126–27.

67 **shared the news:** Todd S. Purdum, *An Idea Whose Time Has Come: Two Presidents, Two Parties, and the Battle for the Civil Rights Act of 1964* (Henry Holt, 2014), 174.

67 **worked for presidential aides:** Gerri Whittington, interview by Michael L. Gillette, June 5, 1990, transcript, LBJ Library Oral Histories, LBJL, https://www.discoverlbj.org/item/oh-whittingtong-19900605-1-06-11.

67 ***What's My Line?:*** "Geraldine 'Gerri' Whittington: A White House First," Spotlight Series, LBJL, accessed March 21, 2025, https://sites.google.com/view/spotlightseries-whittington/home.

67 **Forty Acres Club:** "Faculty Asked to Snub Club," *Austin American*, March 6, 1963.

67 **"Does the president know":** Purdum, *Idea Whose Time Has Come*, 175.

67 **"meant business," "stick-to-itiveness," and "imagination":** Helen Thomas, "LBJ Meant Business When He Pledged to End 'Stag' Gov't, Give Women Top Jobs," *Evening Express* (Portland, ME), August 18, 1964.

Chapter 6

69 **"My God":** Eric F. Goldman, *The Tragedy of Lyndon Johnson* (Alfred A. Knopf, 1969), 361.

69 **"the LBJ-all-the-way":** James Latimer, "State Democrats See Trip as Big Help in Campaign," *Richmond Times-Dispatch*, October 7, 1964.

69 **"still be heard":** "Mrs. Johnson's Visit Is First for Suffolk," *Suffolk News-Herald*, October 7, 1964.

70 **"as far as anyone":** Robertson, "First Lady's Whistle-Stop Tour."

70 **"one of your famous sons":** "Lady Bird's Whistle-Stop: Suffolk, VA: 10/6/64, 12:18 PM," TheLBJLibrary, October 5, 2014, YouTube video, 13:52, https://www.youtube.com/watch?v=HFX6pN8TsZU.

70 **"This is a great day":** "Lady Bird's Whistle-Stop: Suffolk, VA."

70 **caused a commotion:** J. Harvie Wilkinson III, *Harry Byrd and the Changing Face of Virginia Politics 1945–1966* (University Press of Virginia, 1968), 257.

71 **calculated political risk:** Frank B. Atkinson, *The Dynamic Dominion: Realignment and the Rise of Two-Party Competition in Virginia, 1945–1980*, 2nd rev. ed. (Rowman & Littlefield, 2006), 161.

71 ***Brown v. Board of Education* and *Brown II*:** Bryan J. Daugherity, "Desegrega-

NOTES

tion in Public Schools," in *Encyclopedia Virginia*, last updated February 18, 2025, https://encyclopediavirginia.org/entries/desegregation-in-public-schools/.

71 **a term coined by Byrd:** James H. Hershman, "Massive Resistance," in *Encyclopedia Virginia*, last updated February 18, 2025, https://encyclopediavirginia.org/entries/massive-resistance/.

71 **rebrand his image:** Michael Lee Pope, *The Byrd Machine in Virginia: The Rise and Fall of a Conservative Political Organization* (History Press, 2022), 137.

72 **"I don't think there's:** "Lady Bird's Whistle-Stop: Suffolk, VA."

72 **"should make this community":** "Politics Move into High Gear Locally," *Suffolk News-Herald*, October 8, 1964.

72 **"I noticed one or two":** "Lady Bird's Whistle-Stop: Suffolk, VA."

72 **"the high point":** "Politics Move."

72 **"I'm glad that we live":** "Lady Bird's Whistle-Stop: Suffolk, VA."

72 **"The young lady":** "Politics Move."

73 **"truly was in a":** "Signs of a New South Hailed by First Lady, Visible Here," *New Journal and Guide* (Norfolk, VA), October 10, 1964.

73 **"markedly integrated":** "Signs of a New South."

73 **151 Black students:** "School Desegregation in Norfolk, Virginia: The Norfolk 17," Old Dominion University Libraries, accessed February 11, 2025, https://exhibits.lib.odu.edu/exhibits/show/sdinv/the-norfolk-17.

73 **"We had to prove" and "It was hard":** "'Norfolk 17' Reunite Over Integration," *Register* (Danville, VA), December 28, 1981.

73 **her younger brother's hand:** Heather McGinley, "Norfolk 17 Inspires New Generation," *Suffolk News-Herald*, March 1, 2011.

74 **"warmly greeted":** "Signs of a New South."

74 **stop the car:** Obie McCollum, "Lady Bird Sells LBJ All the Way on Visit," *New Journal and Guide* (Norfolk, VA), October 10, 1964.

74 **"grasped outstretched hands":** "Signs of a New South."

74 **"delivered some belts":** Leslie Carpenter, "Lady Bird Cautions South About Future," *Amarillo Globe-Times*, October 6, 1964.

74 **"the word 'yes'":** "Remarks by Mrs. Lyndon B. Johnson, Norfolk, Virginia," press release, October 6, 1964, "Mrs. Johnson—Speeches," Reference File, LBJL, https://www.discoverlbj.org/item/ref-ctjspeeches-19641006-1215.

75 **"These are fairly":** Bruce Phillips, "'Y'Alls' Out in Force to Greet Mrs. Johnson as Lady Bird Special Crosses U.S. South," *Calgary Herald* (Alberta, Canada), October 7, 1964.

75 **"missed the boat" and "If a woman announces":** Pat Saltonstall, "Wife's Crowds Impress Johnson," *Evening Star* (Washington, DC), October 7, 1964.

75 **at a siding outside the city:** McDowell, "First Lady Employs Soft-Sell Approach."

Chapter 7

77 **SWING ALONG and TAR HEELS LOVE:** "Crowds Greet Mrs. Johnson on N.C. Trip," *Daily Tar Heel* (Chapel Hill, NC), October 7, 1964.

78 **"I got up":** Johnson, *White House Diary*, 199.

78 **"settled down to knowing":** Lady Bird Johnson, audio diary and annotated transcript, March 27, 1965, Lady Bird Johnson's White House Diary Collection, LBJL, https://www.discoverlbj.org/item/ctjd-19650327.

78 **"This is the second biggest":** Mary Pakenham, "Carnival Air Attends Tour by Lady Bird," *Chicago Tribune*, October 7, 1964.

78 **"This is the biggest":** "Crowds Greet Mrs. Johnson."

78 **"dashed under the wheels":** Roy Parker Jr., "Mrs. Johnson and Lynda Whistle at State," *News and Observer* (Raleigh, NC), October 7, 1964.

79 **"The Negro voter realizes":** "NAACP Still Quiet on Choice for Governor," *Burlington (NC) Daily Times-News*, October 10, 1964.

79 **"issues involving equality":** "Freedom News," *Crisis* 71, no. 7 (August-September 1964): 457–64, https://www.crmvet.org/docs/640900_naacp_crisis-r.pdf.

79 **"Even more strongly" through "not even made a good Senator":** "Why Lyndon Johnson Must Be Elected," *Saturday Evening Post*, September 19, 1964.

80 **more than two hundred years:** "'Saturday Evening Post' Breaks Tradition to Endorse Johnson," *New York Times*, September 15, 1964, https://www.nytimes.com/1964/09/15/archives/saturday-evening-post-breaks-tradition-to-endorse-johnson.html.

80 **"We are profoundly":** "Episcopalians Decry Goldwater's 'Racism,'" *Indianapolis Recorder*, October 17, 1964.

80 **"She has for us":** "Lady Bird's Whistle-Stop: Ahoskie, NC: 10/6/64, 4:22 PM," TheLBJLibrary, October 5, 2014, YouTube video, 18:02, https://www.youtube.com/watch?v=xeLdGeWYu5E.

81 **"I just can't tell you":** "Lady Bird's Whistle-Stop: Ahoskie, NC."

81 **"got down to":** James Ross, "'Special' Setting Records," *Greensboro Daily News*, October 7, 1964.

81 **"When I look at" through "down the line":** "Lady Bird's Whistle-Stop: Ahoskie, NC."

82 **"Lady Bird special issue," "while he had," and "The time for":** Ross, "'Special' Setting Records."

82 **"This is a thrilling":** "Lady Bird's Whistle-Stop: Ahoskie, NC."

82 **BYE, BYE, BIRDIE:** "Ahoskie 'How Do' Starts Lady Bird's N. Carolina Tour," *News-Herald* (Murfreesboro, NC), October 7, 1964.

Chapter 8

83 **"marvelous welcome":** "Lady Bird's Whistle-Stop: Tarboro, NC: 10/6/64, 5:43 PM," TheLBJLibrary, October 5, 2014, YouTube video, 3:36, https://www.youtube.com/watch?v=pfGV-tru0yM.

NOTES

84 **"I just want" and "Don't let anybody"**: "Lady Bird's Whistle-Stop: Tarboro, NC."

84 **"whoop and holler"**: Jim Nichols and Farnum Gray, "Mrs. Johnson and Daughter Speak Briefly," *Evening Telegram* (Rocky Mount, NC), October 7, 1964.

84 **"the dissenting spectators"**: Ed Hodges, "On Train, Everyone Had a Role," *Durham Morning Herald*, October 7, 1964.

84 **"I was born" through "worked or lived"**: "Lady Bird's Whistle-Stop: Rocky Mount, NC: 10/6/64, 6:14 PM," TheLBJLibrary, October 5, 2014, YouTube video, 13:04, https://www.youtube.com/watch?v=l35npDz8gg8.

85 **"He felt poverty"**: Carpenter, *Ruffles and Flourishes*, 14.

85 **"College was closed"**: "LBJ in Cotulla," LBJ Museum San Marcos, accessed February 12, 2025, https://lbjmuseum.com/exhibits/online-exhibits/lbj-in-cotulla.

85 **"brought many lessons"**: "Lady Bird's Whistle-Stop: Rocky Mount, NC."

85 **"unconditional war on poverty"**: Lyndon B. Johnson, "State of the Union," January 8, 1964, Miller Center, University of Virginia, transcript and audio, 40:33, https://millercenter.org/the-presidency/presidential-speeches/january-8-1964-state-union.

85 **"equip him"**: "Lady Bird's Whistle-Stop: Rocky Mount, NC."

86 **"I'd rather work"**: Sitton, "Mrs. Johnson's Southern Trip."

86 **"all you young people"**: Robertson, "First Lady's Whistle-Stop Tour."

86 **"No one has" and "two lively examples"**: "Remarks by Mrs. Lyndon B. Johnson, Wilson, North Carolina," press release, October 6, 1964, "Mrs. Johnson—Speeches," Reference File, LBJL, https://www.discoverlbj.org/item/ref-ctjspeeches-19641006-1745.

86 **"An urbane man" and "shouting spellbinder"**: Arthur Edson, "Lady Bird Woos South for Mate," *State Journal* (Lansing, MI), October 14, 1964.

86 **"Don't let anybody" through "you name it, we got it"**: Robertson, "First Lady's Whistle-Stop Tour."

87 **"had perfected a tag line"**: Robertson, "First Lady's Whistle-Stop Tour."

87 **"You know what I want?"**: Nan Robertson, *The Girls in the Balcony: Women, Men, and the New York Times* (Random House, 1992), 73.

87 **"You are good enough"**: Robertson, *Girls in the Balcony*, 75.

87 **"It will come as a"**: Robertson, *Girls in the Balcony*, 76.

88 **"quite simply"**: Robertson, *Girls in the Balcony*, 77.

88 **"should not be"**: Marilyn Bender quoted in Marilyn S. Greenwald, *A Woman of the Times: Journalism, Feminism, and the Career of Charlotte Curtis* (Ohio University Press, 1999), 62.

88 **"courts, crimes, storms"**: Robertson, *Girls in the Balcony*, 97.

88 **"like a men's club"**: Robertson, *Girls in the Balcony*, 103.

88 **"the most political"**: Robertson, "Our New First Lady."

88 **"LBJ...all the way"**: "Lady Bird's Whistle-Stop: Selma, NC 10/6/64, 7:38 PM,"

TheLBJLibrary, October 5, 2014, YouTube video, 25:21, https://www.youtube.com/watch?v=TqXKJkSMsjg.
88 **a telegram:** "Lady Bird's Whistle-Stop: Selma, NC."
89 **"May I exact":** "Lady Bird's Whistle-Stop: Selma, NC."
89 **"It had been quite":** Barbour, "Lady Bird Demonstrates."

Chapter 9

91 **to be kept closed:** "Johnson Appeals to NC Farmers, Stresses Price Support Program," Cora Kemp, *Technician* (North Carolina State, Raleigh), October 7, 1964.
91 **"the children all smiling":** Johnson, *White House Diary*, 3.
91 **"a gala air":** Johnson, *White House Diary*, 4.
92 **"Get down!":** Robert A. Caro, *The Passage of Power: The Years of Lyndon Johnson* (Vintage Books, 2013), 313.
92 **"He's hit!":** Caro, *Passage of Power*, 314.
92 **"Lyndon's a good man":** Carpenter, *Ruffles and Flourishes*, 53.
92 **"even on that":** Carpenter, *Ruffles and Flourishes*, 54.
92 **"There is that sense":** Lady Bird Johnson, audio diary and annotated transcript, November 24, 1963, Lady Bird Johnson's White House Diary Collection, LBJL, https://www.discoverlbj.org/item/ctjd-19631124. (Audio and transcript differ slightly; audio cited.)
93 **"At least his man":** Caro, *Passage of Power*, 345.
93 **"In these days":** W. H. Lawrence, "Johnson Is Nominated for Vice President; Kennedy Picks Him to Placate the South," *New York Times*, July 15, 1960, https://archive.nytimes.com/www.nytimes.com/library/politics/camp/600715convention-dem-ra.html.
93 **"Equally surprising":** Lawrence, "Johnson Is Nominated."
93 **"Bird and I talked":** Ruth Montgomery, "LBJ Selects Clothes for His Lady Bird," *Detroit Free Press*, April 29, 1964.
93 **"pledged warm and friendly":** Lawrence, "Johnson Is Nominated."
93 **"Lyndon would never":** Robertson, "Our New First Lady."
93 **"This is a sad time":** "Remarks at Andrews AFB following the Assassination of John F. Kennedy, 11/22/63," TheLBJLibrary, May 15, 2012, YouTube video, 1:12, https://www.youtube.com/watch?v=GsOXuCrQ4g8.
94 **"suddenly on stage":** Smith, "'Don't Fence Me In.'"
94 **"As the shock":** "Our New First Lady," *Winston-Salem Journal*, December 14, 1963.
94 **"an island of peace":** Anne Hannan, "Mrs. Lyndon Johnson Is for Jackie," *Newsday* (Hempstead, NY), October 5, 1960.
94 **"I know he can then":** Anne Hannan, "With Mrs. Johnson LBJ Comes First," *Newsday* (Hempstead, NY), November 23, 1963.

NOTES

- 94 **"The whole country"**: Johnson, *White House Diary*, 16.
- 94 **"committed matrimony"**: Eugenia Boehringer Lasseter, interview by Michael L. Gillette, March 10, 1981, transcript, LBJ Library Oral Histories, LBJL, https://www.discoverlbj.org/item/oh-lassetere-19810310-1-83-31.
- 95 **"a notoriously"**: Robertson, "Our New First Lady."
- 95 **"He was marvelous"**: Mark K. Updegrove, *Indomitable Will: LBJ in the Presidency* (Crown, 2012), 73.
- 95 **"She has made"**: Hannan, "With Mrs. Johnson."
- 95 **"wife, confidante"**: Flora Rheta Schreiber, "Lady Bird Johnson or Emily Lodge: What Kind of Second Lady Would She Be?," *Progress-Index* (Petersburg-Colonial Heights, VA), October 23, 1960.
- 95 **"I never saw her"**: Robertson, "Our New First Lady."
- 95 **"I thought it was fine"**: Robertson, "Our New First Lady."
- 95 **"That's enough"**: Bruce Biossat, "Second Lady of the Land Also Serves Her Country," *Wichita Falls (TX) Times*, June 30, 1963.
- 96 **"Bird would be"**: Robertson, "Our New First Lady."
- 96 **"That's just like Lyndon"**: "Victory Over Communism Big Issue, Says Tower," *Free Lance-Star* (Fredericksburg, VA), October 22, 1964.
- 96 **"Throughout my political career"**: Liz Carpenter, "Women in Government and Politics," box 3, folder 53, Jan Sanders Papers, DeGolyer Library, Southern Methodist University.
- 96 **"the LBJ brand"**: "LBJs Whistlestop in North Carolina," *Wilmington News*, October 6, 1964.
- 96 **"It has been" and "was fresh out"**: "First Lady Arrives Late and Speechless," *News and Observer* (Raleigh, NC), October 7, 1964.
- 96 **"I'm sure we will"**: "First Lady Arrives Late."
- 97 **Dr. Travell always:** Lewine, "Lady Bird Special."
- 97 **"working the fences"**: E. W. Kenworthy, "LBJ Asks Equal Rights," *Austin American-Statesman*, October 10, 1964.
- 97 **"Welcome to" and "We're for you"**: Jim Srodes, "LBJ Gets Warm Hello from Airport Crowds," *Herald-Sun* (Durham, NC), October 7, 1964.
- 97 **"That's what I like"**: Adrian King, "Moore Meets Chief as He Jets in Here," *News and Observer* (Raleigh, NC), October 7, 1964.
- 98 **"It's good to be"**: Charles Craven, "Welcome! The Mob Roared," *News and Observer* (Raleigh, NC), October 7, 1964.
- 98 **"impossible" through "a fellow shaking hands"**: Harold H. Martin, "The Johnson Touch," *Saturday Evening Post*, October 31, 1964.
- 98 **"Hello, there"**: Craven, "Welcome! The Mob Roared."
- 98 **"This is Bill Miller Day"**: Bill Connelly, "N.C. GOP Worked to Stop Upstaging," *Winston-Salem Journal*, October 7, 1964.

99 **"Our teacher said"**: Louisa Craig, "Memories of Train Ride Will Linger Long," *Herald* (Rock Hill, SC), October 8, 1964.

99 **"Kiss her!"**: Craven, "Welcome! The Mob Roared."

99 **"Smile, Dan, smile"**: Annie Lee Singletary, "It's 'Lady's Day' Across the State," *Twin City Sentinel* (Winston-Salem, NC), October 7, 1964.

99 **"How many bands"** through **"what I was doing"**: Reg Murphy, "It's an Hour of Triumph for State's Larry Lloyd," *Atlanta Constitution*, January 18, 1965.

100 **"Need beefing up"** and **"I'll be there"**: Carpenter, interview by Frantz.

100 **"had brought into power"**: Carpenter, *Ruffles and Flourishes*, 152.

100 **"If we lose North Carolina"**: Liz Carpenter to Lyndon B. Johnson, box 1, folder "Lady Bird Johnson's Advance Notebook, 'Lady Bird Special,' Oct. 6–9, 1964 [2 of 3]," Lady Bird Johnson's Advance Notebooks, 1964, White House Social Files, LBJL.

100 **"befitting a lady"**: Carpenter, *Ruffles and Flourishes*, 152.

101 **"they had never seen"**: Robert S. McNeill, "Stunningly Big Carolina Crowd Welcomes LBJ," *Sacramento Bee*, October 7, 1964.

101 **"an unforgettable"**: "Remarks of the President, Mrs. Lyndon B. Johnson, and Miss Lynda Bird Johnson, Coliseum, North Carolina State College of the University of North Carolina," October 6, 1964, box 177, folder "Johnson, Pres.: Campaign Speech, Oct. 6/64," Records of the Democratic National Committee, LBJL.

101 **"This is about"**: "State Democrats Share Platform," *Anderson (IN) Daily Bulletin*, October 7, 1964.

101 **"I knew that Mrs. Johnson"** and **"political business"**: "Remarks of the President, Mrs. Johnson, and Miss Lynda Bird Johnson."

101 **"virtues and flaws"** and **"generally excellent"**: Johnson, *Vantage Point*, 94–95.

101 **"Stay in"**: Johnson, *Vantage Point*, 94.

102 **"the nation would"**: Johnson, *Vantage Point*, 95.

102 **"decision had come"**: Johnson, *Vantage Point*, 97.

102 **the following note:** Johnson, *White House Diary*, 192.

102 **"In a few words"**: Johnson, *Vantage Point*, 98.

103 **a landslide victory:** "Lyndon B. Johnson: Domestic Affairs," Miller Center, University of Virginia, accessed February 13, 2025, https://millercenter.org/president/lbjohnson/domestic-affairs.

103 **"to woo them"**: Peter Lisagor, "Dempsey and Dewey Lessons Spur Johnson's Handshaking," *Chicago Daily News*, October 13, 1964.

103 **"He needed contact"**: Marie Fehmer Chiarodo, interview by Michael L. Gillette, October 29, 1974, transcript, LBJ Library Oral Histories, LBJL, https://www.discoverlbj.org/item/oh-chiarodom-19741029-3-99-32.

103 **"crucial to his"**: Russell Clay, "Johnson, Lady Bird Talk Here," *News and Observer* (Raleigh, NC), October 6, 1964.

NOTES

103 **"Politics is the people's business"**: This and all other quotes from LBJ's Raleigh speech are from "Remarks of the President, Mrs. Johnson, and Miss Lynda Bird Johnson."

104 **"evangelistic fervor"**: "Johnson Asserts Freedom Gaining," *Twin City Sentinel* (Winston-Salem, NC), October 7, 1964.

104 **"The arts of the"**: Perry Morgan, "Raleigh Saw the President and LBJ, Master Politician," *Charlotte News*, October 7, 1964.

105 **"sit down" and "If other people"**: Bill Kirkland, "Attempt to Block Train Threatened," *Durham Morning Herald*, October 7, 1964.

Chapter 10

107 **"snowballing remarkably"**: "Dixie 'Snowball' Thrills Lady Bird," *Evening Press* (Binghamton, NY), October 7, 1964.

107 **"three weeks long"**: Rixie Hunter, "Mrs. Johnson Given Big Welcome on Tour across Piedmont N.C.," *Twin City Sentinel* (Winston-Salem, NC), October 7, 1964.

107 **"were both lassoed"**: James Latimer, "Support for Johnson Voiced in Two States," *Richmond Times-Dispatch*, October 8, 1964.

108 **"Dan Moore Greets Presidential Plane"**: *Daily Tar Heel* (Chapel Hill, NC), October 7, 1964.

108 **"If there is anybody"**: Jesse Poindexter, "Moore Finally Endorses Johnson," *Winston-Salem Journal*, October 8, 1964.

108 **"could take great"**: Alex R. Preston, "Johnson Visit Is Seen as Virginia Hopes Rise," *Evening Star* (Washington, DC), October 7, 1964.

108 **Privately, he now**: "Johnsons Hailed on Trip to South," *New York Times*, October 7, 1964, https://www.nytimes.com/1964/10/07/archives/johnsons-hailed-on-trip-to-south-moore-of-carolina-is-only-leader.html.

108 **estimated 70,000 people**: Helen Thomas, "Lady Bird Stresses Education, Johnsons' Southern Heritage," *Columbia Missourian*, October 7, 1964.

108 **"the surprise"**: Leslie Carpenter, "Lady Bird Cautions South About Future," *Amarillo Globe-Times*, October 6, 1964.

108 **"not-so-secret"**: Roy Parker Jr., "Tar Heel Reception Surprising," *Winston-Salem Journal*, October 8, 1964.

108 **"It would appear"**: Lou Hiner Jr., "Soft Sell Works for Lady Bird on Dixie Tour," *Indianapolis News*, October 7, 1964.

108 **"the first hint"**: "Dixie 'Snowball' Thrills Lady Bird."

108 **"really on the road"**: Cliff Blue, "People & Issues," *Bladen (Elizabethtown, NC) Journal*, October 15, 1964.

109 **"is a part"**: "Democrats Might Find Turning Point in Visit by President," *Daily Times-News* (Burlington, NC), October 7, 1964.

109 **"the President's stock"**: Poindexter, "Moore Finally Endorses Johnson."

109 **"rather special Texas flavor"**: Ozzie Osborne, "First Lady Shows Flair for Touring," *Roanoke World-News*, October 7, 1964.

109 **From a table**: Hunter James, "Wacky World Spins on Campaign Rails," *Greensboro Record*, October 7, 1964.

110 **"The political nature"**: "Cordial Welcome to the First Lady," *Durham Morning Herald*, October 7, 1964.

110 **"We want to make"**: "Cordial Welcome."

110 **"probably more newsworthy"**: Blue, "People & Issues."

110 **"I don't know when"**: "Lady Bird's Whistle-Stop: Durham, NC: 10/7/64, 7:04 AM," TheLBJLibrary, October 5, 2014, YouTube video, 14:40, https://www.youtube.com/watch?v=7fyDOFkmGg8.

111 **"warmed to the fray"**: Thomas, "Lady Bird Stresses Education."

111 **"turned two blind mules"**: "Lady Bird's Whistle-Stop: Durham, NC."

111 **"battle of the placards"**: Dan Donahue, "Record of President Is Cited," *Durham Sun*, October 7, 1964.

111 **"Old Goldwater fools"**: Donnie Moore, "Lynda Is Politician, Too," *Durham Sun*, October 7, 1964.

111 **Zetas Welcome and "She told me"**: Carole Currie, "Personally…," *Durham Morning Herald*, October 8, 1964.

111 **"first in the hearts"**: Bill Kirkland, "'In Our Hearts We KNOW Who's Right,' Says Lynda," *Durham Morning Herald*, October 8, 1964.

111 **"proud of her father"**: Moore, "Lynda Is Politician, Too."

112 **"the problem that"**: Betty Friedan, *The Feminine Mystique* (Dell, 1963), 15.

112 **"burst like a boil"**: Friedan, *The Feminine Mystique*, 17.

112 **"this toothache"**: Friedan, *The Feminine Mystique*, 17.

112 **"In the pre-19th Amendment"**: Friedan, *The Feminine Mystique*, 18–19.

113 **"that a woman"**: Dorothy Stockbridge, "Lady Bird Says Tour Is Success," *Tampa Tribune*, October 10, 1964.

113 **"a wife, mother"**: Goldman, *Tragedy of Lyndon Johnson*, 369.

113 **"a daily working job"**: "Biography of Mrs. Lyndon B. Johnson," n.d., box 11, folder "Whistle-Stop [3 of 6]," Liz Carpenter Subject Files, White House Social Files, LBJL, https://www.discoverlbj.org/item/whsf-lc-subject-b11-f10.

113 **"We now have"**: Richard Wilson, April 1964, cited in "What the Writers Say About Mrs. Lyndon B. Johnson," box 11, folder "Whistle-Stop [3 of 6]," Liz Carpenter Subject Files, White House Social Files, LBJL, accessed February 13, 2025, https://www.discoverlbj.org/item/whsf-lc-subject-b11-f10.

113 **"In an age"**: Margaret Mead, "Mrs. Lyndon B. Johnson: A New Kind of First Lady?," *Redbook*, July 1965, 12.

113 **"Mrs. Johnson is giving"**: Mead, "Mrs. Lyndon B. Johnson."

NOTES

113 **"zest and sanity"**: "Zest and Sanity from Lady Bird," *Life*, July 10, 1964, 4.
113 **"Don't Fear"**: "Lady Bird: Femininity, Brains Mix," *Minneapolis Star*, June 9, 1964.
113 **"Radcliffe Seniors"**: "Radcliffe Seniors Hear Lady Bird Describe the Modern U.S. Woman," *Bennington (VT) Banner*, June 9, 1964.
113 **"Time has brought" and all other quotes from Radcliffe speech**: Lady Bird Johnson, "The Total Woman," baccalaureate address, Radcliffe College, Cambridge, MA, June 9, 1964, transcript, box 11, folder "Whistle-Stop [3 of 6]," Liz Carpenter Subject Files, White House Social Files, LBJL, https://www.discoverlbj.org/item/whsf-lc-subject-b11-f10.
114 **called out laws**: "1st Lady Lauds Wyoming Women in Winning West," *Greeley Tribune*, August 17, 1964.
114 **"Don't hold back" and "potential of strength"**: Lady Bird Johnson, "New Horizons for Women," speech, National Convention of American Home Economics Association, Detroit, MI, June 24, 1964, transcript, box 11, folder "Whistle-Stop [3 of 6]," Liz Carpenter Subject Files, White House Social Files, LBJL, https://www.discoverlbj.org/item/whsf-lc-subject-b11-f10.
114 **"There are no cabinet"**: Lady Bird Johnson, "A Woman's Look at the War on Poverty," speech, Kentucky Federation of Women's Clubs Annual Convention, Lexington, KY, May 21, 1964, transcript, box 11, folder "Whistle-Stop [3 of 6]," Liz Carpenter Subject Files, White House Social Files, LBJL, https://www.discoverlbj.org/item/whsf-lc-subject-b11-f10.
115 **"The women of this"**: "Remarks by Mrs. Lyndon B. Johnson, Reception Given by Miss Frances McGovern, Candidate for Congress, Honoring Mrs. Johnson, Ballroom of the Sheraton Hotel, Akron, Ohio," press release, September 17, 1964, folder "Mrs. Johnson—Speeches," Reference File, LBJL, https://www.discoverlbj.org/item/ref-ctjspeeches-19640917-1500.
115 **"to make the distaff"**: "Lady Bird's White House Plans," *San Francisco Examiner*, January 17, 1964.
115 **"as one of the highlights"**: "Cordial Welcome."

Chapter 11

117 **"Why can't Lady Bird" and all other quotes from this editorial**: "Come and Visit Us, Lady Bird," *Daily Times-News* (Burlington, NC), September 28, 1964.
117 **Elon College**: Now Elon University.
118 **an update**: "Lady Bird to Stop in Burlington During Tour," *Daily Times-News* (Burlington, NC), September 30, 1964.
118 **"With every turn"**: "Lady Bird's Whistle-Stop: Burlington, NC: 10/7/64, 8:10 AM," TheLBJLibrary, October 5, 2014, YouTube video, 5:41, https://www.youtube.com/watch?v=8eXhnmQhG9k.

118 **"We did everything" and "one of the most":** "Elaborate Precautions Taken for Local Visit," *Daily Times-News* (Burlington, NC), October 7, 1964.
119 **"The Goldwater camp":** "Chilled Air of Morning Turns Warm for Lady Bird," *Daily Times-News* (Burlington, NC), October 7, 1964.
119 **"I don't know what":** "Chilled Air of Morning."
119 **"I'm glad it's over":** Connor Jones, "Local Democrats Happy with Event," *Daily Times-News* (Burlington, NC), October 7, 1964.
119 **"Nineteen cars":** Dorothy Ann Benjamin, "Excited Crowd Sees Nation's First Lady," *Greensboro (NC) Record*, October 7, 1964.
120 **signs:** Benjamin, "Excited Crowd"; Gene Whitman, "Color, Noise, Excitement Herald 'Special's' Arrival," *Twin City Sentinel* (Winston-Salem, NC), October 7, 1964.
120 **"We hear about" through "Y-E-E-S":** Hunter, "Mrs. Johnson Given Big Welcome"; "'Lady Bird Special' Rolls South, Meets Enthusiasm," *Oakland (CA) Tribune*, October 7, 1964.
121 **"turned out":** Benjamin, "Excited Crowd."
121 **"Your Greensboro had" through "need you":** "Lady Bird's Whistle-Stop: Greensboro, NC: 10/7/64, 8:53 AM," TheLBJLibrary, October 5, 2014, YouTube video, 13:16, https://www.youtube.com/watch?v=5WbzTd96baY.
121 **"Yes, I'm going":** Benjamin, "Excited Crowd."

Chapter 12

123 **"This is a rough one":** David Cooper, "Crowds Whoop It Up for Lady Bird," *Winston-Salem Journal*, October 8, 1964.
124 **"LBJ for the USA":** Joe Brown, "Lady Bird Special Stops Here—Barely," *High Point (NC) Enterprise*, October 7, 1964.
124 **made headlines:** Almetta Cooke Brooks, "Lunch Counter Strikes Spread to High Point," *Greensboro (NC) Daily News*, February 12, 1960.
124 **continued to peacefully protest:** Kerry Robinson, "High Point High School Students Sit-In for U.S. Civil Rights, 1960," Global Nonviolent Action Database, Swarthmore College, February 2, 2014, https://nvdatabase.swarthmore.edu/content/high-point-high-school-students-sit-us-civil-rights-1960.
124 **another three years:** David Ford, "High Point High Schoolers' 1960 Sit-Ins Helped Pave the Way for Integration," WFDD, February 20, 2023, https://www.wfdd.org/story/high-point-high-schoolers-1960s-sit-ins-helped-pave-way-integration.
124 **"You're running after":** "Lady Bird Rolls Thru Bitter Honeysuckle," *Daily News* (New York City, NY), October 8, 1964.
124 **"They call this":** David Cooper, "Lady Bird Special Leaves 10,000 Agog at Ahoskie," *Winston-Salem Journal*, October 7, 1964.
124 **"I remember how wonderful":** Cooper, "Crowds Whoop It Up."

NOTES

125 **take a seat:** Braxton Younts, "Johnson Climbs Big Chair During Stop in Thomasville," *High Point (NC) Enterprise*, October 11, 1960.
125 **"I am overwhelmed":** Craig, "Memories of Train Ride."
125 **"hardly time to work":** Ed Chaffin, "Lady Bird Special—Like Carolina-Clemson Game on Wheels," *Index-Journal* (Greenwood, SC), October 8, 1964.
125 **"conducting a school play":** Luci Baines Johnson, interview by Michael Gillette, October 18, 2019, transcript, Bess Abell Oral History Project, Louie B. Nunn Center for Oral History, University of Kentucky Libraries, https://kentuckyoralhistory.org/ark:/16417/xt7c650439v80.
126 **"My only wish":** "Lady Bird's Whistle-Stop: Lexington, NC: 10/7/64, 10:22 AM," TheLBJLibrary, October 5, 2014, YouTube video, 3:26, https://www.youtube.com/watch?v=EfWreYiJs6Y.
126 **"Nothing could be finer":** "Lady Bird's Whistle-Stop: Salisbury, NC: 10/7/64, 10:50 AM,"TheLBJLibrary, October 5, 2014, YouTube video, 8:12, https://www.youtube.com/watch?v=scpHfUDqTjM.
126 **"bragged on her husband":** Homer Lucas, "Thousands Greet Lady Bird Special on Arrival Here," *Salisbury (NC) Evening Post*, October 7, 1964.
126 **"If I could vote":** Whitman, "Color, Noise, Excitement."
126 **"Old Prof.":** Dwayne Walls, "Old Prof Came on Special Request to Greet 1st Lady," *Charlotte Observer*, October 8, 1964.
126 **a renowned scholar:** James W. Byrd, "Brewer, John Mason," Handbook of Texas Online, last updated July 29, 2020, https://www.tshaonline.org/handbook/entries/brewer-john-mason.
127 **"I asked her to give":** Walls, "Old Prof."
127 **"I see all these":** "Lady Bird's Whistle-Stop: Salisbury, NC."
127 **lowered slightly the sign:** Ned Cline, "Color Galore at Reception," *Salisbury (NC) Evening Post*, October 7, 1964.
127 **"Who invited":** Cline, "Color Galore at Reception."
127 **"fled down the tracks":** McAden, "Lady Bird, Reporters."
127 **"Oh, darn":** Peter C. Kohler, "Hometown Boy Rides into Concord with Lady Bird, Lynda," *Charlotte Observer*, October 8, 1964.
128 **"With every stop":** "Lady Bird's Whistle-Stop: Concord, NC: 10/7/64, 11:23 AM," TheLBJLibrary, October 5, 2014, YouTube video, 3:28, https://www.youtube.com/watch?v=A2m63X7Sx7U.

Chapter 13

129 **"Is there gonna be":** John Kilgo, "'I Think Charlotte Likes My LBJ,' Says Lady Bird," *Charlotte News*, October 7, 1964.
129 **USE YOUR HEAD:** "Happy Pandemonium Rings for Lady Bird," *Charlotte Observer*, October 8, 1964.

130 **"I think Charlotte"**: Kilgo, "'I Think Charlotte Likes.'"
130 **Welcome Lady Bird**: "Happy Pandemonium Rings."
130 **"from all parts"**: Mildred Schroeder, "The First Family's Girl Friday," *San Francisco Examiner*, March 11, 1964.
130 **"heaped upon"**: Lee Winfrey, "Soft-Voiced Luci Emerges as Star," *Sunday Press* (Binghamton, NY), October 11, 1964.
131 **"hush-puppy grin"**: Lee Winfrey, "Boggs Plays Picador Role Well for 1st Lady," *Charlotte Observer*, October 8, 1964.
131 **"We had grits"**: Cooper, "Crowds Whoop It Up."
131 **"It was an unlawful"**: Roy Covington, "Fire Alarm at Square GOP Stunt?," *Charlotte Observer*, October 8, 1964.
131 **"We're running so strong"**: Kilgo, "'I Think Charlotte Likes.'"
131 **"wearing a red"**: Bob Saunders, "Thousands Line Route of Caravan," *Charlotte News*, October 7, 1964.
131 **"I am pleased"**: "Lady Bird's Whistle-Stop: Charlotte, NC: 10/7/64, 11:50 AM," TheLBJLibrary, October 5, 2014, YouTube video, 6:38, https://www.youtube.com/watch?v=-uD2JoEHAXU.
132 **"wisely"**: "That Southern First Lady," *Charlotte News*, October 8, 1964.
132 **"Your goals here"**: "Lady Bird's Whistle-Stop: Charlotte, NC."
132 **"merely another weapon" and he would give:** Walter R. Mears, "Barry Has Question: Is Rocky a Republican?," *Sacramento Bee*, October 25, 1963.
132 **"Make no mistake"**: "No Conventional A-Weapon: LBJ," *Register* (Santa Ana, CA), September 8, 1964.
133 **"unhesitatingly" and "We are convinced"**: "As We See It: The Case for Lyndon B. Johnson," *Kansas City Star*, August 30, 1964.
133 **"Who do you want"**: *Encyclopaedia Britannica*, s.v. "United States Presidential Election of 1964," by Michael Levy, last updated October 27, 2024, https://www.britannica.com/event/United-States-presidential-election-of-1964.
133 **The Daisy ad:** Robert Mann, "How the 'Daisy' Ad Changed Everything About Political Advertising," *Smithsonian*, April 13, 2016, https://www.smithsonianmag.com/history/how-daisy-ad-changed-everything-about-political-advertising-180958741/.
133 **"gave a lesson"**: Jim Srodes, "7,000 Greet Mrs. Johnson in 15-Minute Durham Visit," *Durham Herald*, October 8, 1964.
133 **"Lady Bird was the star" through "everybody gains"**: Joe Doster, "What It Was Up There on Platform Was Politicking," *Charlotte Observer*, October 8, 1964.
134 **"The President's chief emissary"**: "That Southern First Lady."

Chapter 14

135 **"Friendship Nine"**: Guha Shankar, "'Jail, No Bail': Tactics of Protest in the

NOTES

Freedom Struggle in Rock Hill, South Carolina," *Folklife Today* (blog), February 13, 2023, https://blogs.loc.gov/folklife/2023/02/jail-no-bail-tactics-of-protest-in-the-freedom-struggle-in-rock-hill-south-carolina/.

136 **garnered widespread publicity:** Eleanor Roosevelt, "Negroes Prefer Jail to Segregated Society," *Dayton Daily News*, February 6, 1961.

136 **A week later:** "Rock Hill Sit-Ins and Jail-No-Bail," Digital SNCC Gateway, accessed February 14, 2025, https://snccdigital.org/events/rock-hill-sit-ins-and-jail-no-bail.

136 **TO THE FREEDOM FIGHTERS:** *The Papers of Martin Luther King, Jr.*, ed. Clayborne Carson, vol. 7, *To Save the Soul of America, January 1961–August 1962*, ed. Tenisha Armstrong (University of California Press, 2014), 167–68.

137 **Freedom Riders:** "Freedom Rides," Martin Luther King, Jr. Research and Education Institute, Stanford University, accessed February 15, 2025, https://kinginstitute.stanford.edu/freedom-rides; "We Were Prepared to Die: Freedom Riders," Civil Rights Museum, accessed February 15, 2025, https://civilrightsmuseum.org/we-were-prepared-to-die-freedom-riders/.

137 **pulled into Rock Hill:** "John Lewis and Two Others Attacked at South Carolina Greyhound Bus Terminal," Equal Justice Initiative, accessed February 15, 2025, https://calendar.eji.org/racial-injustice/may/9.

137 **"I could tell":** John Lewis with Michael D'Orso, *Walking with the Wind: A Memoir of the Movement* (Harcourt Brace, 1998), 137.

137 **"standing square":** Lewis, *Walking with the Wind*, 138.

138 **"That was offensive":** Lady Bird Johnson, interview by Harry Middleton, August 1994, transcript, LBJ Library Oral Histories, LBJL, https://www.discoverlbj.org/item/oh-ctj-199408xx-38-11-46.

138 **"We work 'em":** Zephyr Wright, interview by Michael L. Gillette, December 5, 1974, transcript, LBJ Library Oral Histories, LBJL, https://www.discoverlbj.org/item/oh-wrightz-19741205-1-81-1.

138 **studied home economics:** "Black History Month at Wiley University," Wiley University, accessed March 1, 2025, https://www.wileyc.edu/black-history-month-february-2025. (Wiley College is now Wiley University.)

138 **"Mr. President, how did":** James Farmer, *Lay Bare the Heart: An Autobiography of the Civil Rights Movement* (Plume, 1986), 293.

139 **would no longer:** "Recipes from the President's Kitchen," NPR, February 19, 2008, https://www.npr.org/2008/02/19/19085244/recipes-from-the-presidents-kitchen.

139 **"They drove through":** Harry C. McPherson, interview by T. H. Baker, December 5, 1968, transcript, LBJ Library Oral Histories, LBJL, https://www.discoverlbj.org/item/oh-mcphersonh-19681205-1-74-210-a.

139 **"You deserve this":** "Recipes from the President's Kitchen."

140 **"They've never had"**: Eva Edelsburg, "Lady B. Johnson Stirs Rock Hill," *Evening Herald* (Rock Hill, SC), October 8, 1964.
140 **Signs proclaimed**: J. Walter Johnson Jr., "Signs Don't Bother the Johnson Party," *Evening Herald* (Rock Hill, SC), October 8, 1964.
140 **"I've got a chemistry test"**: Edelsburg, "Lady B. Johnson Stirs Rock Hill."
140 **The tempo picked up**: Events in Rock Hill are compiled from numerous newspaper articles, all dated October 8, 1964, including Herbert Johnson, "Rock Hill Security Is Noted," *Greenville (SC) News*; Pat J. McDonnell, "Lady B Wows 'Em in RH and Chester," *Evening Herald* (Rock Hill, SC); Edelsburg, "Lady B. Johnson Stirs Rock Hill"; Johnson, "Signs Don't Bother."
141 **"a Democrat—without prefix" and "the lone loyal"**: "Lady Bird's Whistle-Stop: Rock Hill, SC: 10/7/64, 1:37 PM," TheLBJLibrary, October 5, 2014, YouTube video, 12:32, https://www.youtube.com/watch?v=fbCn-74zPV4.
141 **"which always sounds"**: McDonnell, "Lady B Wows 'Em."
141 **"I know what South Carolina"**: "Lady Bird's Whistle-Stop: Rock Hill, SC."
142 **"My grandmother"**: "Lady Bird's Whistle-Stop: Rock Hill, SC."
142 **"left no doubt," "there was thunderous," and "some eyes turned"**: Claudia Howe, "All Eyes Focused on Her," *Charlotte Observer*, October 8, 1964.
142 **confided in Kara Burney and "getting reckless"**: Kara Burney to Liz Carpenter, folder "Report to the President and Mrs. Johnson on the 'Lady Bird Special' at Charleston, South Carolina," Papers of Cecil E. Burney, LBJL.
142 **"had given the whistle-stop workers"**: "The Charleston Story," folder "Report to the President and Mrs. Johnson on the 'Lady Bird Special' at Charleston, South Carolina," Papers of Cecil E. Burney, LBJL.
142 **"flowing, soft-toned"**: McDonnell, "Lady B Wows 'Em."
142 **"No matter their reason"**: Craig, "Memories of Train Ride."
142 **"I just want to let them"**: Edelsburg, "Lady B. Johnson Stirs Rock Hill."
143 **"I wanted to hear"**: Edelsburg, "Lady B. Johnson Stirs Rock Hill."
143 **public schools**: "Equalization Schools: South Carolina's History of Unequal Education," Lowcountry Digital History Initiative, accessed February 15, 2025, https://ldhi.library.cofc.edu/exhibits/show/equalization-schools/public-schools-desegregate.
143 **"I don't like Goldwater's" and "I've seen state"**: Rosalie Spaniel, "School Students Turn Out to Greet Lady Bird," *Evening Herald* (Rock Hill, SC), October 8, 1964.
143 **"I like that daughter"**: Edelsburg, "Lady B. Johnson Stirs Rock Hill."
143 **"Don't you dare eat that"**: Johnson, "Rock Hill Security Is Noted."

Chapter 15

145 **"became as southern"**: Sam Wood, "A Squelch by Lady Bird," *Austin American*, October 8, 1964.

NOTES

145 **"We want Lady Bug"**: Ted Shelton, "'Want Lady Bug,' Little Tyke Shouts," *Charlotte Observer*, October 8, 1964.

145 **"I'm very happy"**: "Lady Bird's Whistle-Stop: Chester, SC: 10/7/64, 2:16 PM," TheLBJLibrary, October 5, 2014, YouTube video, 12:31, https://www.youtube.com/watch?v=NdZlMBEqWH8.

146 **"In a pleasant departure"**: "New Note in Dixie."

146 **to which everyone and the first integrated:** Donald S. Russell, interview by Herbert S. Hartsook and Marcia Synnott, July 6, 1992, transcript, South Carolina Political Collections Oral History Project, University of South Carolina, https://digital.tcl.sc.edu/digital/collection/scpcot/id/41.

146 **"It's as easy to plan"** and **open-house policy:** "Virginia U. Russell."

146 **"I don't mind telling you"** through **"traveling through the South"**: "Lady Bird's Whistle-Stop: Chester, SC."

147 **"you could still detect"**: Craig, "Memories of Train Ride."

147 **"rail hopping"**: Craig, "Memories of Train Ride."

147 **recalled the gauntlet:** McLendon and Smith, *Don't Quote Me!*, 77.

147 **"It was physically"**: McLendon and Smith, *Don't Quote Me!*, 77.

147 **"there was too much"**: McLendon and Smith, *Don't Quote Me!*, 78.

148 **locate a runner:** Dickerson, *Among Those Present*, 127.

148 **"feed the story" and "protectively"**: Marlene Sanders and Marcia Rock, *Waiting for Prime Time: The Women of Television News* (Perennial, 1990), 52–53.

148 **toss copy:** Frances Lewine, interview by Anne S. Kasper, November 1991 to April 1993, transcript, Washington Press Club Foundation Oral History Project, Rare Book and Manuscript Library, Columbia University.

148 **"rather colorful language"**: John C. Goolrick, "LBJ Ladies Obvious Asset," *Free Lance-Star* (Fredericksburg, VA), October 6, 1964.

149 **"tried to think of"**: Carpenter, *Ruffles and Flourishes*, 160.

149 **"the classic trip"**: McLendon and Smith, *Don't Quote Me!*, 77.

149 **"grueling, grimy"**: Thomas, *Front Row at the White House*, 255.

149 **"the most incredible"**: Thomas, *Front Row at the White House*, 254.

149 **"fetching coffee" and "Being in a newsroom"**: Thomas, *Front Row at the White House*, 29.

150 **"kitchen sink"**: Thomas, *Front Row at the White House*, 35.

150 **"a brutal" through "tonic to them"**: Carpenter, *Ruffles and Flourishes*, 159.

150 **"hectic time ahead" and warning memo:** Carpenter, *Ruffles and Flourishes*, 157.

150 **"Mrs. Johnson was still talking"** through **"once in a while"**: Gloria Negri, "Meanwhile, Back at the Station," *Boston Globe*, October 11, 1964.

152 **several days earlier:** "'Lady Bird Special' Sets 6 S.C. Stops," *Salisbury (NC) Evening Post*, October 5, 1964.

152 **"turned politician" and "Vote Democratic"**: Robert McHugh, "Columbia Crowds Prove Receptive," *State* (Columbia, SC), October 8, 1964.

Chapter 16

153 **"jostling together" and "It's something like"**: Ed Chaffin, "Lady Bird Special—Like Carolina-Clemson Game on Wheels," *Index-Journal* (Greenwood, SC), October 8, 1964.

153 **Here in Columbia:** Events in Columbia are based on a compilation of sources: Liz Carpenter's *Ruffles and Flourishes*; newspaper articles, including Mont Morton, "And Some Came Just to Heckle," *State* (Columbia, SC), October 8, 1964, and Lewis Lord, "Handful of Youths Boo, Heckle Nation's First Lady in Columbia," *Greenville (SC) News*, October 8, 1964; and the audio recording "Lady Bird's Whistle-Stop: Columbia, SC: 10/7/64, 3:58 PM," TheLBJLibrary, October 5, 2014, YouTube video, 19:35, https://www.youtube.com/watch?v=6crN4jL1uCo.

154 **"It was so surprisingly"**: Carpenter, *Ruffles and Flourishes*, 160.

154 **"I am proud to be" through "proceed with this meeting"**: "Lady Bird's Whistle-Stop: Columbia, SC."

154 **"We want Strom"**: Lord, "Handful of Youths Boo."

154 **"I'm proud to have"**: "Lady Bird's Whistle-Stop: Columbia, SC."

155 **"You need manners"**: Morton, "And Some Came."

155 **"a beloved daughter" through "reelected President"**: "Lady Bird's Whistle-Stop: Columbia, SC."

155 **"I have learned something" through "the same coin"**: "Lady Bird's Whistle-Stop: Columbia, SC."

156 **"South Carolina wants Goldwater"**: "Hecklers Taunt Lady Bird in Sen. Thurmond Territory," *Patriot* (Harrisburg, PA), October 8, 1964.

156 **"Shocked, the crowd"**: Carpenter, *Ruffles and Flourishes*, 160.

156 **"She was a formidable foe"**: Boggs, *Washington Through a Purple Veil*, 191.

156 **"the real cold hostility"**: Lady Bird Johnson, audio diary and annotated transcript, April 19, 1965, Lady Bird Johnson's White House Diary Collection, LBJL, https://www.discoverlbj.org/item/ctjd-19650419.

156 **"My friends" through "thank you"**: "Lady Bird's Whistle-Stop: Columbia, SC."

157 **"We could weep"**: Nan Robertson, "First Lady Booed in South Carolina," *New York Times*, October 8, 1964.

157 **"deepest apologies"**: "USC President Sends Apology to Mrs. Johnson for Heckling," *Index-Journal* (Greenwood, SC), October 10, 1964.

157 **"GOP's Youthful Hecklers"**: Wood, "Squelch by Lady Bird."

157 **"Booing the First Lady"**: Robert McHugh, "Columbia Crowds Prove Receptive," *State* (Columbia, SC), October 8, 1964.

157 **"The Republican movement"**: McHugh, "Columbia Crowds Prove Receptive."

157 **"They were rude"**: "Hecklers Taunt Lady Bird."

157 **"do not live up"**: McHugh, "Columbia Crowds Prove Receptive."

NOTES

157 **"I think the crowds"**: McHugh, "Columbia Crowds Prove Receptive."
158 **"we had been advised"**: Carpenter, *Ruffles and Flourishes*, 160.
158 **"the most racially troubled"**: I. A. Newby, *Black Carolinians: A History of Blacks in South Carolina from 1895 to 1968* (University of South Carolina Press, 1973), 345.
158 **South Carolina State College**: Now South Carolina State University.
158 **Civil rights activists**: Details on Orangeburg history are from Newby, *Black Carolinians*, and "National Register of Historical Places Multiple Property Documentation Form: Resources Associated with the Civil Rights Movement in Orangeburg County, South Carolina," National Park Service, April 7, 1995, https://npgallery.nps.gov/GetAsset/8b8c7389-4166-461f-b403-15ee6 15e44be.
158 **"If put into effect"**: "Threats and Intimidations Reported Here," *Times and Democrat* (Orangeburg, SC), October 10, 1963.
159 **"reputed to be" and "animal life"**: Drew Gilpin Faust, *Necessary Trouble: Growing Up at Midcentury* (Farrar, Straus and Giroux, 2023), 181.
159 **attempted to approach**: Frank K. Myers, "Mostly Negro Youth Present for Occasion," *Times and Democrat* (Orangeburg, SC), October 8, 1964.
159 **"a sprinkling"**: Myers, "Mostly Negro Youth Present."
159 **Orangeburg Massacre**: Sam Watson, "SC State to Commemorate 57th Anniversary of Orangeburg Massacre on Saturday, Feb. 8," *Bulldog News*, SC State University, January 23, 2025, https://scsu.edu/news/2025_orangeburg_massacre _preview_01_23_25.php.
160 **"It all had the aura" and "We want them for"**: Amelia Speth, "It Sounded Like a College Rally," *Times and Democrat* (Orangeburg, SC), October 8, 1964.
160 **"whether one has"**: "Mrs. Johnson Visits Today," *Times and Democrat* (Orangeburg, SC), October 7, 1964.
160 **"incidents" and "particularly the"**: "T&D Readers Forum," *Times and Democrat* (Orangeburg, SC), October 18, 1964.
160 **"Keeping at a distance"**: Carpenter, *Ruffles and Flourishes*, 161.
160 **ORANGEBURG FOR GOLDWATER**: "Lady Bird Arrives Late But Loud," *Times and Democrat* (Orangeburg, SC), October 8, 1964.
160 **BLACK BIRD SPECIAL**: "Puts More Vigor into Voters," *Salisbury (NC) Evening Post*, October 8, 1964.
160 **erected a billboard**: Edson, "First Lady Real Pro."
160 **"I wanted to come here"**: "Lady Bird's Whistle-Stop: Orangeburg, SC: 10/7/64, 5:48 PM," TheLBJLibrary, October 7, 2014, YouTube video, 15:39, https://www .youtube.com/watch?v=5zBEPPpGvNQ.
161 **"We're glad we have"**: "Lady Bird's Whistle-Stop: Orangeburg, SC."
161 **"For the Negroes and"**: Myers, "Mostly Negro Youth Present."

Chapter 17

163 **You will work:** Instructions to Advance Women.
164 **"primarily heard reports":** "Charleston Story."
164 **"Are we going to have" through "shopping center":** Carpenter, *Ruffles and Flourishes*, 151.
165 **"Local Democrats were discouraged":** "Charleston Story."
165 **vandalized and "We are disturbed":** Charles Hunter, "Vandals Hit Democrats," *Charleston Evening Post*, October 5, 1964.
165 **"The three of us":** "Charleston Story."
166 **"obvious that we":** "Charleston Story."
166 **After graduating:** "Biography of Mrs. Cecil E. Burney (Kara)," press release, September 1964, box 11, folder "Whistle-Stop [4 of 6]," Liz Carpenter Subject Files, White House Social Files, LBJL, https://www.discoverlbj.org/item/whsf-lc-subject-b11-f11.
166 **"strongly Goldwater" and "one encounters":** "Charleston Story."
166 **"in a most decisive manner":** "Charleston Story."
167 **"hot beat" and "Jim Konduros lived":** "Charleston Story."
167 **white convertible:** "LBJ Supporters," *Charleston Evening Post*, October 6, 1964; "Thank-You Letters," folder "Report to the President and Mrs. Johnson on the 'Lady Bird Special' at Charleston, South Carolina," Papers of Cecil E. Burney, LBJL.
168 **"a hard time" and "built a respectable":** Burney to Carpenter.
168 **"will probably receive":** "Thank-You Letters."
168 **"This is to be their show":** Martha Carson, "Home-Grown Talent Rehearses," *News and Courier* (Charleston, SC), October 2, 1964.
169 **"Don't buy the line":** Instructions to Advance Women.
169 **"Another thing":** Instructions to Advance Women.
169 **"She cannot expect":** "First Lady in Politics," *News and Courier* (Charleston, SC), October 6, 1964.
169 **"not to 'be bashful'":** "Charleston Story."
169 **some two hundred talks:** "Biography of Mrs. Cecil E. Burney (Kara)."
170 **"most content," "out front," and "I am sure":** "Charleston Story."
170 **"We've got 4,000 balloons":** "Democrats Guessing on Crowd," *News and Courier* (Charleston, SC), October 7, 1964.
170 **about fifty young people:** Charles Pou, "Lady Bird at Savannah, Stresses Southern Ties," *Atlanta Journal*, October 8, 1964.
170 **"The hecklers came again":** Carpenter, *Ruffles and Flourishes*, 161.
170 **issued a statement:** "GOP Asks for Restraint During First Lady's Visit," *Charleston Evening Post*, October 1, 1964.
170 **"We question the propriety":** "Democrats Paving Way for Lady Bird," *News and Courier* (Charleston, SC), October 2, 1964.

170 **"While we deplore"**: "GOP Asks for Restraint."
171 **"more reminiscent"**: "Lady Bird's Whistle-Stop: Charleston, SC: 10/7/64, 7:29 PM," TheLBJLibrary, October 16, 2014, YouTube video, 46:29, https://www.youtube.com/watch?v=X3Vx8S-eDCQ.
171 **"'blackmail' editorial"**: "Charleston Story."
171 **"We say to the" and "The occasion may"**: "Time to Be Identified," *News and Courier* (Charleston, SC), October 7, 1964.
171 **"I don't know where"**: "Lady Bird's Whistle-Stop: Charleston, SC."
171 **"political spotlight"**: "Hitting at Meal Ticket," *Index-Journal* (Greenwood, SC), October 13, 1964.
172 **"I'm going to tell you this"**: "Lady Bird's Whistle-Stop: Charleston, SC."
172 **"However much this type"**: "Hitting at Meal Ticket."
172 **"Just holler on" and "Folks, I want to say"**: "Lady Bird's Whistle-Stop: Charleston, SC."
172 **"LBJ for the USA"**: Laurens H. Irby, "Lady Bird Makes Pitch for Democratic Victory," *News and Courier* (Charleston, SC), October 8, 1964.
172 **"Lady Bird, fly away," "What's the matter?" and "Oh, shut up"**: Hortense Roach, "Hecklers a Small But Noisy Group," *Charleston Evening Post*, October 8, 1964.
172 **"bread and butter"**: Carpenter, *Ruffles and Flourishes*, 161.
173 **"Mrs. Johnson should have" and "she maintained"**: Ashton Gonella, interview by Dorothy Pierce McSweeny, February 19, 1969, transcript, LBJ Library Oral Histories, LBJL, https://www.discoverlbj.org/item/oh-gonellaa-19690219-1-74-114.
173 **"its roots in the traditions" through "and their hopes"**: "Lady Bird's Whistle-Stop: Charleston, SC."
173 **"honored"**: "Charleston Story."
173 **"that people had changed"**: "Charleston Story."
173 **could do differently**: Lynda Johnson Robb, in discussion with the author, September 12, 2024.
174 **"knights in shining"**: Wauhillau La Hay, "Lady Bird Trades Lace for Iron Glove," *Pittsburgh Press*, October 9, 1964.
174 **"I will never forget"**: Lady Bird Johnson, audio diary and annotated transcript, April 19, 1965, Lady Bird Johnson's White House Diary Collection, LBJL, https://www.discoverlbj.org/item/ctjd-19650419.
174 **"This is a political year"**: La Hay, "Lady Bird Trades Lace."
174 **"Tell me about," "held up," and "Didn't you know?"**: Michael R. Beschloss, *Reaching for Glory: Lyndon Johnson's Secret White House Tapes, 1964–1965* (Touchstone, 2002), 47.
175 **"You want to listen" and all other quotes cited from this conversation**: Beschloss, *Taking Charge*, 272–73.

175 **"through every yard" and "called three or four":** Lyndon B. Johnson, "Remarks at a Fundraising Dinner," New Orleans, LA, October 9, 1964, transcript, LBJL, https://www.lbjlibrary.org/object/text/remarks-fundraising-dinner-new-orleans-10-09-1964.

175 **"just gave them hell" through "see you on Friday":** Beschloss, *Reaching for Glory*, 48–49.

Chapter 18

177 **"chilling" and "somewhat reluctantly":** Carpenter, *Ruffles and Flourishes*, 162.

177 **"grinned sheepishly" and "Well, not":** "Cheers Greet Lady Bird on Tour of Charleston," *Index-Journal* (Greenwood, SC), October 8, 1964.

178 **"They didn't say":** Carpenter, *Ruffles and Flourishes*, 162.

178 **"apparently had been":** Sam Wood, "Lady Bird Given Savannah Cheers," *Austin Statesman*, October 8, 1964.

178 **did not dissuade:** Maxine Cheshire, "Luci Gets the Youth Vote," *Washington Post*, October 9, 1964.

178 **"Join the Teenage":** "Cheers Greet Lady Bird."

178 **Nathaniel Russell House:** "Nathaniel Russell House," Historic Charleston Foundation, accessed April 14, 2025, https://www.historiccharleston.org/house-museums/nathaniel-russell-house.

179 **"practically everyone" and "She's probably trying":** Montgomery, "Capital Letter."

179 **Dock Street Theatre:** "Dock Street Theatre," Charleston Stage, accessed April 14, 2025, https://charlestonstage.com/about-us/dock-street-theatre.

179 **"the roof fell in":** Charles Hunter, "First Lady Spends 8 Quiet Minutes in St. Michael's," *Charleston Evening Post*, October 8, 1964.

179 **"Machiavellian technique" and "I don't think you ever":** Abell, interview by Baker, June 13, 1969.

179 **a man spit:** Ruth Cupp, "Lady Bird's Whistle-Stop Tour Gets Less Than Warm Welcome," *News and Courier* (Charleston, SC), September 27, 1990.

179 **"How terribly sorry":** Lady Bird Johnson to Ruth Williams, November 30, 1964, Ruth Williams Cupp Papers, Accession 467, box 1, folder 3, Louise Pettus Archives and Special Collections, Winthrop University.

180 **"You are mighty nice":** Ruth Williams to Lady Bird Johnson, December 8, 1964, Ruth Williams Cupp Papers, Accession 467, box 1, folder 3, Louise Pettus Archives and Special Collections, Winthrop University.

180 **"We're for Lyndon Johnson":** Montgomery, "Capital Letter."

180 **"So glad you came":** Jack Roach, "Mrs. Johnson Tours Town, Heads South," *Charleston Evening Post*, October 8, 1964.

180 **"What did you think?" through "a little bit sorry":** Carpenter, *Ruffles and Flourishes*, 162.

181 **"I was disappointed"**: "Lady Bird Sends Apologies to Area," *Beaufort (SC) Gazette*, October 15, 1964.
181 **"We've got something"**: Montgomery, "Capital Letter."

Chapter 19

183 **"U.S. Senators were"**: Montgomery, "Capital Letter."
183 **run over:** Dallek, *Lyndon B. Johnson*, 163.
183 **"It takes women"**: Montgomery, "Capital Letter."
184 **"How could I make" through "the Democratic ticket"**: Celestine Sibley, "Mrs. Herman Talmadge Makes Clear Her Position on LBJ," *Atlanta Constitution*, October 19, 1964.
184 **"It was the first time"**: Sibley, "Mrs. Herman Talmadge."
184 THIS IS GOLDWATER TERRITORY: Charles Pou, "Lady Bird's Trip Elates Sanders," *Atlanta Journal*, October 9, 1964.
184 **"sardine-can-like"**: Jim Sheppard, "First Lady Is Speaker at Rally," *Savannah Morning News*, October 9, 1964.
185 **"We were never certain"**: Boggs, *Washington Through a Purple Veil*, 192.
185 **kept a record:** Miller and Miller, interview by Frantz.
185 **"were rough"**: Clipping from an unidentified newspaper, box 3, folder 44, Jan Sanders Papers, DeGolyer Library, Southern Methodist University.
185 KHRUSCHEV LOVES LBJ: Maxine Cheshire, "Luci Gets the Youth Vote," *Washington Post*, October 9, 1964.
185 **"ought to welcome"**: Clipping from unidentified newspaper.
185 **concerned that violence:** Robb, discussion.
185 **In fact, one fight:** Wood, "Squelch by Lady Bird."
185 **"Johnson advance men" through "that's going to change"**: Mary Pakenham, "Mrs. Johnson Gets Mixed Reception in Tour of Georgia," *Chicago Tribune*, October 9, 1964.
186 **"First Lady Day"**: "First Lady Day Here Should Run Smoothly, Thanks in Part to Her," *Savannah Morning News*, October 4, 1964.
186 **"There is more custom"**: "Former Suffragette Now Battles in UN," *Florence (SC) Morning News*, February 21, 1966.
186 **an interview:** "First Lady Day Here."
186 **"not even during"**: Clipping from unidentified newspaper.
186 **"as having made" and "put the machinery"**: Junius Griffin, "Dr. King Pledges Aid for Johnson," *New York Times*, September 30, 1964, https://www.nytimes.com/1964/09/30/archives/dr-king-pledges-aid-for-johnson-says-negro-effort-to-defeat.html.
187 **"This can mean the balance"**: Griffin, "Dr. King Pledges Aid."
187 **"The role that is mine"**: Martin Luther King Jr., "Statement on Presidential

Endorsement," press release, November 1, 1960, Martin Luther King, Jr. Research and Education Institute, Stanford University, https://kinginstitute.stanford.edu/king-papers/documents/statement-presidential-endorsement.

187 **"I have had a philosophy" through "on even him"**: Alvin Adams, "SCLC Convention Bears Down," *Jet*, October 15, 1964.

188 **"The future is here too" through "flood of change"**: "Lady Bird's Whistle-Stop, Savannah, GA: 10/8/64, 11:50 AM," TheLBJLibrary, October 7, 2014, YouTube video, 7:16, https://www.youtube.com/watch?v=H7DmM7CU7RQ.

188 **"raucous and loud"**: Charles Pou, "Luci's the Star of Mom's Show," *Atlanta Journal*, October 9, 1964.

188 **"It seems to me" through "hands of government"**: "Lady Bird Special," ABC News, October 12, 1964, Assign #A082P15, ABCNews VideoSource, https://www.abcnewsvsource.com.

189 **"That young 'un"**: Celestine Sibley, "They Loved Luci on the Tour, and It Was Easy to See Why," *Atlanta Constitution*, October 14, 1964.

189 **LADY BIRD, LADY BIRD FLY AWAY and JOHNSON IS FOR KING**: "Lady Bird Ignores Catcalls," *Daily News* (NY, NY), October 9, 1964.

189 **"fifteen or twenty kids"**: Celestine Sibley, "It's a Bandwagon Now, Sanders Says as State Cheers for Lady Bird," *Atlanta Constitution*, October 9, 1964.

189 **"some of it pure hate"**: Jack Nelson, "Southeast Georgia Leans GOP but There's a Huge Silent Vote," *Atlanta Constitution*, October 27, 1964.

190 **THE GOLDWATER CLUB**: "Big Georgia Crowds Greet First Lady; Goldwater Backers Polite," *San Bernardino (CA) Daily Sun*, October 9, 1964.

190 **YOUNG MEN FOR LUCI**: Ann Waldron, "Down by the Station," *St. Petersburg (FL) Times*, October 9, 1964.

190 **"It's just wonderful"**: "Lady Bird's Whistle-Stop: Jesup, GA: 10/8/64, 2:27 PM," TheLBJLibrary, October 7, 2014, YouTube video, 12:14, https://www.youtube.com/watch?v=-8MFtcU0Z8Q.

190 **"You couldn't have"**: "Lady Bird's Whistle-Stop: Jesup, GA."

191 **"Operation Skyhook" through "drive the car to town"**: "Operation Skyhook for the Lady Bird Special," box 1, folder "Lady Bird Special—Whistlestop Tour [1 of 2]," Personal Papers of Lindy Boggs, LBJL.

191 **"never made a jollier"**: Celestine Sibley, "Has 'Lady Bird Special' Set Pattern for Presidents' Wives?," *Atlanta Constitution*, October 13, 1964.

192 **"strong Goldwater flavor"**: "Cheers, Heckling Greet Lady Bird," *Macon Telegraph*, October 9, 1964.

192 **Welcome First Lady**: "Lady Bird Finds Georgians Friendly," *Greenville (SC) News*, October 9, 1964.

192 **"one of the most trying"**: Marie Smith, "Lady Bird Combs Mob Right Out of Hair," *Washington Post*, November 5, 1960.

NOTES

192 **significant margins:** Gary A. Donaldson, *The First Modern Campaign: Kennedy, Nixon, and the Election of 1960* (Rowman & Littlefield, 2007), 136.

192 **largely women and "counterfeit Confederate":** Donaldson, *First Modern Campaign*, 136.

193 **"Mink Coat Mob":** Woods, *LBJ: Architect of American Ambition*, 373.

193 **LET'S GROUND LADY BIRD:** Donaldson, *First Modern Campaign*, 136.

193 **"It came upon me":** Woods, *LBJ: Architect of American Ambition*, 374.

193 **"admirable coolness":** Rowland Evans and Robert Novak, *Lyndon B. Johnson: The Exercise of Power* (Signet, 1966), 320.

193 **"be just like Marie Antoinette":** Gould, *Lady Bird Johnson*, 19.

193 **"If the time has come":** Woods, *LBJ: Architect of American Ambition*, 373.

193 **ran the headline:** Smith, "Lady Bird Combs Mob."

193 **"spite and spittle":** "LBJ Discovers 'America the Ugly,'" *Boston Globe*, March 29, 1968.

193 **in a new light:** Evans and Novak, *Lyndon B. Johnson*, 320.

194 **since 1944:** Evans and Novak, *Lyndon B. Johnson*, 320.

194 **"Lady Bird Johnson Day":** Lady Bird Johnson to Mayor Tom Gattis, October 8, 1964, box 1329, folder "Lady Bird Special—G," Alphabetical Files, White House Social Files, LBJL.

194 **"I heard so much":** "Lady Bird Barnstorms through South Georgia," *Patriot* (Harrisburg, PA), October 9, 1964.

194 **"We think we have" through "still in need":** "Lady Bird's Whistle-Stop: Waycross, GA: 10/8/64, 3:23 PM," TheLBJLibrary, October 7, 2014, YouTube video, 19:58, https://www.youtube.com/watch?v=AHzvxjjrzm0.

195 **"Not at all":** Sibley, "It's a Bandwagon Now."

195 **"people have better manners":** Pou, "Luci's the Star."

195 **"My friends of Valdosta":** "Lady Bird's Whistle-Stop: Valdosta, GA, 10/8/64, 4:56 PM," TheLBJLibrary, October 7, 2014, YouTube video, 11:23, https://www.youtube.com/watch?v=LRdx_9f5BPQ.

195 **Goldwater 315:** "Big Georgia Crowds."

195 **results of a poll:** "Goldwater Tops Johnson in a Georgia Union Poll," *New York Times*, September 13, 1964, https://www.nytimes.com/1964/09/13/archives/goldwater-tops-johnson-in-a-georgia-union-poll.html.

196 **"what a fine":** "Lady Bird's Whistle-Stop: Valdosta, GA."

196 **"And they loved it":** Earl Braswell, "Daughter Luci Scores Big Hit," *Valdosta Daily Times*, October 9, 1964.

196 **"the ride of a lifetime" and "charmed":** Virginia Culpepper, "Valdostans Thrilled by 60-Mile Ride," *Valdosta Daily Times*, October 9, 1964.

196 **"Tell me, how do":** Culpepper, "Valdostans Thrilled by 60-Mile Ride."

197 **"Right now, we're hunting":** "Lady Bird's Whistle-Stop: Thomasville, GA:

10/8/64, 6:02 PM," TheLBJLibrary, October 7, 2014, YouTube video, 13:19, https://www.youtube.com/watch?v=zUiCaWl0U8E.
197 **"started out as a":** Sibley, "It's a Bandwagon Now."
197 **"Mrs. Johnson is cutting":** "Cheers, Heckling Greet Lady Bird."

Chapter 20

199 **unmarked on state highway maps:** "Lady Bird's Off," *St. Petersburg (FL) Times*, October 6, 1964.
199 **"You could get in":** Gordon Payne, "Many Engineers Handling 'Special,'" *Charleston Evening Post*, October 8, 1964.
199 **"This proved successful":** Report on Whistle-Stop Plans in Florida, box 3, folder 51, Jan Sanders Papers, DeGolyer Library, Southern Methodist University.
200 **"We were glad":** Boggs, *Washington Through a Purple Veil*, 192.
200 **front-page announcement:** "Johnson Girls Needed," *Florida Flambeau* (Florida State University), October 2, 1964.
200 **dividing line:** Glenda Alice Rabby, *The Pain and the Promise: The Struggle for Civil Rights in Tallahassee, Florida* (University of Georgia Press, 1999), 95.
200 **on one side:** Angelique Fullwood and TyLisa C. Johnson, "Across the Tracks: A Story About the Railroad Dividing Line Between FAMU and FSU, Parts 1–3," *Famuan* (Florida A&M University), February 16, 2017, https://www.thefamuanonline.com/2017/02/16/across-the-tracks-a-story-about-the-railroad-dividing-line-between-famu-and-fsu-parts-1-3/.
201 **bus boycott:** "The Tallahassee Bus Boycott 1956–57," Florida Memory: State Library and Archives of Florida, accessed February 17, 2025, https://www.floridamemory.com/learn/classroom/learning-units/civil-rights/tallahasseebusboycott; Sadie Uhl and Hope Evans, "Black History Month: The Story of the Tallahassee Bus Boycott," Department of History, College of Arts and Sciences, Florida State University, February 6, 2021, https://history.fsu.edu/article/black-history-month-story-tallahassee-bus-boycott.
201 **"placing themselves":** Charles U. Smith and Lewis M. Killian, *Tallahassee, Florida: The Tallahassee Bus Protest*, Field Reports on Desegregation in the South (Antidefamation League of B'nai Brith, 1958), https://www.bjpa.org/search-results/publication/19571.
201 **"We would not pay a fine":** Tananarive Due and Patricia Stephens Due, *Freedom in the Family: A Mother-Daughter Memoir of the Fight for Civil Rights* (One World, 2003), 69–70.
202 **"courageous willingness":** Due and Due, *Freedom in the Family*, 75–76.
202 **"very meaningful":** Due and Due, *Freedom in the Family*, 75.
202 **"We cannot be contented":** Due and Due, *Freedom in the Family*, 73.
202 **"perennial show stealer":** "The Best Band in the Land," *Ebony*, November 1963.
202 **"The band members seem":** "Best Band in the Land."

NOTES

202 **"seemingly inexhaustible"**: "Best Band in the Land."
203 **"get a look at"**: "More About—Lady Bird Special," *Tallahassee Democrat*, October 9, 1964.
203 **"Cover that Goldwater sign"**: "More About—Lady Bird Special."
203 **one of three front-page articles**: Frances Lewine, "Lady Bird Hears Cheers En Route"; "Mrs. LBJ's Address Slated Here Tonight: Key Talk of Tour"; "Plans Made to Receive Lady Bird," *Tallahassee Democrat*, October 8, 1964.
203 **"really let go"**: Hallie Boyles, "Throngs Welcome Lady Bird, Luci," *Tallahassee Democrat*, October 9, 1964.
203 **"Johnson Women Score Hit at FSU"**: *Cocoa (FL) Tribune*, October 9, 1964.
203 **"campus commies and pinks"**: Martin Waldron, "Lady Bird Late, But All Waited," *St. Petersburg (FL) Times*, October 9, 1964.
203 **"mortified" through "it was flawless"**: Patricia Pendergast to Lady Bird Johnson, October 11, 1964, box 293, folder "Campaign (Florida)," White House Social Files, LBJL.
204 **"Anybody who says" through "the right to speak"**: "More About—Lady Bird Special."
204 **"key talk"**: "Mrs. LBJ's Address Slated Here."
205 **"the key to freedom" through "moon from Florida"**: "Remarks by Mrs. Lyndon B. Johnson, Florida State University, Tallahassee," press release, October 8, 1964, "Mrs. Johnson—Speeches," Reference File, LBJL, https://www.discoverlbj.org/item/ref-ctjspeeches-19641008-1930.
205 **"Cape Kennedy is not" through "human storms"**: "Lady Bird Special in Tallahassee," ABC News, October 10, 1964, Assign #A081P96, ABC News VideoSource, https://www.abcnewsvsource.com.
205 **"We want Luci"**: Frances Lewine, "Vote-Hunting Lady Bird Isn't Joking: 'I've Been Working on the Railroad,'" *Miami Herald*, October 10, 1964.
206 **"Suddenly it's teensville"**: *Life*, May 15, 1964.
206 **"LUCI WILL BE HERE TOO"**: *Florida Flambeau*, October 7, 1964.
206 **"for Luci and her mother"**: "Luci Made HC Court Member," *Florida Flambeau*, October 9, 1964.
206 **"threw some"**: Boyles, "Throngs Welcome Lady Bird, Luci."
206 **"I'm thrilled to death"**: "Lady Bird Special in Tallahassee."
206 **"leaning forward"**: Boyles, "Throngs Welcome Lady Bird, Luci."
206 **"She opens her mouth"**: Arthur Edson, "Never Before Has Wife of President Hit Trail So Hard," *Pensacola Journal*, October 12, 1964.
206 **Goldwater formula**: "Luci Gets Souvenirs, But FSU...," *Pensacola Journal*, October 10, 1964.
206 **"farsighted enough"**: Carpenter, *Ruffles and Flourishes*, 164.
207 **Press stinks**: Carpenter, *Ruffles and Flourishes*, 164.
207 **"The press that bathes"**: Tony Knight, "Good Morning!," *Pensacola Journal*, October 10, 1964.

207 **"The gratitude of"**: Carpenter, *Ruffles and Flourishes*, 164.

Chapter 21

209 **"I never talk politics"**: "Travel-Weary First Lady Winds Up Tour Today," *Dispatch* (Lexington, NC), October 9, 1964.

209 **"surprisingly large"**: Sam Wood, "Lady Bird Charms Cool Demo Rebels," *Austin American-Statesman*, October 10, 1964.

210 **"I did not ignore"**: Report on Whistle-Stop Plans in Florida, box 3, folder 51, Jan Sanders Papers, DeGolyer Library, Southern Methodist University.

210 **"interested in Lady Bird's visit"**: Report on Whistle-Stop Plans in Florida, box 3, folder 51, Jan Sanders Papers, DeGolyer Library, Southern Methodist University.

210 **The success of the Whistle-Stop:** Instructions to Advance Women.

210 **"folks of the South" through "to ignore it"**: "Lady Bird's Whistle-Stop: Chipley, FL: 10/9/64, 7:45 AM," TheLBJLibrary, October 7, 2014, YouTube video, 6:45, https://www.youtube.com/watch?v=cFds9hsigvk.

211 **"This man began" through "But he stopped"**: E. W. Carswell, "Chipley Councilman's Wife Bopped Heckler," *Pensacola News-Journal*, October 11, 1964.

211 **obstructing the view and "Heck, I'm for Barry"**: "Barry Sign Irks Mother, She Rips It Into Pieces," *Pensacola Journal*, October 10, 1964.

212 **"raised a shower" and "open insult"**: Percy Hamilton, "State Desk," *Pensacola News*, October 13, 1960.

212 **"and the whole"**: Helen Thomas, "Lady Bird Gets 'Enemy' Posies," *Fort Lauderdale News and Sun-Sentinel*, October 10, 1964.

Chapter 22

213 **Coast Guard vessel:** Darrell Eiland, "U.S. Coast Guard: They're in Lifesaving Business," *Pensacola News-Journal*, March 7, 1965.

213 **an attempt would be made:** Darrell Eiland, "Hoopla Flavors Train Stop Here," *Pensacola News*, October 9, 1964.

214 **PENSACOLA LOVES LADY BIRD:** Eiland, "Hoopla Flavors Train Stop Here."

214 **"This is slow campaigning"**: Report on Whistle-Stop Plans in Florida, box 3, folder 51, Jan Sanders Papers, DeGolyer Library, Southern Methodist University.

215 **"I really love politics"**: "Biography of Mrs. Barefoot Sanders (Jan)," press release, September 1964, box 11, folder "Whistle-Stop [4 of 6]," Liz Carpenter Subject Files, White House Social Files, LBJL, https://www.discoverlbj.org/item/whsf-lc-subject-b11-f11.

215 **"her hard-hitting"**: Untitled Report, box 3, folder 49, Jan Sanders Papers, DeGolyer Library, Southern Methodist University.

216 **"Lady Bird Johnson came to town"**: Eiland, "Hoopla Flavors Train Stop Here."

216 **"unsightly grass"**: Knight, "Good Morning!"
216 **NAS ORNITHOLOGISTS**: Eiland, "Hoopla Flavors Train Stop Here."
216 **"blip" through "The hazards of travel"**: Lewine, interview by Kasper.
216 **stood and waited**: "Welcome Lady Bird—to Goldwater Country," *Pensacola Journal*, October 10, 1964.
217 **"really cut loose" and "Look, there she is"**: Mac Harris, "They Came to See Lady Bird, Luci," *Pensacola Journal*, October 10, 1964.
217 **"Once more"**: "Lady Bird's Whistle-Stop: Pensacola, FL: 10/9/64, 11:22 AM," TheLBJLibrary, October 7, 2014, YouTube video, 14:05, https://www.youtube.com/watch?v=IxS5IGaMshQ.
217 **"All in all"**: Harris, "They Came to See."
217 **"will help return"**: Thomas, "Lady Bird Gets 'Enemy' Posies."
217 **"sprinkling their conversation"**: Pat Lloyd, "Panhandle Gives 'Lady Bird' 'Southern Hospitality' Hello," *Pensacola Journal*, October 10, 1964.
218 **"conversational English"**: Edgar Poe, "Lady Bird Special Press Gets 'Dixie Dictionary,'" *Times-Picayune* (New Orleans, LA), October 8, 1964.
218 **"Everyone got a laugh" through "filed a complaint"**: Carpenter, *Ruffles and Flourishes*, 157.
218 **"Dixie Dictionary"**: Poe, "Lady Bird Special Press."
218 **"Is this next stop going to be"**: Boggs, *Washington Through a Purple Veil*, 192.

Chapter 23

219 **"the land of cousins"**: "Lady Bird's Whistle-Stop: Flomaton, AL: 10/9/64, 12:51 PM," TheLBJLibrary, October 7, 2014, YouTube video, 14:44, https://www.youtube.com/watch?v=Sxt0m2bhsxQ.
219 **"wonderful visit" through "my childhood"**: Lady Bird Johnson, audio diary and annotated transcript, July 25, 1964, Lady Bird Johnson's White House Diary Collection, LBJL, https://www.discoverlbj.org/item/ctjd-19640725.
220 **"Long ago I"**: Robertson, "Our New First Lady."
220 **"Old South begins"**: Antonio J. Taylor quoted in Robertson, "Our New First Lady."
220 **"passion and"**: Gillette, *Lady Bird Johnson*, 9.
220 **"My life there"**: Gillette, *Lady Bird Johnson*, 9.
221 **"We're so proud" and "Welcome home"**: "Lady Bird's Whistle-Stop: Flomaton, AL."
221 **"a thawing of the chill"**: Wood, "Lady Bird Charms."
221 **"political enemies"**: Thomas, "Lady Bird Gets 'Enemy' Posies."
221 **"He didn't want to"**: Carpenter, *Ruffles and Flourishes*, 166.
222 **"Where are Governor" through "give than to receive"**: Carpenter, *Ruffles and Flourishes*, 165–66.

222 **"I don't think" through "the State of Alabama":** Maryon Pittman Allen, "Lt. Governor's Wife Former Newshen Advises Cohorts Never Turn Down Any Political Assignment," *Alabama Journal* (Montgomery, AL), October 15, 1964.

222 **"the state must show":** "Mrs. Allen Named Lady Bird Greeter," *Dothan (AL) Eagle*, October 5, 1964.

223 **"full approval" through "holiday mood":** Allen, "Lt. Governor's Wife."

223 **"was a happy event":** Lady Bird Johnson to Virginia Durr, October 20, 1964, Liz Carpenter Alphabetical Files, box 124, folder "Whistle-Stop Tour (Only)," LBJL.

223 **"white backlash" and "Mobile gave":** Gloria Negri, "Mrs. Johnson 'Comes Home' to Alabama," *Boston Globe*, October 10, 1964.

223 **favorite stop:** Helen Thomas, "She Won't Brood About Hecklers," *Miami Herald*, October 19, 1964.

224 **"I'm home":** Negri, "Mrs. Johnson 'Comes Home.'"

224 **"Everywhere I look":** Helen Thomas, "…But It Was a Political Success," *St. Petersburg (FL) Times*, October 10, 1964.

224 **"seeing you and Cliff":** Johnson to Durr.

224 **"terrible sight":** Virginia Foster Durr, *Outside the Magic Circle* (University of Alabama Press, 1994), 280.

224 **"Black Bird, go home":** "Lady Bird's Whistle-Stop: Mobile, AL: 10/9/64, 2:36 PM," TheLBJLibrary, October 7, 2014, YouTube video, 23:45, https://www.youtube.com/watch?v=4Z_oixDuCkw.

224 **"proved herself":** Negri, "Mrs. Johnson 'Comes Home,'"

225 **"I read in the paper" through "we may belong to":** "Lady Bird's Whistle-Stop: Mobile, AL."

225 **"John, you really":** Virginia Foster Durr, interview by Mary Walton Livingston, October 17, 1967, transcript, LBJ Library Oral Histories, LBJL, https://www.discoverlbj.org/item/oh-durrv-19671017-1-68-14.

225 **"fusing the best" through "the way I say it":** "Lady Bird's Whistle-Stop: Mobile, AL."

226 **"I'm sure that these":** Durr, interview by Livingston.

226 **"Doesn't it mean anything":** Mary McGrory, "The First Family Visits in Dixie," *Sunday Star* (Washington, DC), October 11, 1964.

226 **"not a single boo":** McGrory, "First Family Visits in Dixie."

226 **assigned to the beat:** Mary McGrory, interview by Kathleen Currie, August 1991 to July 1992, transcript, Washington Press Club Foundation Oral History Project, Rare Book Manuscript Library, Columbia University.

226 **"The most intelligent" through "First Lady's harassment":** McGrory, "First Family Visits in Dixie."

226 **"Standing here today":** "Lady Bird's Whistle-Stop: Mobile, AL."

227 **"Just a moment, please":** "Lady Bird's Whistle-Stop: Mobile, AL."

NOTES

227 **"Mrs. Johnson was the most":** Negri, "Mrs. Johnson 'Comes Home.'"
227 **"won her campaign diploma":** Wood, "Lady Bird Charms."
228 **Some three hundred people:** Wauhillau La Hay, "First Lady's Tour Was Vote-Getter," *Memphis Press-Scimitar*, October 10, 1964.
228 **"We saw you go by" through "I love you":** Gary L. Southern to Lady Bird Johnson, October 9, 1964, box 297, folder "Campaign (Mississippi)," White House Social Files, LBJL.

Chapter 24

229 **"dominated by the race question":** Louis Harris, "Harris Survey: Only One Issue for Voters in Mississippi Race," *Winona (MN) Daily News*, November 23, 1964.
229 **"Anti-Johnson sentiment was strong":** Drew Pearson, "LBJ Backers in Mississippi Quiet," *Bismarck (ND) Tribune*, July 26, 1965.
229 **"the nation's most segregated":** John Herbers, "Mississippi: A Profile of the Nation's Most Segregated State," *New York Times*, June 28, 1964, https://www.nytimes.com/1964/06/28/archives/mississippi-a-profile-of-the-nations-most-segregated-state-through.html.
229 **"greatest political triumph":** Mary McGrory, "LBJ, Lady Bird Make Formidable Team," *Hammond (IN) Times*, October 16, 1964.
230 **"the most dangerous":** "Elect Goldwater, Mississippi Demos Told by Governor," *Miami Herald*, September 10, 1964.
230 **"a real sense of pleasure" through "in our state":** "Lady Bird's Whistle-Stop: Biloxi, MS," TheLBJLibrary, October 7, 2014, YouTube video, 20:18, https://www.youtube.com/watch?v=lGshyEJukK0.
230 **"No campaign is":** "Lady Bird's Whistle-Stop: Biloxi, MS."
230 **"Good luck":** "Lady Bird's Whistle-Stop: Biloxi, MS."
230 **so entrenched:** Herbers, "Mississippi: A Profile"; Kate Ellis and Stephen Smith, hosts, *State of Siege: Mississippi Whites and the Civil Rights Movement*, podcast, American RadioWorks, January 20, 2011, https://americanradioworks.publicradio.org/features/mississippi/e1.html; "The Present-Day Ku Klux Klan Movement," Report by the Committee On Un-American Activities, December 11, 1967, House of Representatives, 90th Congress, 2nd Session.
230 **originally founded:** "Confederate Veterans Establish the Ku Klux Klan," Equal Justice Initiative, accessed April 14, 2025, https://calendar.eji.org/racial-injustice/dec/24.
231 **larger percentage:** Herbers, "Mississippi: A Profile."
231 **"emotional session" and "brutality and terror":** E. W. Kenworthy, "Rival Delegations from Mississippi Bid for Seats at the Convention," *New York Times*, August 23, 1964, https://www.nytimes.com/1964/08/23/archives/rival-delegations-from-mississippi-bid-for-seats-at-the-convention.html.

231 **Fannie Lou Hamer:** Unless otherwise noted, the account of what took place in the hearing, including Hamer's testimony and all other quotes, is drawn from "Proceedings of the Democratic National Convention Credentials Committee," Atlantic City, NJ, August 22, 1964, box 102, DNC Papers Series 2, LBJL, https://www.discoverlbj.org/item/pp-dnc-s2-b102-credentialsreport.

233 **reject the Committee's decision:** Tom Wicker, "Mississippi Delegates Withdraw, Rejecting a Seating Compromise," *New York Times*, August 26, 1964, https://www.nytimes.com/1964/08/26/archives/mississippi-delegates-withdraw-rejecting-a-seating-compromise.html.

233 **"We didn't come all":** "Mississippi Freedom Democratic Party (MFDP)," SNCC Digital Gateway, accessed February 20, 1964, https://snccdigital.org/inside-sncc/alliances-relationships/mfdp.

233 **Only four of the:** "Mississippi Issue Decided," *Congressional Quarterly Weekly Report*, No. 35, week ending August 28, 1964, p. 1960.

234 **"Don't you tell me" and "She told me she was":** Margaret McMullan, "60 Years Ago, Courage Confronted Racism at the Democratic Convention," *Bulwark*, August 21, 2024, https://www.thebulwark.com/p/1964-democratic-convention-racism-courage.

234 **targeted by the KKK:** Charles M. Hills, "Affairs of State," *Clarion-Ledger* (Jackson, MS), April 28, 1965.

234 **He received:** Cliff Sessions, "Berger Says Refusal Brings Harassment," *Clarion-Ledger* (Jackson, MS), July 22, 1965.

234 **"They threatened his life":** Lyndon B. Johnson and Nicholas Katzenbach, telephone conversation, August 31, 1964, audio recording and transcript, Recordings and Transcripts of Telephone Conversations and Meetings, LBJL, https://www.discoverlbj.org/item/tel-05294.

234 **continued to campaign:** "Berger Gives Talk for LBJ," *Clarion-Ledger* (Jackson, MS), October 18, 1964.

235 **Mary Love Bailey:** Marie Ridder, "Lady Bird Special Called 'Phenomenal Success,'" *Independent Star-News* (Pasadena, CA), October 11, 1964; Kay Powers, "Class Feed," *Austin Statesman*, October 7, 1964.

235 **"How proud":** Lady Bird Johnson to Thelma McMullan, December 9, 1964, box 297, folder "Campaign (Mississippi)," White House Social Files, LBJL.

235 **"happy encounters":** "Lady Bird's Whistle-Stop: Biloxi, MS."

235 **Mrs. Forest A. Miller:** "Former Teacher Awaits Arrival of First Lady," *Asheville (NC) Times*, October 9, 1964.

235 **"dollars-and-cents" through "found faith":** "Lady Bird's Whistle-Stop: Biloxi, MS."

236 **Leo P. Hays wrote:** Leo P. Hays to Lady Bird Johnson, October 9, 1964, box 297, folder "Campaign (Mississippi)," White House Social Files, LBJL.

NOTES

Chapter 25

237 **"How are you baby?":** James McLean, "LBJ Dazzles Thousands in New Orleans Talks," *Hattiesburg (MS) American*, October 10, 1964.

237 **"I was terribly proud":** Johnson, *Vantage Point*, 108.

238 **"as if they had been":** Mary Pakenham, "Mrs. Johnson, Lyndon Embrace in New Orleans," *Chicago Tribune*, October 10, 1964.

238 **"radiant," "jovial," and "greeted the throngs":** Negri, "Mrs. Johnson 'Comes Home.'"

238 **"[She] had real guts":** McGrory, "First Family Visits in Dixie."

238 **"It was a hot and steamy night":** Russell, *Lady Bird: A Biography*, 263.

238 **"a valiant woman":** Gene Barnes, "Move Forward, Says Lady Bird," *Times-Picayune* (New Orleans, LA), October 10, 1964.

238 **"This has been four":** "Remarks of the President, Mrs. Lyndon B. Johnson, and Miss Luci Johnson upon Arrival of the 'Lady Bird Special' at Union Station, New Orleans, Louisiana," October 9, 1964, box 177, folder "Johnson, Pres.: Campaign Speech, Oct. 9/64," Records of the Democratic National Committee, LBJL.

239 **"roared its approval":** "Predicts Victory, Backs Peace, Prosperity," *Times-Picayune* (New Orleans, LA), October 10, 1964.

239 **"We feel we're honoring":** "Thousands Hail Johnson on Crowded Ride Route," *Times-Picayune* (New Orleans, LA), October 10, 1964.

239 **memo outlining strategy:** "New Orleans Speech," October 9, 1964, box 26, folder "New Orleans," Office Files of Bill Moyers, Papers of Lyndon Baines Johnson, President, 1963–1969, LBJL.

239 **hedged when asked:** C. M. Hargroder, "McKeithen May Not Meet LBJ in N. O.," *Times-Picayune* (New Orleans, LA), September 24, 1964.

239 **"We are for Johnson":** "New Orleans Gives Welcome to Long-Praising President Johnson," *Advertiser* (Lafayette, LA), October 11, 1964.

240 **"I just touched":** "Predicts Victory, Backs Peace, Prosperity."

240 **"a lesson about people" and "It was part":** Peter Lisagor, "Dempsey and Dewey Lessons Spur Johnson's Handshaking," *Chicago Daily News*, October 13, 1964.

240 **"fandangled him":** Sid Davis, interview by Michael L. Gillette, August 1, 1990, transcript, LBJ Library Oral Histories, LBJL, https://www.discoverlbj.org/item/oh-daviss-19900801-4-99-38.

240 **"The motorcade was just about":** "Police Chase Roof Viewers," *Times-Picayune* (New Orleans, LA), October 10, 1964.

241 **"Thank you for coming":** "Predicts Victory, Backs Peace, Prosperity."

241 **"Come on up":** "New Orleans Gives Welcome."

241 **"There is always":** William K. Wyant Jr., "Campaigning's a Joyful Task for President," *St. Louis Post-Dispatch*, October 30, 1964.

241 **"Are you Democrats?":** "New Orleans Gives Welcome."

241 **"Well," he said:** "Thousands Hail Johnson."
241 **"I see we have":** "Thousands Hail Johnson."
241 **"She still thinks:"** "Thousands Hail Johnson."
242 **"strained forward":** "President Halts Parade for Curbstone Parleys," *Shreveport Times*, October 10, 1964.
242 **"Go, Goldwater":** "Predicts Victory, Backs Peace, Prosperity."
242 **"This is unbelievable":** "Thousands Hail Johnson."
242 **endorsed him:** Roman Heleniak, "Lyndon Johnson in New Orleans," *Louisiana History: The Journal of the Louisiana Historical Association* 21, no. 3 (Summer 1980): 263–75, https://www.jstor.org/stable/4232006.
242 **"Mardi Gras-sized crowd":** "President Says He Won't Veer Right or Left," *Tampa Tribune*, October 10, 1964.
242 **the limousine's roof:** "Lady Bird, Lyndon Welcomed by Governors," *Times-Picayune* (New Orleans, LA), October 10, 1964.
242 **"I've got to go":** "President Halts Parade."
242 **"shooting pictures like mad":** Howard Jacobs, "Illegal Interference," *Times-Picayune* (New Orleans, LA), October 14, 1964.
243 **"We're on the wrong side":** "Predicts Victory, Backs Peace, Prosperity."
243 **"Hello, folks":** "Thousands Hail Johnson."
243 **"You have brought":** "Remarks at Union Station."
244 **"lace mitts" and "iron gloves":** La Hay, "Lady Bird Trades Lace."
244 **"I am aware":** "Remarks at Union Station."
244 **"I had the privilege":** "Remarks at Union Station."
245 **"Damn, that Luci's got it":** Lyndon B. Johnson and George Reedy, telephone conversation, October 10, 1964, audio recording and transcript, Recordings and Transcripts of Telephone Conversations and Meetings, LBJL, https://www.discoverlbj.org/item/tel-05857.
245 **"It was a heady time":** Johnson, interview by Gillette.
245 **"You have heard from":** "Remarks at Union Station."
245 **"before going off to":** "New Orleans Speech."
245 **"the races were packed together":** Chalmers M. Roberts, "LBJ's Talk on Rights Applauded in South," *Washington Post*, October 11, 1964.
245 **"to be President of all":** "Remarks at Union Station."
246 **"went wild":** Carpenter, *Ruffles and Flourishes*, 167.
246 **"beating the bushes":** Adras LaBorde, "Talk of the Town," *Alexandria (LA) Daily Town Talk*, October 7, 1964.
246 **"All the way with LJB":** McLendon and Smith, *Don't Quote Me!*, 78.
246 **"the most dramatic moment":** Jack Valenti, *A Very Human President* (W. W. Norton, 1975), 206.
246 **"If our position in the world":** This and all other quotes in this speech cited from

NOTES

Lyndon B. Johnson, "Speech at the Jung Hotel, New Orleans," October 9, 1964, Miller Center, University of Virginia, transcript and audio, https://millercenter.org/the-presidency/presidential-speeches/october-9-1964-speech-jung-hotel-new-orleans.

247 **"You have the election," "also cautious," and "blandly"**: Valenti, *Very Human President*, 206.
247 **"the racial issue"**: Referencing Sam Lubell, Johnson, *The Vantage Point*, 109.
247 **"The Issues"**: "New Orleans Speech."
247 **"I had confidence"**: Johnson, *Vantage Point*, 109.
248 **"only one rather" and "people who had been"**: Johnson, *Vantage Point*, 109.
248 **"not in New York"**: Johnson, *Vantage Point*, 109.
248 **"I spoke off the cuff"**: Johnson, *Vantage Point*, 109.
248 **"began, in evangelical"**: Valenti, *Very Human President*, 206.
249 **"was less than" through "detriment of the people"**: Johnson, *Vantage Point*, 109.
249 **Joe Bailey**: Johnson, *Vantage Point*, 110.
250 **"the applause was there"**: Valenti, *Very Human President*, 207.
251 **"never heard anything like it"**: McGrory, "First Family Visits in Dixie."
251 **"dynamic" through "particularly of the South"**: James H. Gillis, "Speech Lauded by Politicians," *Times-Picayune* (New Orleans, LA), October 10, 1964.
251 **"You know, I never"**: Valenti, *Very Human President*, 208.
251 **"I'm glad I did" through "something else in the South"**: Dickerson, *Among Those Present*, 129–30.
252 **"make a grand finale"**: Lindy Boggs to Lady Bird Johnson, September 19, 1964, box 1, folder "Lady Bird Johnson's Advance Notebook, 'Lady Bird Special,' Oct. 6-9, 1964, [2 of 3]), Lady Bird Johnson's Advance Notebooks, 1964, White House Social Files, LBJL.
252 **"like cooked spaghetti" through "run a railroad!"**: Carpenter, *Ruffles and Flourishes*, 168.
252 **"he will hardly" through "political history"**: McGrory, "First Family Visits in Dixie."

Epilogue

253 **"a virtuoso"**: "After Lady Bird," *Greensboro (NC) Daily News*, October 13, 1964.
253 **"was not a stunt"**: Max Freedman, "Lady Bird Is a Smart Campaigner," *Kokomo (IN) Morning Times*, October 15, 1964.
253 **primary Democratic campaign effort**: "U.S. First Lady Enjoys Spotlight," *Hamilton (Ontario, Canada) Spectator*, November 4, 1964.
253 **"brought evidence"**: Sitton, "Mrs. Johnson's Southern Trip."
253 **received the landslide**: "1964: Statistics: Data Archive Elections," American Presidency Project, UC Santa Barbara, accessed February 21, 2025, https://www.presidency.ucsb.edu/statistics/elections/1964.

254 **"only a miracle"**: Sweig, *Lady Bird Johnson*, 118.
254 **42,599 votes:** "1964: Statistics: Data Archive Elections," American Presidency Project, UC Santa Barbara, accessed February 21, 2025, https://www.presidency.ucsb.edu/statistics/elections/1964.
254 **Women voted:** Lois Duke Whitaker, ed., *Women in Politics: Outsiders or Insiders?: A Collection of Readings*, 3rd ed. (Prentice-Hall, 1999), 69.
254 **94 percent of the Black vote:** Simeon Booker with Carol McCabe Booker, *Shocking the Conscience: A Reporter's Account of the Civil Rights Movement* (University Press of Mississippi, 2013), 249.
254 **"We're certainly all"**: Beschloss, *Reaching for Glory*, 134.
254 **"There will be a renewal"**: "Dr. King Tells Plans to Resume Demonstrations," *Los Angeles Times*, October 27, 1964.
254 **"She took on"**: Beschloss, *Reaching for Glory*, 134.
254 **"sweet, friendly letter"**: Lady Bird Johnson to Gary L. Southern, October 19, 1964, box 297, folder "Campaign (Mississippi)," White House Social Files, LBJL.
254 **surprise birthday party:** Isabelle Shelton, "Bliss in Your Future, Ladies," *Baltimore Sun*, February 21, 1965.
255 **"day on day"**: Thomas, *Front Row at the White House*, 255.
255 **"never had any doubt"**: Thomas, *Front Row at the White House*, 255.
255 **"perhaps it took" through "on this reaction":** Ed Minteer, "Our Slant," *Albuquerque Journal*, October 14, 1964.
255 **"Woman Newsmaker":** Mary Campbell, "Annual Poll Winners: LBJ Chosen 'Newsmaker of Year,'" *Victoria (TX) Advocate*, December 27, 1964.
255 **"She may have set":** Sibley, "Has 'Lady Bird Special' Set."
255 **"Perhaps this marks":** Max Freedman, "Mrs. Johnson's Tour a Success," *Atlanta Constitution*, October 14, 1964.
256 **"There were moments" through "my political life":** Johnson, *White House Diary*, 198.

Index

A

ABC, 148
Abell, Bess, 9, 13–15, 19–20, 125, 179
Adolphus Hotel, 192–194
Ahoskie, North Carolina, 10, 77–78, 80–82
Air Force One, 92, 97, 105, 238, 239
Alabama stops
    Flomaton, 219, 221–223
    Mobile, 223–227
Alexandria, Virginia, 23–25, 30–32, 36
Allen, Maryon, 221–223
Alley, John, 118
American Folklore Society, 127
American Home Economics Association, 114
Anne-Marie of Denmark, 47
Ashe, Victor J., 74

Ashland, Virginia, 44–47
Associated Press, 24, 54, 216, 218, 255
Atlanta Constitution (periodical), 184
Aucoin, Erby, 242–243
Aulander, North Carolina, 83
Austin American-Statesman, 227
Austin American-Statesman (periodical), 11
Avery, Johnnie Mae, 143

B

Bailey, Joe, 249
Bailey, Mary Love, 235
Bates, Emma, 142
Beatlemania, 42
Belknap, Paul, 170
Berger, Fred, 234

Bigelow, Al, 137
Biloxi, Mississippi, 229–230, 235–236
Black Americans
    Black-owned businesses, 73
    employment, 86
    Lady Bird Special tour attendees, 70, 74, 110, 124, 134, 159–161, 185, 245, 249
    on Lady Bird's staff, 138
    Mississippi population, 231
    Norfolk 17, 73–74
    as Republican voters, 78
    segregation, xiv, 70–71, 78, 137, 158–159, 201
    voter registration, xv, 187, 231
    votes for LBJ, 254
    voting rights, 4, 70–71, 233
    working in Johnson administration, 67
Blackshear, Georgia, 191–192
Bleecker, John M., Jr., 170
Boggs, Hale, 16, 62, 70, 78, 84, 86–87, 120, 131, 171, 217, 238, 254
Boggs, Lindy, 16–17, 18, 43, 46, 96, 156, 164, 185, 200, 215, 254
Boston Globe (periodical), 61, 150
Boynton v. Virginia, 137
Brewer, J. Mason, 126–127
Brothers Four, 15
Brown v. Board of Education, 71, 158
Bryant, Farris, 29, 200, 204, 217
Bryant, Julia, 29
Burke, Edmund, 121
Burlington, North Carolina, 117–119
Burney, Kara, 142, 163–166, 168–171, 173
Burns, Hayden, 203
bus boycotts, 201
Byrd, Harry, 26, 61, 70–71, 73
Byrd Organization, 70–71

C

Cape Kennedy, 205
Carpenter, Les, 149
Carpenter, Liz, 7, 154, 156, 160, 172, 177–178, 183, 246, 252
    on Charleston stop, 181
    Dixie Dictionary, 217–218
    on Dr. Travell, 51, 148
    education, 11
    as executive assistant, 12, 65–66, 93–94
    on the Johnson girls, 47
    journalism career, 11–13, 63
    Kennedy assassination, 92
    on Lady Bird, 33, 34, 40, 41
    as press secretary, 11, 12–13
    tour planning, xiii, xiv, xvii, 5–6, 7, 9–11, 17–19, 100, 164, 207, 215
    on tour press, 54–55, 150, 169
    on Wallace's roses, 221–222
Cater, Douglass, 8
CBS, 55
Chaney, James, xv–xvi, 76, 79, 231
Charleston, South Carolina, 163–174, 177–181

INDEX

Charlotte, North Carolina, 129–134
Chattahoochee, Florida, 209
Chester, South Carolina, 145–147
Chiarodo, Maria Fehmer, 103
Chicago Sun (periodical), 62–63
Chicago Tribune (periodical), 175
Chipley, Florida, 209–211
church burnings, xv, xvi
Cincinnati Enquirer (periodical), 63
Civil Rights Act (1957), 3
Civil Rights Act (1960), 3
Civil Rights Act (1964)
    Democratic opposition to, 3–4, 25
    filibusters, 3, 26, 28
    Lady Bird's support for, 31–32
    passage of, 4, 101, 138
    public accommodation requirement, 219–220
    signing of, 2, 30, 139, 159, 236
    Southern compliance with, xiv, 139
civil rights movement
    bus boycotts, 201
    Freedom Riders, 137
    "jail, no bail" tactic, 135–136, 201
    learning tours, 159
    lunch-counter sit-ins, 124, 135–137, 201–202
    SCLC St. Paul convention, 187
    violence toward workers, xiv–xvi, 137–138, 158–159, 231
Claflin University, 158, 160, 161
Clay, Cecil D., 165
Cleveland, Grover, 133

Columbia, South Carolina, 153–157
Commentator (periodical), 56
Concord, North Carolina, 127–128
Congress of Racial Equality, xv, 138
Connelly, Dave, 129
Constantine of Greece, 47
Cornell University Medical College, 49
Cornwallis, Charles, 131–132
Craig, Louisa, 105, 125, 142, 146
Crestview, Florida, 210, 211
cross burnings, xiii, xv, 201
Crow Reservation, 8
Current, Gloster B., 79

D

Daisy ad, 133
Dealey Plaza, 91
Democratic Campaign Steering Committee, 222
Democratic National Committee, 22
Democratic National Convention, 5, 7, 29–30, 93, 101, 230, 231–234
Democrats and Democratic Party
    candidate endorsements, 79–80, 107–108, 133
    Charleston campaign headquarters vandalized, 165
    opposition to Civil Rights Act, 3–4, 25, 26
    party unity, 25
    responses to Lady Bird Special tour, 25–30
    Southern, 2–4, 30

Southern hostility toward, xiv
Thurmond's defection from, 27, 59–60, 171
Democrats for Election of the Johnson-Humphrey Ticket, 74
Dempsey, Jack, 240
Department of Labor, Women's Bureau, 65
Department of State, 66
Depression, 84–85, 194
Derby, Minnie Wade, 219
Derby, Patsy, 219
desegregation, xiv, 4, 71, 124, 143, 158, 201, 220
Dewey, Tom, 103
Dickerson, Nancy, 55–56, 62, 148, 237–238, 251–252
Dirksen, Everett, 3
discrimination, xiv, 78, 138, 186
Dixie (dog), 167–168
Dixie Dictionary, 218
Dock Street Theatre, 179
dogs, as supporters, 167–168
Doster, Joe, 133
Drifton, Florida, 199–200
Duke, Washington, 111
Duke University, 111
Durham, North Carolina, 109–115
Durham Morning Herald (periodical), 105, 110
Durland, William, 43, 44
Durr, Clifford, 224
Durr, Virginia, 223, 224, 225–226

E

Eastland, James, xv, 29, 230
economic protests, 201
Edson, Arthur, 24
Edwards, India, 6
Ellender, Allen, 30, 246
Elon College, 117
Ervin, Sam, 26
Evening Star (periodical), 17, 62, 63, 226
Evers, Medgar, 79
Everything to Live For (Horgan), 41

F

Fair, S. Clyde, 159
farm subsidy program, 104
Farmer, James, 138, 187
FBI, 6, 98, 234
The Feminine Mystique (Friedan), 112
Field, Marshall, III, 62
Finch, Billy, 143
First Lady Day, 186
Flaming Gorge Dam, 8
Fleeson, Doris, 148–149
Flomaton, Alabama, 219, 221–223
Florida A&M University (FAMU), 200–202
Florida Flambeau (periodical), 200, 206
Florida State University (FSU), 200–204
Florida stops
  Chattahoochee, 209
  Chipley, 209–211
  Crestview, 210, 211

Drifton, 199–200
Milton, 212
Pensacola, 213–218
Tallahassee, 200–207
Forty Acres Club, 67
Fredericksburg, Virginia, 37–39, 41–44
Freedman, Max, 255
Freedom Democratic Party, 231–233
Freedom Riders, 137–138
Freedom Summer Project, xv
Freeman, Mrs. Arthur T., 74
Friedan, Betty, 112, 113
Friendship Junior College, 135
Friendship Nine, 135–137

G

Gaillard, J. Palmer, Jr., 166, 177
Garner, Alfred, 118–119
Gavin, Robert L., 98
gender roles, 112–113
George, Lucy, 64
Georgia stops
    Blackshear, 191–192
    Homerville, 195
    Jesup, 189–190
    Savannah, 183–189
    Thomasville, 197
    Valdosta, 195–196
    Waycross, 192–195
Girl Scouts, 188, 189
Godwin, Mills, 38, 46, 70–72, 73, 74
Goldwater, Barry
    endorsements, 175
    Goldwater formula (AUH2O), 206, 209
    NAACP resolution against nomination of, 79
    nuclear weapons support, 132–133, 143
    presidential campaign, xvi, 4, 226, 252
    proposal to cut off farm price supports, 40
    public denunciations of, 80
    right-leaning views, 71
    "Southern strategy," 78, 120, 124
    supporters of, 23, 27, 38, 44, 46, 56, 61, 70, 72, 84, 86, 97, 99, 105, 110, 111, 119, 124, 126–127, 130, 131, 141, 142, 154–157, 160–161, 166, 170–172, 178–179, 184–186, 188–189, 190, 195–196, 203–204, 211, 216–217, 224–226, 235–236
Goldwater Youth Group, 204
Gonella, Ashton, 173, 221
Goodman, Andrew, xv–xvi, 76, 79, 231
Graham, Katharine, 238
Great Society agenda, 71, 85, 194
Greensboro, North Carolina, 119–121
Gulf of Tonkin, 80

H

Hamer, Fannie Lou, 231–233
"Happy Days Are Here Again" (song), 38, 151, 191
Harper's Bazaar (periodical), 112

Harrison, Albertis S., Jr., 26, 46, 51–52, 57, 61, 70, 74, 107–108
Hays, Leo P., 236
Hays, Sara Ann, 236
"Hello, Lyndon!" (song), 38, 47, 124, 176, 200, 214
Hepburn, Katharine, 45
Herald (periodical), 82, 142
Herald-Progress (periodical), 46
Herman, Jerry, 38
High Point, North Carolina, 123–124
Hight, Jack, 164–166
Hill, Lister, 225
Hobgood, North Carolina, 83
Hodges, Luther, 38, 60–61, 62, 86, 157, 196
Hodges, Martha, 196
Holland, Spessard, 28
Homerville, Georgia, 195
Hoover, J. Edgar, xvi
Horgan, Paul, 41
Hotel Duval, 206–207
housewives, 112
Howar, Barbara, 22
Hubbard, Charlotte Moton, 66
Hughes, Genevieve, 137
Hughes, Sarah T., 92
Hugo, Victor, 3
Humphrey, Hubert, 10–11, 16, 43

I

Independence Square, 129, 131
Index-Journal (periodical), 171–172
integration, 29, 30, 73, 146, 159, 186

interstate travel, 137–139

J

Jackson, A. B., 74
Jackson, Estelle, 53–54
"jail, no bail" tactic, 135–136, 201
Jakes, Wilhelmina, 201
Jefferson, Thomas, 43, 45, 244
Jesup, Georgia, 189–190
Jim Crow laws, 70–71
John Birch Society, 79, 190
Johnson, Augustus C., 25
Johnson, Dot, 230
Johnson, Lady Bird. *see also* Lady Bird Special whistle-stop tour
   appreciation for the South, xvi, 29, 30–32, 84–85, 142, 146, 220–221
   birth and early years, 220
   Black household staff, 138
   Carpenter and, 12, 33, 34, 40, 41
   Civil Rights Act, 3–4
   cousins, 219–220, 224
   as First Lady, 7–9, 11, 32, 40–41, 93–94, 96, 113, 169
   journalism background, 13, 34
   Kennedy assassination, 91–94
   "land and people" tour, 8, 114
   LBJ Special whistle-stop tour, 7, 123
   LBJ's congressional career, 32–35
   LBJ's vice presidency, 35–36, 65
   marriage to LBJ, 32, 94–95
   media coverage, 8, 13, 35, 41, 54, 169, 174

personality, 95
speaking style, 41–42
speeches, 113–114
"spit and spittle" incident, 192–194
tour planning, xiii, xiv, xvi–xvii, 10–11, 39–40
whistle-stop tour, 1–2
Johnson, Luci, 20, 46–47, 130, 173, 181–182, 184, 188–189, 196, 203, 205–206, 217, 224–225, 236, 237, 244–245
Johnson, Lynda, 20, 25, 43, 44, 46–47, 53, 57, 72, 74, 83, 99, 105, 111, 115, 120, 124, 130, 143, 152, 161, 173, 176
Johnson, Lyndon B.
   animosity toward, 4
   childhood, 85
   Civil Rights Acts, xiv, 2–4, 30, 101, 139, 159, 236, 248–249
   civil rights views, 138–139, 247–248
   congressional career, 12, 32–35, 85
   education, 85
   election win, 253–254
   endorsements, 51–52, 79–80, 82, 108, 133, 186
   Freedom Summer murders, xv–xvi
   Great Society agenda, 71, 85, 194
   health issues, 101–102
   Kennedy assassination, 2–3, 91–94, 102
   Kennedy presidential campaign, 64, 192–194
   Lady Bird Special tour appearances, 25, 32, 36, 96–105, 237–252
   LBJ Special whistle-stop tour, 6–7, 10, 18, 21, 123
   marriage to Lady Bird, 32, 94–95
   media coverage, 67, 241
   military service, 33
   personality, 95
   presidency, 92–94
   reelection campaign, xiii, 2, 5, 43, 101–104, 174–175, 239–243, 246–251
   security measures, 5, 96–97, 98
   speaking style, 42, 175
   support for tour, 9–10
   vice presidency, 35–36, 93
Johnson, Paul, 29–30, 230, 232
Johnson Girls, 24, 73, 74, 167, 172, 200, 202–203
Johnston, Elizabeth, 155
Johnston, Gladys, 172
Johnston, Olin, 27, 30, 141, 154–155, 171–172
Jones, Thomas F., 157
Jordan, Everett, 26
journalism. *see also* media coverage
   Carpenter's background, 11–13, 63
   Lady Bird's background, 13, 34
   women in, 53–56, 61–63, 87–88, 148–150, 216
Jung Hotel, 246–252

K

Kansas City Star (periodical), 133
Katzenbach, Nicholas, 234

Kenmore, 39
Kennedy, Bobby, 35
Kennedy, Ethel, 65
Kennedy, Jackie, 35, 92
Kennedy, John F.
    assassination, 2–3, 4–5, 43, 76, 91, 102
    civil rights agenda, 2–3, 30
    health issues, 50
    media coverage, 61
    presidency, 9, 16, 150
    presidential campaign, 6, 12, 35, 64–65, 93, 166, 192–193
Kennedy, Rose, 64–65
Kentucky Federation of Women's Clubs, 114
King, Martin Luther, Jr., xvi, 136–137, 186–187, 189, 202, 232–233, 254
Kleberg, Richard, 32
Konduros, Jim, 165, 167
Kopp, John, 192
Ku Klux Klan (KKK), xiv, xv, xvi, 6, 79, 138, 230–231, 234

L

Ladies for Lyndon, 1, 21–22, 24, 38, 47, 181, 185, 219, 230, 238
Lady Bird Special whistle-stop tour. *see also specific cities and states*
    advance teams, 18–20, 43–44, 163–169, 185–186, 199–200, 209–210, 214–216, 235

bathing facilities, 206–207
Black attendees, 70, 74, 110, 124, 134, 159–161, 185, 245, 249
campaign swag, 24
Car #3, 20–21, 196, 221
customized speeches for, 39–40
dining cars, 22
Goldwater supporters at, 23, 38, 44, 46, 56, 61, 70, 72, 84, 86, 99, 105, 111, 119, 124, 126–127, 130, 131, 141, 142, 178, 190, 203–204, 216–217, 235–236
guest accommodations, 20–21
hecklers, 72, 154–157, 160, 170–175, 184–186, 188–189, 192, 195–196, 200, 204, 211, 224–226, 236, 258
itinerary, 10–11
LBJ's appearances, 25, 32, 36, 96–105, 237–252
living and working quarters, 20
media coverage, xiv, 2, 17, 18, 21, 24, 41, 42, 44, 45–46, 51, 52–56, 61–63, 69–70, 75, 82, 87, 107, 109, 110, 117–118, 126, 133–134, 142, 147–152, 160, 169–172, 175–176, 196, 203, 206–207, 216–218, 227, 237–238, 253, 255
medical services on, 49, 50–51, 147, 148–149
menu, 15, 17, 22, 109
miles covered, 2
Operation Skyhook, 191

opposition to, 9
parlor-observation car, 1, 19–20
planning for, xiii, xiv, xvi–xvii, 5–6, 7, 9–11, 15–17, 39–40, 100
plots and threats against, 6, 75–76, 131, 202–203, 213–214
proposal for, 7
protesters at, 154–157
security measures, xiv, 5–6, 20, 22, 37–38, 43, 56, 78, 96–97, 118–119, 127, 213–214, 224
sleeping quarters, 22
states visited, xiv
success of, 253–256
support team, 21–22
train car adornments, 1, 20
LBJ Special whistle-stop tour, 6–7, 10, 18, 21, 46, 123, 212
League of Women Voters, 186
Lee, Robert E., 31, 247
Lewine, Frances, 216, 218
Lewis, Betty, 39
Lewis, Fielding, 39
Lewis, John, 137
Lexington, North Carolina, 125–126
Life (magazine), 113, 205–206
Lloyd, Larry, 99–100
Lloyd, Nancy, 129
Lodge, Henry Cabot, Jr., 65
Long, Dewey, 10
Long, Russell, 30, 238
Louisiana State University, 239

Louisiana stop, 237–252
Low, Juliette Gordon, 188, 189
lunch-counter sit-ins, 124, 135–137, 201–202

M

Marching 100, 202
Mary Washington College, 42
Mass, Henry, 143
McAden, Barbara, 127, 150
McAteer, Rhoda, 143
McClure, Bette, 44, 164
McDowell, Charles, Jr., 53, 57
McGovern, Frances, 115
McGrory, Mary, 226, 252
McKeithen, John, 30, 239, 240
McMillan, John L., 108
McMullan, Margaret, 234
McMullan, Milton, 234
McMullan, Thelma, 234, 235
McMullen, JoAnne, 143
Mead, Margaret, 113
Mecklenburg Declaration of Independence, 132
media coverage
  of Abell, 14
  of Dr. Travell, 50, 51
  of Johnson's endorsements, 52, 108
  of Lady Bird, 8, 13, 35, 41, 54, 113, 169, 174
  of Lady Bird Special tour, xiv, 2, 17, 18, 21, 24, 41, 42, 44, 45–46, 51,

52–56, 61–63, 69–70, 75, 82, 87, 107, 109, 110, 117–118, 126, 133–134, 142, 147–152, 160, 169–172, 175–176, 196, 203, 206–207, 216–218, 227, 237–238, 253, 255
of LBJ, 67, 241
of Luci, 205–206
newspaper endorsements of Goldwater, 175
newspaper endorsements of Johnson, 79–80, 133
of Russell, 146
Miami Herald (periodical), 202
Miller, Mrs. Forest A., 235
Miller, Scooter, 21–22, 185
Miller, William, 80, 98
Milton, Florida, 212
Mississippi stop, 229–230, 235–236
Mobile, Alabama, 223–227
Monroe James, 39
Moore, Dan K., 27, 81–82, 85, 97, 99, 100, 107–108
Moore, Jeanelle, 27, 82, 89, 96, 99, 134
Moran, Joe, 20
Moyers, Bill, 67

N

NAACP, 79, 158
Nash, Diane, 136
Nathaniel Russell House, 178–179
National Geographic Society, 39
National Youth Administration, 32

Native American reservations, 8
NBC, 55, 56, 148, 237
Negri, Gloria, 61–62, 150–152, 223, 227, 238
New Deal, 30, 32, 33
New Journal and Guide (periodical), 73, 74
New Orleans, Louisiana, 237–252
News and Courier (periodical), 169, 171, 179–180
New York Times (periodical), xiv, 87, 88, 253
New York Times Magazine (periodical), 55
Nineteenth Amendment, 11
Nixon, E. D., 224
Nixon, Richard, 192–193
Norfolk 17, 73–74
Norfolk, Virginia, 60, 69, 72–75
North Atlantic Treaty Organization, 132
North Carolina stops
　Ahoskie, 10, 77–78, 80–82
　Burlington, 117–119
　Charlotte, 129–134
　Concord, 127–128
　Durham, 109–115
　Greensboro, 119–121
　High Point, 123–124
　Lexington, 125–126
　Raleigh, 36, 82, 91, 96–105, 109, 148
　Rocky Mount, 84–86
　Salisbury, 126–127

Selma, 88–89
Tarboro, 83–84
Thomasville, 124–125
Wilson, 86–87
Northington, Etta Belle, 43–44
Northwestern University, 87
nuclear weapons, 132–133
Nunnery, William L., 151

O

O'Donnell, Kenneth, 9
Operation Skyhook, 191
Operation Whistle-stop, 10, 11, 15, 18. *see also* Lady Bird Special whistle-stop tour
Orangeburg, South Carolina, 158–161
Orangeburg Massacre, 159
Oswald, Lee Harvey, 91

P

Pakenham, Mary, 175–176, 206, 238
Parks, Rosa, 224
Pascagoula, Mississippi, 228, 254
Patterson, Carrie, 201
peace movement, 132–133
Pearson, Drew, 229
Pendergast, Patricia, 203–204
Pensacola, Florida, 213–218
Pensacola Journal (periodical), 216
Petersburg, Virginia, 60–62
Peterson, Barbara, 105, 142
Peterson, Esther, 65–66
Phoenix Fire Station, 227

Pinehaven Shopping Center, 166–168, 170, 173
police brutality, 4, 159, 201
poll taxes, 71

R

racial justice, 67
racism, 80, 138
Radcliffe College, 113–114
Raleigh, North Carolina, 36, 82, 91, 96–105, 109, 148
Randolph, A. Philip, 187
Randolph-Macon College, 45, 46
Rather, Mary, 221–222
Rauh, Joseph L., Jr., 233
Rayburn, Sam, 34, 55, 249
Redbook (periodical), 113
Ree, Otha, 138
Reedy, George, 102, 245
religious leaders, opposition to Goldwater, 80
Republicans and Republican Party
    NAACP resolution against Goldwater's nomination, 79
    position on tour demonstrations, 170
    Thurmond's defection to, 27, 59–60, 171
Reston, June, 93
Reynolds Coliseum, 91, 97, 99, 110
Richmond, Virginia, 46, 49, 51–53
Richmond Times-Dispatch (periodical), 51, 52–53, 56

Ridgeland, South Carolina, 181–182
Riley, Kathleen, 168
riots, 4
Rivers, Mendel, 171–172, 175, 177, 179
Robertson, A. Willis, 26
Robertson, Nan, 87–88, 146, 149
Rock Hill, South Carolina, 135, 139–143
Rockefeller, Nelson, 133
Rocky Mount, North Carolina, 84–86
Rook, Tom, 56
Roosevelt, Eleanor, 7, 8, 13, 41, 63, 96
Roosevelt, Franklin D., 30, 32, 33, 38, 40–41, 45, 92–93
Ross, Nellie Tayloe, 8
Russell, Donald, xiii, 17, 27, 141, 145–146, 154–155
Russell, Richard, 28, 183, 194, 195
Russell, Virginia, 16, 17, 27, 43, 125, 142, 145–146, 155, 157, 164, 215
Ryan, Leo B., 186

S

Salem Church Dam, 42
Salisbury, North Carolina, 126–127
Sanders, Barefoot, 215–216
Sanders, Betty Foy, 28
Sanders, Carl, 28, 184, 189, 194–195, 197
Sanders, Jan, 199–200, 209–210, 214–216
Sanders, Marlene, 148
Sanford, Terry, 26, 80–81, 98, 100–101, 110, 127
Saturday Evening Post (periodical), 79, 88

Savannah, Georgia, 183–189
Savannah Press Club, 189
schools, desegregation and integration, xiv, 29, 71, 73–74, 143, 158, 159
Schwerner, Michael, xv–xvi, 76, 79, 231, 232
Schwerner, Rita, xv, 232
Seaboard Air Line Railroad, 199
Secret Service, xiv, 5–6, 20, 38, 75–76, 78, 91, 92, 97–98, 118–119, 125, 140, 152, 159, 177–178, 240
segregation, xiv, 71, 78, 137, 158–159, 201
Sellers, Wayne C., 142
Selma, North Carolina, 88–89
sexism, 88
Shelton, Isabelle, 17, 62–63
Sherrod, Charles, 136
Shriver, Eunice, 65
Sibley, Celestine, 184, 191–192, 255
Sitton, Claude, 253
Smathers, George, 28
Smathers, Rosemary, 28
Smith, Jean Kennedy, 65
Smith, Margaret Chase, 75
Smith, Wilma, 155
Snake River, 8
Snoopie (dog), 167–168
Sommer, Pete, 165
the South
    compliance with Civil Rights Act, xiv, 139
    hostility toward Democrats, xiv

Lady Bird's appreciation for, xvi, 29, 30–32, 84–85, 142, 146, 220–221
"New South," 72–73, 74
political landscape, 26
Southern Democrats, 2–4, 30
unpopularity of Civil Rights Act, xiv
violence toward civil rights workers, xiv–xvi, 137–138, 158–159, 231
votes for LBJ, 254
South Carolina State College, 158, 159, 160, 161
South Carolina stops
    Charleston, 163–174, 177–181
    Chester, 145–147
    Columbia, 153–157
    Orangeburg, 158–161
    Ridgeland, 181–182
    Rock Hill, 135, 139–143
    Winnsboro, 151, 152
    Yemassee, 181
Southern, Gary, 228, 254
Southern, Michael, 228
Southern Christian Leadership Conference (SCLC), 186–187
Southern Governors Conference, 221
Southmayd, Carol, 111
Southwest Texas State Teachers College, 85
space exploration, 205
Sparkman, John, 225, 226
Sputnik, 169
St. Michael's Church, 179
"states' rights," 4

Stennis, John, 29, 139, 230
Stephens, Patricia, 201
Stephens, Priscilla, 201
Stewart, Terry, 143
Student Nonviolent Coordinating Committee, 136, 231
Suffolk, Virginia, 60, 69–72, 75–76

T

Taft, Helen, 205
Taft, William Howard, 45
Tallahassee, Florida, 200–207
Tallahassee Democrat (periodical), 203, 204
Talmadge, Betty, 28, 183–184, 187, 190, 195
Talmadge, Herman, 28, 183, 195
Tarboro, North Carolina, 83–84
Texas Folklore Society, 126
Texas Institute of Letters, 126–127
Texas School Book Depository, 91
Thomas, Helen, 8, 46, 67, 149–150, 206, 216, 255
Thomasville, Georgia, 197
Thomasville, North Carolina, 124–125
Thurmond, Strom, 27, 59–60, 72, 171
Tidewater Voter Registration Project, 74
Tillett, Gladys Avery, 186
Time (magazine), 50, 146
Times and Democrat (periodical), 159, 161
Tower, John, 96
Travell, Janet, 49–51, 97, 105, 146, 148
Trawick, Mrs., 211
Truman, Bess, 64, 169

Truman, Harry, 6–7, 10, 30, 64, 92–93, 103
Truman, Margaret, 64
Tufty, Esther Van Wagoner, 11
Turner, Patricia, 73–74
Twenty-Fourth Amendment, 70–71

U

Udall, Stewart, 8
UN Commission on the Status of Women, 186
Union Passage Terminal, 237, 245
Union Station (Washington, DC), 1
United Press International, 8
University of Alabama, 224
University of North Carolina, Chapel Hill, 109
University of North Carolina, Greensboro, 119
University of North Carolina, Raleigh, 91
University of South Carolina, 154, 157
University of Utah, 8
U.S. Army, 22
U.S. Marine Corps, 38
US Senate, 34–35

V

Valdosta, Georgia, 195–196
Valdosta Daily Times (periodical), 196
Valenti, Jack, 67, 246, 248, 250–251
Virginia stops
  Alexandria, 23–25, 30–32, 36
  Ashland, 44–47
  Fredericksburg, 37–39, 41–44
  Norfolk, 60, 69, 72–75
  Petersburg, 60–62
  Richmond, 46, 49, 51–53
  Suffolk, 60, 69–72, 75–76
voter registration, xv, 187, 231
voting rights, 4, 70–71, 112–113
Voting Rights Act, 254

W

Waagner, Harry, 177–178
Wallace, George, 4, 29, 221–222, 232
Warren Commission Report, 5, 98
Washington, George, 39
Washington, Mary, 39
Washington County News (periodical), 210
Washington Daily News (periodical), 149
Washington Post (periodical), 14, 42, 238
Waycross, Georgia, 192–195
What's My Line? (game show), 67
whistle-stop tours. *see also* Lady Bird Special whistle-stop tour
  defined, 2
  LBJ Special, 6–7, 10
  tradition of, 6–7
  Truman's, 6–7, 10
White, William E., 2
white citizens councils, 158, 220
White House
  physician, 50
  press secretary, 11, 12–13

INDEX

    social secretary, 13–15
    state visits, 40–41
White Knights of the KKK, xvi, 231
white supremacy, 230–231
Whitney, Eli, 187–188
Whittington, Geraldine, 66–67
Wiggs, Hayden, 88–89
Wilkins, Roy, 67
William Randolph Hearst Foundation, 47
Williams, Ruth, 165, 167, 179
Wilson, North Carolina, 86–87
Wilson, Richard, 113
Wilson, Woodrow, 45
Winnsboro, South Carolina, 151, 152
Wirtz, Alvin J., 33
women
    campaigning by, 63–65
    gender roles, 112–113
    Johnson administration appointees, 65–67
    journalists, 53–56, 61–63, 87–88, 148–150, 216
    judges, 92
    in politics, 75, 114–115, 165, 179–180
    votes for LBJ, 254
    voting rights, 112–113
    women's rights, 113–114, 186
Wood, Sam, 227
Woodyard, Nettie Mason, 220
World War I, 60
World War II, 33, 38, 50, 63, 240

Wright, Zephyr, 138, 139
Wynn, Douglas, 230
Wynn, Leila, 230, 234

Y

Yemassee, South Carolina, 181
Young, Thomas W., 74
Young, Whitney, 67
Young Citizens for Johnson, 46
Young Republicans, 204

Z

Zeta Tau Alpha sorority, 111

About the Author

Shannon McKenna Schmidt is the author of *The First Lady of World War II: Eleanor Roosevelt's Daring Journey to the Frontlines and Back*. She is also the coauthor of *Novel Destinations: A Travel Guide to Literary Landmarks from Jane Austen's Bath to Ernest Hemingway's Key West* and *Writers Between the Covers: The Scandalous Romantic Lives of Legendary Literary Casanovas, Coquettes, and Cads*.

In addition, Shannon has written for *National Geographic Traveler*, *Shelf Awareness*, and other websites and publications. She has been a guest on radio and television programs including MSNBC's *Morning Joe*, and she has spoken at the FDR Presidential Library and Museum, the Roosevelt House Public Policy Institute at Hunter College, the National World War II Museum, and many other venues. An avid traveler, she spent a seven-year stretch on the road full-time, first trekking the United States by RV and then backpacking around the globe.

Shannon lives in Hoboken, New Jersey.

shannonmckennaschmidt.com